목차
CONTENTS

성동구
SEONGDONG-GU
광진구
GWANGJIN-GU
강남구
GANGNAM-GU
송파구
SONGPA-GU
Bongeunsa Temple
Seonjeongneung
Lotte World Adventure Seoul
Olympic Park
Urban Hive
GT Tower East
Seoul Arts Center

미쉐린 가이드

THE MICHELIN GUIDE

서울 | 부산

SEOUL | BUSAN

2025

독자 여러분께

서울 미쉐린 가이드가 어느덧 아홉 번째, 부산은 두 번째 발간을 맞이했습니다. 시간이 참 빠르게 흐릅니다.

서울과 부산의 미식 문화는 끊임없이 발전하며 새롭게 변화하고 있습니다. 한식의 다양한 스타일은 물론, 전 세계의 다채로운 요리와 음료를 접할 수 있는 기회가 더욱 확대되는 것을 실감합니다. 특히, 부산에서는 미식을 즐기려는 소비층이 점점 넓어지고 있어, 미쉐린 가이드가 이러한 흐름에 작은 보탬이 되었다면 기쁘게 생각합니다.

앞으로도 독자 여러분께 훌륭한 레스토랑을 소개하기 위해 끊임없는 여정을 이어가겠습니다.

맛있는 식사 되세요!

TO OUR DEAREST READERS

The ninth edition of the Seoul Guide and the second edition of the Busan Guide have been published. Time truly flies!

Both Seoul and Busan continue to evolve and expand, offering a wider array of culinary experiences. From diverse styles of Korean cuisine to a vast selection of international dishes and beverages, the dining scene is growing rapidly. It's also exciting to see Busan's food culture expanding, with an increasing number of people embracing gastronomy. We are delighted that the Michelin Guide has played a small part in this culinary journey.

Our mission remains the ame—to continue seeking out outstanding restaurants for +our readers.

Enjoy your meal!

한국에서 먹기...
용어사전
EATING IN KOREA...
GLOSSARY

출처 : 국립국어원
Source: National Institute of Korean Language

KOREAN	ROMANIZATION	ENGLISH
(돼지)수육	Suyuk	Boiled Pork Slices
(돼지)양념갈비	Yangnyeomgalbi	Marinated Grilled Pork Ribs
간장	Ganjang	Soy Sauce
간장게장	Ganjang-Gejang	Soy Sauce Marinated Crab
갈비구이	Galbi-gui	Grilled Ribs
갈치구이	Galchi-Gui	Grilled Cutlassfish
감자전	Gamja-jeon	Potato Pancake
감자탕	Gamjatang	Pork Back-bone Stew
계란찜	Gyeranjjim	Steamed Eggs
고추장	Gochujang	Red Chili Paste
고추전	Gochujeon	Pan-fried Battered Chili Pepper
골뱅이무침	Golbaengi-Muchim	Spicy Sea Snail Salad
곰국시	Gomguksi	Beef Noodles
곰장어	Gomjangeo	Sea Eel
곰탕	Gomtang	Beef Bone Soup
곱창구이	Gopchang-Gui	Grilled Beef Small Intestine
구절판	Gujeolpan	Platter of Nine Delicacies
굴국밥	Gul-Gukbap	Oyster and Rice Soup
김	Gim	Laver
김치	Kimchi	Kimchi
깍두기	Kkakdugi	Diced Radish Kimchi
꽃게탕	Kkotgetang	Spicy Blue Crab Stew
녹두전	Nokdujeon	Mung Bean Pancake
누룽지닭백숙	Nurungji Dak-Baeksuk	Whole Chicken Soup with Scorched Rice
닭갈비	Dakgalbi	Spicy Stir-fried Chicken

Pakorn Khantiyaporn/Getty Images Plus

KOREAN	ROMANIZATION	ENGLISH
닭백숙	Dak-Baeksuk	Whole Chicken Soup
대구맑은탕	Daegu-Malgeun-Tang	Codfish Soup
대창구이	Daechang-Gui	Grilled Beef Large Intestine
도가니탕	Doganitang	Ox Knee Soup
도토리묵	Dotorimuk	Acorn Jelly Salad
돌솥비빔밥	Dolsot-Bibimbap	Hot Stone Pot Bibimbap
동치미	Dongchimi	Radish Water Kimchi
돼지국밥	Dwaeji-Gukbap	Pork and Rice Soup
된장	Doenjang	Soybean Paste
된장국	Doenjang-Guk	Soybean Paste Soup
된장찌개	Doenjang-Jjigae	Soybean Paste Stew
두부	Dubu	Bean Curd
두부전	Dubu-Jeon	Pan-fried Battered Bean Curd
떡갈비	Tteok-Galbi	Grilled Short Rib Patties
떡국	Tteokguk	Sliced Rice Cake Soup
막걸리	Makgeolli	Unrefined Rice Wine
막국수	Makguksu	Buckwheat Noodles
막창구이	Makchang-Gui	Grilled Beef Reed Tripe
만두	Mandu	Dumpling

WizData/Getty Images Plus

KOREAN	ROMANIZATION	ENGLISH
만둣국	Mandutguk	Dumpling Soup
매운탕	Maeuntang	Spicy Fish Stew
멍게 비빔밥	Meongge-Bibimbap	Sea Pineapple Bibimbap
메밀국수	Memil-Guksu	Buckwheat Noodles
메밀전	Memil-Jeon	Buckwheat Pancake
메밀전병	Memil-Jeonbyeong	Buckwheat Crepe
묵은지찜	Mugeunji-Jjim	Braised Meat with Aged Kimchi
물냉면	Mul-Naengmyeon	Cold Buckwheat Noodles
물회	Mulhoe	Cold Raw Fish Soup
미역국	Miyeokguk	Seaweed Soup
바싹불고기	Bassakbulgogi	Thin-sliced Bulgogi
밥	Bap	Steamed Rice
배추나물	Baechunamul	Cabbage Salad/Napa Cabbage Salad
백김치	Baekkimchi	White Kimchi
보쌈	Bossam	Napa Wraps with Pork
복국	Bokguk	Puffer Soup
부각	Bugak	Vegetable and Seaweed Chips
불고기	Bulgogi	Bulgogi

KOREAN	ROMANIZATION	ENGLISH
불고기	Bulgogi	Bulgogi
비빔냉면	Bibim-Naengmyeon	Spicy Buckwheat Noodles
비빔밥	Bibimbap	Bibimbap
빈대떡	Bindaetteok	Mung Bean Pancake
삼겹살	Samgyeopsal	Grilled Pork Belly
삼계탕	Samgyetang	Ginseng Chicken Soup
선짓국	Seonjitguk	Beef Blood Soup
설렁탕	Seolleongtang	Ox Bone Soup
수제비	Sujebi	Hand-pulled Dough Soup
순대	Sundae	Blood Sausage
순댓국	Sundae-Guk	Blood Sausage Soup
순두부찌개	Sundubu-Jjigae	Soft Bean Curd Stew
신선로	Sinseollo	Royal Hot Pot
쌈밥	Ssambap	Leaf Wraps and Rice
아귀찜	Agwijjim	Spicy Braised Monkfish
양념갈비	Yangnyeom-Galbi	Yangnyeom-Galbi
얼갈이김치	Eolgari-Kimchi	Winter Cabbage Kimchi
육개장	Yukgaejang	Spicy Beef Soup
육전	Yukjeon	Pan-fried Battered Beef
육회	Yukhoe	Beef Tartare
잡채	Japchae	Stir-fried Glass Noodles and Vegetables
전복죽	Jeonbokjuk	Abalone Porridge
족발	Jokbal	Braised Pigs' Feet
주꾸미볶음	Jukkumibokkeum	Stir-fried Webfoot Octopus
청국장찌개	Cheongukjang-Jjigae	Rich Soybean Paste Stew
추어탕	Chueotang	Loach Soup
칼국수	Kalguksu	Noodle Soup
콩나물국밥	Kongnamul-Gukbap	Bean Sprout and Rice Soup
콩국수	Kong-Guksu	Noodles in Cold Soybean Soup
평양냉면	Pyeongyang-Naengmyeon	Pyeongyang Cold Buckwheat Noodles
한정식	Han-Jeongsik	Korean Table d'hote
함흥냉면	Hamheung-Naengmyeon	Hanmheung Cold Buckwheat Noodles
헛제삿밥	Heotjesatbap	Bibimbap with Soy Sauce
호박전	Hobakjeon	Pan-fried Battered Zucchini
호박죽	Hobakjuk	Pumpkin Porridge

미쉐린 가이드의 약속

미쉐린 평가원들은 그들이 방문하는 레스토랑과 호텔이 어디에 있든 항상 체계적이고 동일한 기준을 적용해 일관된 방법으로 평가를 진행합니다.

<미쉐린 가이드>는 그 명성에 걸맞게 독자 여러분께 다음과 같이 약속드립니다.

평가원들은 철저히 익명성을 유지하며 레스토랑과 호텔의 정기적인 방문을 통해 일반 고객과 동일한 서비스하에서 평가를 진행합니다. 이들은 모든 음식값을 지불함으로써 공정성을 유지하고, 필요한 경우 평가를 모두 마친 후에야 본인 소개와 함께 레스토랑이나 호텔에 대한 자세한 정보를 문의할 수 있습니다.

독자를 최우선으로 생각하는 <미쉐린 가이드>는 공정성 유지를 위해 모든 평가를 독립적으로 진행하며, 가이드에 등재된 레스토랑과 호텔은 미쉐린에 그 어떤 비용이나 대가를 지불하지 않습니다. 모든 결정은 평가원 팀의 토의를 거쳐 이루어지며, 세계적인 기준을 동일하게 적용합니다.

독자들이 신뢰할 수 있는 정보 제공을 위해 <미쉐린 가이드>에 소개하는 모든 정보와 등급 부여는 매년 재평가 후 새롭게 갱신합니다.

전 세계에 발간되는 <미쉐린 가이드>는 어느 곳이나 동일한 평가 기준을 적용하기 때문에 그에 대한 동일한 가치를 느낄 수 있습니다.

모든 나라의 문화와 음식은 각기 다르지만, 그 음식의 가치와 퀄리티에 대한 기준은 미쉐린 스타 선성 과정에 있이 가장 중요한 원칙입니다. 미쉐린의 목표는 독자 여러분의 '이동성의 향상'입니다.

여러분의 미식 여행이 안전하고 즐거운 여정이 될 수 있도록 최선의 노력을 다하겠습니다.

THE MICHELIN GUIDE'S COMMITMENTS

Whether they are in Japan, the USA, China or Europe, our inspectors apply the same criteria to judge the quality of each and every restaurant and hotel that they visit. The MICHELIN guide commands a **worldwide reputation** thanks to the commitments we make to our readers - and we reiterate these below:

Our inspectors make regular and **anonymous visits** to restaurants and hotels to gauge the quality of products and services offered to an ordinary customer. They settle their own bill and may then introduce themselves and ask for more information about the establishment.

To remain totally objective for our readers, the selection is made with complete **independence**. Entry into the guide is free. All decisions are discussed with the Editor and our highest awards are considered at an international level.

The guide offers a **selection** of the best restaurants and hotels in every category of comfort and price. This is only possible because all the inspectors rigorously apply the same methods.

All the practical information, classifications and awards are revised and updated every year to give the most **reliable information** possible.

In order to guarantee the **consistency** of our selection, our classification criteria are the same in every country covered by the MICHELIN guide. Each culture may have its own unique cuisine but **quality** remains the **universal principle** behind our selection.

Michelin's mission is to **aid your mobility**. Our sole aim is to make your journeys safe and pleasurable.

STARS

전 세계적으로 유명한 '미쉐린 ✿ 1스타 ✿✿ 2스타 ✿✿✿ 3스타'는 요리의 재료의 수준과 맛의 조화, 기술과 창의성 그리고 언제나 변함없는 맛의 일관성을 충족하는 레스토랑에 주어집니다.

✿✿✿ 요리가 매우 훌륭하여 특별히 여행을 떠날 가치가 있는 레스토랑

✿✿ 요리가 훌륭하여 찾아갈 만한 가치가 있는 레스토랑

✿ 요리가 훌륭한 레스토랑

BIB GOURMAND

합리적인 가격에 훌륭한 음식을 제공하는 레스토랑

이 심볼은 합리적인 가격에 훌륭한 음식을 제공하는 레스토랑을 나타냅니다. 빕 구르망 등급을 받은 레스토랑 에서는 1인당 45,000원 혹은 그 이하의 가격에 식사를 즐기실 수 있습니다.

THE MICHELIN GREEN STAR

지속가능한 미식

미쉐린 가이드 레스토랑 목록의 녹색 심볼은 지속가능성의 가치를 적극 실천하고 있는 레스토랑을 나타냅니다.

업계의 롤모델로서 지속가능한 미식을 앞장서 실천해 온 레스토랑은, 셰프의 말을 인용하여 그 비전을 소개하였습니다. 새로운 심볼은 앞으로 지속가능성 활동에 동참하는 레스토랑을 소개하는데 활용됩니다.

미쉐린 가이드 셀렉션

미쉐린 가이드는 도쿄와 샌프란시스코는 물론 파리와 코펜하겐에 이르기까지 세계 최고의 레스토랑 발굴이라는 사명에 늘 충실해 왔습니다.

종류를 가리지 않는 요리와 전통, 무한한 창의성이 숨쉬는 요리를 비롯해 다양한 장소에서 경험할 수 있는 갖가지 스타일의 요리까지, 미쉐린 가이드의 평가원들은 우수한 퀄리티와 노하우, 풍미를 소개하는 데 많은 노력을 기울이고 있습니다.

또 하나 놓치지 말아야 할 것이 바로 감동입니다. 한 끼 식사가 주는 즐거움이야말로 미쉐린 스타 레스토랑의 백미라 할 수 있습니다. 짧은 미식의 순간이 일류 셰프들의 손길을 거쳐 잊지 못할 기억으로 바뀌는 경험을 할 수 있기 때문입니다. 미쉐린 가이드에 선정된 뛰어난 레스토랑에는 등급이 부여됩니다. 첫째는 '스타' 등급입니다. 손님을 최상의 미식의 세계로 안내하는 곳에는 1스타와 2스타, 3스타 등급이 부여되고, 합리적인 가격에 훌륭한 요리를 선보이는 곳에는 '빕 구르망' 등급이 주어집니다.

끝으로 친환경적이고 지속 가능한 미식에 앞장서는 레스토랑에 부여되는 '그린 스타' 등급이 있습니다. 우리가 즐길 수 있는 미식의 세계는 그야말로 무궁무진합니다. 미쉐린 가이드는 이처럼 무한한 미식의 세계를 여러분께 하나하나 소개하고자 합니다.

STARS

Our famous One ✿, Two ✿✿ and Three ✿✿✿ Stars identify establishments serving the highest quality cuisine - taking into account the quality of ingredients, the mastery of techniques and flavours, the levels of creativity and, of course, consistency.

✿✿✿ Exceptional cuisine, worth a special journey!
✿✿ Excellent cuisine, worth a detour!
✿ High quality cooking, worth a stop!

BIB GOURMAND

Good quality, good value cooking.
'Bibs' are awarded for simple yet skilful cooking.
These restaurants offer quality cooking for ₩45,000 or less (price of a 3-course meal excluding drinks).

THE MICHELIN GREEN STAR

GASTRONOMY AND SUSTAINABILITY

The Green Star highlights role-model establishments actively committed to sustainable gastronomy.

A quote by the chef outlines the vision of these trail-blazing establishments. Look out for the MICHELIN Green Star in our restaurant selection!

THE MICHELIN GUIDE'S SELECTION

From Tokyo to San Francisco, Paris to Copenhagen, the mission of the MICHELIN Guide has always been the same: to uncover the best restaurants in the world.

Cuisine of every type; prepared using grand traditions or unbridled creativity; whatever the place, whatever the style.. the MICHELIN Guide Inspectors have a quest to discover great quality, know-how and flavours.

And let's not forget emotion.. because a meal in one of these restaurants is, first and foremost, a moment of pleasure: it is experiencing the artistry of great chefs, who can transform a fleeting bite into an unforgettable memory.

From all of the restaurants selected for the Guide, the most remarkable are awarded a distinction: first there are the Stars, with up to Three awarded for those which transport you to the top of the gastronomic world. Then there is the Bib Gourmand, which cleverly combines quality with price.

And finally, another Star, not red but green, which shines the spotlight on establishments that are committed to producing sustainable cuisine.

There are so many culinary experiences to enjoy: the MICHELIN Guide brings you all these and more!

미쉐린 가이드 심볼

최고의 레스토랑을 전문적으로 발굴해 온 미쉐린이 무궁무진한 미식의 세계를 탐험하는 여정에 여러분을 초대합니다. 미쉐린은 레스토랑의 요리는 물론이고 데코레이션과 서비스, 분위기 등 요리와 관련한 경험을 다방면으로 평가합니다.

이탤리언 • *Italian*

시설 및 서비스

	훌륭한 와인 리스트
	훌륭한 전통술
	장애인 편의 시설
	야외 테라스
	좌식 테이블
	훌륭한 전망
	발렛 파킹
	별실 보유
	카운터 테이블
N	새롭게 추가된 레스토랑

가격 범위

₩	50,000원 이하
₩₩	50,000원-150,000원
₩₩₩	150,000원-250,000원
₩₩₩₩	250,000원 이상

THE MICHELIN GUIDE'S SYMBOLS

Michelin are experts at finding the best restaurants and invite you to explore the diversity of the gastronomic universe. As well as evaluating a restaurant's cooking, we also consider its décor, the service and the ambience - in other words, the all-round culinary experience.

A keyword help you make your choice more quickly:

이탈리언 • *Italian*

FACILITIES & SERVICES

🍇	Interesting wine list
🍶	Interesting Korean liquor or Sake
♿	Wheelchair access
⛱	Terrace dining
👟	Shoes off
⩽	Interesting view
🚗	Valet parking
⊡	Private rooms
⋯	Counter
N	New entry in the guide

PRICE RANGE

₩	under 50,000 KRW
₩₩	50,000-150,000 KRW
₩₩₩	150,000-250,000 KRW
₩₩₩₩	over 250,000 KRW

서울

SEOUL

Mlenny/Getty Images Plus

서울
SEOUL
0 1km
0 1/2 mile
N
서대문구
SEODAEMUN-GU
종로구
JONGNO-GU
마포구
MAPO-GU
용산구
YONGSAN-GU
중구
JUNG-GU
영등포구
YEONGDEUNGPO-GU
동작구
DONGJAK-GU
서초구
SEOCHO-GU
경복궁
GYEONGBOKGUNG PALACE
북촌
BUKCHON
창덕궁
CHANGDEOKGUNG PALACE
서울역사박물관
Seoul Museum of History
종로
동대문디자인프라자 (DDP)
DONGDAEMUN DESIGN PLAZA
서울시립미술관
Seoul Museum of Art (SEMA)
남산
Namsan
리움미술관
Leeum Museum of Art
전쟁기념관
The War Memorial of Korea
국립박물관
NATIONAL MUSEUM OF KOREA
월드컵경기장
World Cup Stadium
선유도공원
Seonyudo Park
한강공원
Hangang Park
국립서울현충원
SEOUL NATIONAL CEMETERY
Tongil-ro 통일로
Susaek-ro 수색로
World Cup-ro 월드컵로
Seongsan-ro 성산로
Sinchon-ro 신촌로
Baekbeom-ro 백범로
Mapo-daero 마포대로
Jong-ro
Toegye-ro 퇴계로
Wonhyoro 원효로
Hangang-daero 한강대로
Seobinggo-ro 서빙고로
서강대교 Seogangdaegyo Bridge
마포대교 Mapodaegyo Bridge
Gukhoe-daero 국회대로
여의대방로
Gyeongin-ro 경인로
Yeouidaebang-ro
Sangdo-ro 상도로
Dongjak-daero 동작대로
Banpo-daero 반포대로
시흥대로
Nambusunhwan-ro 남부순환로
Siheung-daero
Hangang
30
70
88
94
15
1

성북구
SEONGBUK-GU
동대문구
DONGDAEMUN-GU
성동구
SEONGDONG-GU
광진구
GWANGJIN-GU
강남구
GANGNAM-GU
송파구
SONGPA-GU
동소문로
Dongsomun-ro
망우로
Mangu-ro
왕산로
Wangsan-ro
Cheonho-daero
천호대로
Wangsimni-ro 왕십리로
Achasan-ro
아차산로
Apgujeong-ro
압구정로
Dosan-daero
도산대로
Eonju-ro
언주로
Bongeunsa-ro
봉은사로
Teheran-ro
테헤란로
Samseong-ro
삼성로
Gangnam-daero
강남대로
Nambusunhwan-ro
남부순환로
양재대로
Yangjae-daero
Olympic-ro
올림픽로
Songpa-daero
송파대로
봉은사
Bongeunsa Temple
선정릉
Seonjeongneung
어반하이브
Urban Hive
GT타워
GT Tower East
예술의전당
Seoul Arts Center
롯데월드 어드벤처
Lotte World Adventure Seoul
올림픽파크
Olympic Park
서울 암사동 유적
Amsa-dong prehistoric site
NA
61
30
70
88
29
AH1
31
1
51
309
100

tawatchaiprakobkit/Getty Images Plus

강남구
GANGNAM-GU

밍글스
MINGLES

한식 • *Korean*

02-515-7306

강남구 도산대로 67길 19, 2층

2F, 19 Dosan-daero 67-gil, Gangnam-gu

www.restaurant-mingles.com

■ 가 격 PRICE: ₩₩₩₩

따뜻한 여백의 미가 돋보이는 밍글스. 실내 디자인, 한국 음식의 정갈한 멋을 한층 더 살려 주는 한국 작가들의 기물, 여기에 주방을 이끄는 강민구 셰프의 젊고 감각적인 재능까지, 다양한 전문가들의 감각과 감성이 하나의 공간에 모여 있다. 초창기부터 뚜렷한 한국적 색채를 기반으로 전통과 현대의 경계를 자유롭게 넘나들며 밍글스만의 맛과 멋을 창조해온 강민구 셰프는 매번 방문 시 한 걸음 더 진화된 요리를 선보인다. 밍글스만의 독특한 매력은 전복 배추선과 어만두처럼 경계를 허무는 요리에서 정점을 이룬다. 김민성 매니저가 이끄는 서비스 팀의 배려 깊은 고객 응대 역시 레스토랑의 가치를 한층 더 높여 준다.

Chef Kang Min-goo's keen eye for detail shines with warm minimalism takes center stage at Mingles, where the interior design highlights the understated elegance of Korean aesthetics. Complementing this ambiance are exquisite tableware and decor crafted by Korean artisans, further enhancing the refined charm of traditional Korean cuisine. From the beginning, Kang has marched to the beat of his own drum, breaking down barriers by marrying the old with the new, but always with a deep respect for tradition. His journey and evolution continues, with dishes like Abalone and Cabbage Seon and Fish Mandu showcasing the creativity of the chef and his talented team.

강남구

권숙수
KWONSOOKSOO

'전문 조리사'를 뜻하는 '숙수'에서 착안해 이름 지은 '권숙수'는 권우중 셰프의 한식 레스토랑이다. 이곳에선 한식의 기본 맛을 좌우하는 장, 젓갈, 식초 등을 직접 담가 사용하는데, 이러한 정성이 권숙수만의 기품 있는 요리를 완성한다. 제철 식재료 중에서도 좀 더 진귀한 재료를 선별하고, 흔한 식재료일지라도 창의적인 조합을 통해 새로운 요리로 탄생시키는 권 셰프의 노력과 열정을 곳곳에서 발견할 수 있다. 좋은 음식을 위해서라면 일절 타협하지 않는 '숙수'의 고집이 고스란히 녹아 있는 이곳에서 한식의 깊은 맛을 느껴보길.

Chef Kwon Woo-joong's homage to tradition is evident in every facet of Kwonsooksoo, even in the name itself (sooksoo is an archaic term for professional cook). Inspired by time-honored methods of cooking, Kwon digs deep into his own roots. He tirelessly scours the country for rare finds that best represent each of the seasons and transforms even the most mundane ingredients into something special. What the diners get to experience is passion on a plate, coupled with a good dose of ingenuity.

한식 • *Korean*

02-542-6268

강남구 압구정로 80길 37, 4층

4F, 37 Apgujeong-ro 80-gil, Gangnam-gu

www.kwonsooksoo.com

■ 가격 PRICE: ₩₩₩₩

컨템퍼러리 •
Contemporary

02-6985-7214

강남구 테헤란로 231, 센터필드 East 2층 E205호

2F Center field EAST E205, 231 Teheran-ro, Gangnam-gu

www.restaurantallen.com

■ 가 격 PRICE: ₩₩₩₩

레스토랑 알렌

RESTAURANT ALLEN

레스토랑 알렌은 서현민 셰프의 정교함과 정성이 빚어낸 현대적 퀴진의 세련미를 두루 경험할 수 있는 곳이다. 한국의 제철 식재료를 연구하고 활용하며 얻은 셰프의 노하우가 요리에 고스란히 담겨 있어 무척 매력적인 맛을 선사한다. 복잡한 맛을 표현하기보다 식재료의 특성을 쉽고 정확하게 전달하는 셰프의 감각과 스킬은 알렌만의 강점이자 흥미로운 다이닝 포인트이다. 아울러 일사분란한 키친 팀과 서비스 팀이 만들어내는 팀워크 덕분에 고객들은 편안한 분위기에서 다이닝을 즐길 수 있다. 요리에 계절을 담아내는 알렌만의 스타일에서 남다른 즐거움을 경험하게 될 것이다.

Restaurant Allen is where Chef Allen Suh's meticulous culinary craft and dedication translate into a contemporary cuisine with a refined flair. Chef Suh's dishes embody his expertise in local seasonal ingredients and their application. Their alluring flavors are not complex; rather, they are straightforward and true to the ingredients. Such attention to the basics makes Allen stand out from the rest. Plus, the exceptional teamwork of the efficient kitchen and service staff allows customers to enjoy dining amidst a relaxed atmosphere. Allen's distinctive means of hinting at the time of year through its cuisine is a truly exclusive delight.

✿✿

미토우
MITOU

미토우는 제철 식재료를 이용해 자신들만의 방식으로 일본 전통 요리를 표현하는 권영운, 김보미 셰프의 재능이 돋보이는 공간이다. 이들은 미토우의 요리에 계절감을 담기 위해 끊임없이 정진한다. 이런 노력은 품질 좋은 식재료를 고르는 데에서도 드러난다. 미토우의 요리에 쓰이는 닭과 달걀, 쌀과 채소는 모두 셰프의 가족이 운영하는 농장에서 공급받고 있다. 셰프들의 손을 거쳐 미토우의 식탁에 오르는 요리는 이런 정성 어린 노력의 결정체라 할 수 있다. 미토우의 요리에서는 셰프가 요리를 공부하며 얻었다는 수련자의 진중함과 겸손함, 정진하는 마음가짐이 고스란히 느껴진다. 계절이 바뀔 때마다 미토우의 식탁을 기대하는 하는 이유다.

일식 • *Japanese*

010-7286-9914

강남구 도산대로 70길 24

24 Dosan-daero 70-gil, Gangnam-gu

■ 가 격 PRICE: ₩₩₩₩

At Mitou, the prowess and ingenuity of the chef duo Kwon Young-woon and Kim Bo-mi are showcased through authentic Japanese cuisine prepared with fresh seasonal ingredients. Indeed, their relentless struggle to incorporate seasonality into the menu starts with a careful selection of quality ingredients. In particular, chicken, eggs, rice and vegetables used at this establishment are sourced from Chef Kwon's family farm. A culmination of such painstaking effort, the fare at Mitou genuinely reflects a sense of earnestness, modesty and dedication harbored by the two chefs as eternal students of culinary art. It thus comes as no surprise that customers eagerly anticipate Mitou's new offerings every season.

GANGNAM-GU

스와니예
SOIGNÉ

이노베이티브 •
Innovative

02-3477-9386

강남구 강남대로 652 신사스퀘어 2층 201호

#201, 2F Sinsa square, 652 Gangnam-daero, Gangnam-gu

www.soigneseoul.com

■ **가 격 PRICE: ₩₩₩₩**

'Contemporary Cuisine of Seoul'이라는 슬로건 아래 이준 셰프와 그의 팀이 선사하는 창의적인 요리를 만날 수 있는 스와니예. 전 세계 음식으로부터 영감을 얻은 요리를 선보이지만, 기본 바탕은 한국적인 것이 특징이다. 매장 중앙에 보이는 오픈 키친을 중심으로 다이닝룸과 프라이빗 룸, 비스포크 다이닝 레드룸을 운영한다. 주기적으로 바뀌는 메뉴를 '에피소드'라고 표현하는데, 고유한 주제의 각 에피소드는 마치 기승전결이 있는 한 편의 시를 감상하는 듯하다. 또한 각 에피소드에 맞는 와인 페어링도 세심하게 준비되어 있다.

Soigné, under the slogan "Contemporary Cuisine of Seoul," is a culinary destination where Chef Lee Jun and his team present creative and refined dishes. While drawing inspiration from global cuisines, the restaurant stays rooted in the essence of Korean flavors and ingredients. At the heart of the restaurant is an open kitchen, offering guests a dynamic view of the cooking process. Soigné also features a main dining room, private rooms, and a bespoke dining space known as the Red Room, catering to diverse dining experiences.The menu is uniquely referred to as "Episodes" and is regularly refreshed. Each episode revolves around a distinct theme, creating a poetic dining journey with a sense of beginning, climax, and resolution. To enhance the experience, thoughtfully curated wine pairings accompany each episode, ensuring a harmonious and memorable meal.

알라 프리마
ALLA PRIMA

늘 과감하고 창의적인 요리로 미식가들의 발길을 유혹하는 알라 프리마. 오픈된 주방이 한눈에 들어오는 넓은 카운터 테이블과 쾌적한 다이닝 홀, 그리고 프라이빗 다이닝 공간이 모던하게 펼쳐진다. 재료를 생명으로 여기는 김진혁 셰프의 요리는 깔끔한 소스, 맛의 밸런스, 그리고 계절 식재료들의 향연이라 할 수 있다. 와인뿐만 아니라 사케와도 잘 어울리는 이 곳의 모던 퀴진을 경험하려면 예약은 필수다.

Chef Kim Jin-hyuk continues to attract discerning gourmets with his whimsically creative and modern offerings. His reverence for seasonal ingredients, his attention to balance, and his delicate yet assertive sauces come together like a symphony that pairs well with both wine and sake. The L-shaped counter with ample seating, the gleaming open kitchen, the spacious dining hall, and the private dining room each do their part to make the diners feel comfortable. Be sure to reserve ahead.

이노베이티브 •
Innovative

02-511-2555
강남구 학동로 17길 13
13 Hakdong-ro 17-gil, Gangnam-gu
www.allaprima.co.kr

■ 가 격 PRICE: ₩₩₩₩

GANGNAM-GU

이노베이티브 •

Innovative

070-4231-1022

강남구 도산대로 45길 10-5

10-5 Dosan-daero 45-gil, Gangnam-gu

www.restaurantevett.com

■ 가격 PRICE: ₩₩₩₩

에빗
EVETT

식재료를 야생에 나가 채집하고 메주를 손수 띄워 장을 담그는 조셉 리저우드 셰프의 레스토랑 에빗. 조셉 리저우드 셰프에게 뻔하고 식상한 재료는 존재하지 않는다. 직접 잡은 개미로 산미를 더한 녹차식혜 소르베부터 우지 타르트와 깻잎 주스까지 에빗의 메뉴에는 셰프의 감각으로 재해석된 창의적 요리로 가득하다. 한국의 계절감을 살리면서 셰프의 독특한 해석을 가미한 에빗의 요리는 구색을 잘 갖춘 와인과 함께할 때 한층 더 빛을 발한다.

To the adventurous owner-chef Joseph Lidgerwood, who ventures out into the wild to pick ingredients or makes his own soy sauce and soybean paste from scratch, there is no such thing as an obvious or humdrum ingredient. From sikhye (sweet rice punch) sorbet with green tea syrup, which is garnished with handpicked ants for a touch of sour flavor, to tallow tart and perilla leaf juice, Evett's menu brims with inventive dishes reimagined by the chef that perfectly reflect the seasonal sensibilities of Korea. When paired with its impressive selection of wines, those dishes become even more irresistible.

정식당
JUNGSIK

모던 한식 파인 다이닝을 개척한 장본인이라 평가받는 임정식 셰프는 자신의 이름을 내건 정식당 서울과 정식당 뉴욕을 통해 새롭고 창의적인 한식을 세계에 알리고 있다. 김밥, 비빔밥, 구절판, 보쌈 등 대중들이 친근하게 여기는 다양한 한식 요리에서 영감을 얻어 재해석한 독창적인 메뉴는 한국인에게 익숙한 맛을 기발하게 풀어내는 방식으로 한식의 맛과 멋을 동시에 만족시킨다. 독특한 디저트와 훌륭한 구성의 와인 리스트, 그리고 배려심 깊은 서비스 등 즐거운 식사를 위한 요소들이 두루 갖춰진 곳이다.

Touted as a pioneer of modern Korean fine dining, Chef Yim Jung-sik — with his Seoul and New York restaurants - is credited for introducing Korean cuisine to the world with an innovative flair that is entirely his own. What Yim does best is drawing inspiration from the familiar — gimbap, bibimbap, platter of nine delicacies and napa wraps with pork — and creating something unexpected yet surprisingly evocative and authentic. Whimsical desserts, a good wine list and attentive service — Jungsik has it all.

컨템퍼러리 • *Contemporary*

02-517-4654

강남구 선릉로 158길 11

11 Seolleung-ro 158-gil, Gangnam-gu

www.jungsik.kr

■ **가 격 PRICE: ₩₩₩₩**

GANGNAM-GU

코지마
KOJIMA

스시 • *Sushi*

02-2056-1291

강남구 압구정로 60길 21, 분더샵 6층

6F Boon the Shop, 21 Apgujeong-ro 60-gil, Gangnam-gu

■ 가 격 PRICE: ₩₩₩₩

최상급 자연산 재료를 숙성시킨 부드러운 네타와 단단한 샤리의 절묘한 조화를 우아한 공간에서 즐길 수 있는 곳. 오랜시간 일본에서 수련한 김우태 셰프는 재료에 대한 친절한 설명을 곁들이며 손님과 교감하는 스타일이다. 또한 그날 쓰는 생선의 종류에 따라 도수와 맛을 조절해 사케를 페어링 하는 실력이 뛰어나 함께 맛보며 좋은 맛의 밸런스를 만나볼 수 있다. 다양한 츠마미, 쉽게 접할 수 없는 사케와 함께 김우태 셰프의 오마카세를 더욱 맛있게 즐겨 보시기 바란다.

Chef Kim Woo-tae offers omakase crafted from seasonal Korean wild seafood and high-quality ingredients, emphasizing their fresh, natural flavors. The chef's friendly and calm demeanor adds a distinct vibe to Kojima. The chef, who trained in the Edomae sushi philosophy, remains dedicated to improving his craft. The strength of Team Kojima lies in their ability to transform high-quality ingredients into an exquisite selection of tsumami and nigiri. They also recommend the best sake to pair with the food for a more vibrant dining experience.

강남구

강민철 레스토랑
KANG MINCHUL RESTAURANT

거장이라 불릴 만한 경지에 오른 요리사들과 함께했던 시간은 강민철 셰프에게 요리에 대한 열정과 철학, 자부심은 물론 자신이 나아가야 할 방향에 대한 큰 동기를 부여했다. 이렇듯 그의 이름을 내건 레스토랑의 요리에는 그가 진중하게 걸어온 요리사로서의 자세와 방향성이 오롯이 담겨져 있다. 묵직한 풍미의 다양한 클래식 프렌치 소스를 기반으로 변화무쌍하게 맛의 조합을 이끌어 내는 강민철 레스토랑의 요리는 세련된 프렌치 퀴진의 다양한 스타일을 보여주면서도 중심이 잘 잡힌 프렌치 퀴진 본연의 깊이 있는 맛의 흐름도 잘 표현하고 있다. 공간이 넓지 않아 예약이 쉽지는 않지만 그만큼의 멋진 다이닝 경험을 얻을 수 있을 것이다.

Chef Kang Min-chul has been greatly inspired by time spent with master chefs, instilling in him a pride and passion for cuisine and culinary philosophy. It's also helped him find his own direction and the fare at this namesake restaurant genuinely reflects his attitude toward gastronomy. The menu comprises dishes offering a kaleidoscope of flavors while highlighting the diversity of refined French cuisine. The restaurant's small space makes reservations a challenge, but once you secure a table, prepare to be rewarded with an unforgettable dining experience.

프렌치 • *French*

02-545-2511

강남구 도산대로 68길 18, 지하 1층

B1F, 18 Dosan-daero 68-gil, Gangnam-gu

www.kangminchul.com

■ 가 격 PRICE: ₩₩₩₩

GANGNAM-GU

고료리 켄
GORYORI KEN

요리에 매진하는 셰프의 움직임 하나하나를 지켜볼 수 있는 여덟 석의 한정된 공간. 직접 발로 뛰어 선별한 신선한 재료에 창의적인 아이디어와 현대적인 조리법이 더해진 김건 셰프의 요리에는 고료리 켄이 꾸준히 지향해온 정체성이 담겨 있다. 늘 신선한 양질의 재료를 고객에게 제공하기 위해 모든 재료를 당일 소진한다는 셰프의 원칙에서 신뢰감을 느낄 수 있다. 한결같은 맛과 정성이 손님을 맞는 기본 자세라고 생각하는 김건 셰프, 그의 요리를 즐기기 위해 예약은 필수이다.

This intimate setting, with the main bar seating only eight, allows patrons to watch the chef's every movement. While preserving its unassuming façade on the second floor of the premises, Chef Kim Geon showcases highly seasonal ingredients in creations inspired by the freshness of the produce and his own creative intuition. Consistency and care are things Kim takes very seriously when serving his customers. The drinks menu features an impressive variety of sake produced by small Japanese breweries.

컨템퍼러리 •
Contemporary

02-511-7809

강남구 언주로 152길 15-3, 2층

2F, 15-3 Eonju-ro 152-gil, Gangnam-gu

■ 가 격 PRICE: ₩₩₩₩

GANGNAM-GU

라미띠에
L'AMITIÉ

프렌치 • French

02-546-9621
강남구 도산대로 67길 30, 2층
2F, 30 Dosan-daero 67-gil, Gangnam-gu

■ 가 격 PRICE: ₩₩₩

2006년부터 '정성의 온기가 담긴 프렌치 퀴진'을 선보여온 장명식 셰프의 '라미띠에'. 변함없는 안정감을 보여주는 이 곳은 촉촉하게 쪄낸 완도산 전복에 전복 내장 에스푸마와 향긋한 마늘 퓨레, 셀러리 피클을 곁들인 전복 요리, 그리고 샤프란 향이 매력적인 리소토에 빵가루를 입혀 바삭하게 튀겨낸 아란치니는 라미띠에의 요리가 가진 특징을 잘 보여주는 시그니처 메뉴다. 오랜 시간이 흘러도 한결같은 셰프의 열정을 라미띠에의 요리에서 경험해 보기를 바란다.

Since 2006, Chef Jang Myoung-sik has welcomed diners with his consistently warm and comforting French cuisine. At this new location, Jang continues to serve up his passion for French cooking on a plate. Signature dishes include steamed Wando abalone served with abalone intestine espuma, fragrant garlic purée and pickled celery as well as crispy saffron arancini.

레귬
LÉGUME

오직 채소만으로 품격 있고 매력적인 요리를 만드는 건 결코 쉬운 일이 아니다. 하지만 레귬의 성시우 셰프는 이 어려운 일을 능숙하게 해 내고 있다. 어린 시절부터 채소 식단을 즐겨 채식에 대한 이해가 높았고, 새로운 시각으로 자신만의 채식 요리를 추구한 덕분이다. '100% 비건 요리'를 지향하는 레귬은 단순한 한 끼의 채식을 넘어 세련된 채식 다이닝의 스타일을 완성했고, 이를 통해 한국적인 채식의 다양성과 방향성을 보여 준다. 감각적인 모던 퀴진에 셰프의 능숙한 역량이 접목된 채식 기반의 비건 요리는 뚜렷한 정체성을 드러내며 창의적인 맛을 선사한다. 분명한 사실은, 레귬의 비건 요리가 채식주의자만이 아닌 모든 대중의 입맛을 사로잡을 수 있는 요리라는 점이다.

비건 • Vegan

050-71365-1567

강남구 강남대로 652, 신사 스퀘어 2층

2F, Sinsa Square, 652 Gangnam-daero, Gangnam-gu

www.legume.kr

■ 가격 PRICE: ₩₩

It's no easy feat to invent dignified and alluring cuisine that is based only on plant ingredients. Yet, Chef Sung Si-woo at Légume pulls it off with panache. The chef's fondness for veggies since childhood has led to a deeper understanding of vegetarian diets, which, coupled with his unique perspective, has given birth to his one-of-a-kind delicacies. In pursuit of 100 percent vegan cuisine, this eatery has perfected a refined vegetarian dining style that transcends the provision of mere plant-based meals, thereby highlighting the diversity and direction of Korean vegetarian cuisine. At Légume, sensorial contemporary cuisine meets the chef's seasoned skills and is transformed into a vegan menu with a distinct identity and imaginative flavors. The evident truth is that the kitchen's vegan fare not only appeals to vegetarians but also to people with a wide range of palates.

GANGNAM-GU

무니

MUNI

강남구

일식 • *Japanese*

02-511-1303

강남구 도산대로 72길 16

16 Dosan-daero 72-gil, Gangnam-gu

■ 가 격 PRICE: ₩₩₩₩

화려한 청담동의 뒷골목에서 무심코 지나치기 십상인 일본 요리 전문점 '무니'. 현실적인 이유로 주방에서 일을 하기 시작했다는 김동욱 셰프는 처음부터 오로지 일식에만 집중했고, 나날이 커져가는 요리에 대한 갈증을 해소하기 위해 일본으로 떠났다. 가이세키의 정석이라고 표현하기에는 한계가 있는 것이 사실이다. 하지만 자신이 부지런히 수집해온 그릇에 제철 요리를 담아 계절감을 뚜렷하게 표현해 내는 등 그의 요리에는 전통적인 요소들이 녹아 있다. 일본 니혼슈 소믈리에(키키사케시) 자격증을 취득한 그에게 요리와 어울릴 만한 사케를 추천받는다면 한층 더 풍성한 다이닝을 경험할 수 있을 것이다.

Tucked away in a back alley of glitzy Cheongdam-dong, Muni is helmed by Chef Kim Dong-wook, who started working in kitchens to make ends meet. To quench his growing thirst for knowledge in Japanese cuisine, Kim left for Japan to hone his skills, which would one day lay the foundation for this restaurant. To describe his style of cooking as textbook kaiseki is overkill, but his respect for tradition is evident, including in the way he utilizes seasonal ingredients and the way he plates his creations. The chef is a certified sake sommelier (Kikisake-shi), so ask for recommendations.

무오키
MUOKI

남아프리카 공화국 방언으로 '참나무'를 뜻하는 '무오키'는 박무현 셰프의 우직한 성격을 그대로 반영한 곳이다. 세계 다양한 지역에서 요리 경험을 쌓은 박 셰프는 본인만의 스타일을 녹여낸 음식을 제공하고자 이곳을 오픈했다. 새로운 조리법으로 뻔하지 않은 맛과 질감의 조화를 표현해내는 것을 즐기는 그의 메뉴엔 재료에 대한 깊은 이해 없인 만들 수 없는 재미있는 요리들이 포함되어 있다. 7가지 방법으로 조리한 토마토, 5가지 방식으로 만든 당근 디저트, 그리고 제주식 갈치 호박국을 자신만의 방식으로 재해석한 요리 등이 그러한 예다. 그의 요리 세계가 궁금하다면 예약 후 들러볼 것.

South African dialect for oak tree, Muoki is Chef Park Moo-hyun's restaurant. The name is a nod to the chef's cosmopolitan background as well as his straightforward attitude when it comes to cooking. Park has a knack for incorporating new cooking methods into creating a mélange of unpredictable flavors and textures. Tomatoes seven ways, five different kinds of carrot-based desserts, and his take on Jeju-style hairtail and pumpkin soup are good examples of his creativity and insight. Be sure to book ahead.

컨템퍼러리 •
Contemporary

010-2948-4171

강남구 학동로 55길 12-12, 2층

2F, 12-12 Hakdong-ro 55-gil, Gangnam-gu

www.muoki.kr

■ **가격 PRICE: ₩₩₩**

빈호
VINHO

컨템퍼러리 •
Contemporary

010-9677-2302

강남구 학동로 43길 38, 논현웰스톤 162호

#162 Wellstone Bldg, 38 Hakdong-ro 43-gil, Gangnam-gu

www.restaurantvinho.kr

■ 가격 PRICE: ₩₩₩

전성빈 셰프와 김진호 소믈리에가 의기투합해 만든 빈호는 탁 트인 통창과 오픈된 주방에 길쭉한 테이블이 마치 여럿이 함께 식사하며 와인을 즐기는 듯한 느낌을 준다. 방대한 와인 리스트는 기본이고, 세심한 서비스와 음식의 페어링, 제철 재료와 절묘하게 어울리는 진한 소스 등을 통해 현대적인 요리의 진수를 맛볼 수 있다. 특히 방어 타르타르는 사워도우 크럼블과 수란으로 버무린 후 살짝 구운 로메인으로 둘러 가츠오 크림과 파슬리 오일, 레몬즙을 넣은 소스와 함께 나오는데 고소한 풍미와 산뜻한 방어의 맛이 잘 어울린다. 와인과 함께 한다면 음식의 매력이 배가 된다는 것을 잘 보여주는 곳이다.

Co-helmed by Chef Jeon Seong-bin and Sommelier Kim Jin-ho, Vinho features expansive window walls and an open kitchen fronted by an elongated counter. This spatial harmony creates a lively communal wine-and-dine ambiance. The vast wine list, coupled with careful service and food pairing, as well as deep-flavored sauces that exquisitely complement seasonal ingredients, makes the eatery a perfect venue to savor the pinnacle of contemporary cuisine. Its yellowtail tartare, which features dices of yellowtail mixed with sourdough crumbs and poached eggs and then wrapped with slightly grilled romaine, is served with a sauce featuring katsuobushi cream, parsley oil and lemon juice. The sweet and nutty flavor of the sauce provides the ideal accompaniment to the yellowtail's fresh flavors. Vinho delights in showcasing how wine can heighten the allure of fine cuisine.

세븐스도어

7TH DOOR

김대천 셰프의 요리는 시간이 흐를수록 더욱 다양해지고 그 깊이를 더해 간다. 7th Door의 요리에서는 셰프가 지향하는 한식의 방향성을 경험할 수 있다. 그는 한식의 특징인 발효와 숙성을 주제로 삼아 자신만의 노하우와 정성을 담아 요리에 쓰일 재료를 준비한다. 이러한 과정을 거쳐 음식이 고객의 테이블에 오르기까지 김대천 셰프의 집중력과 아이디어가 요리에 재치 있게 녹아들고, 셰프의 이런 재치와 위트가 식사와 식사 사이에 재미를 더한다. 맛의 5가지 표현과 요리의 주제인 발효와 숙성 그리고 셰프의 감각, 이 7가지 테마의 어우러짐은 미식의 즐거움을 기대하게 한다.

Chef Kim Dae-chun's cooking continues to diversify and deepen over time. The menu at this restaurant embodies the culinary direction he wishes to pursue, largely thanks to his modern Korean preparations. Under the theme of fermentation and aging, the essential attributes of Korean gastronomy, the chef prepares ingredients with care and expertise. The 7th Door symbolises a gastronomic entrance to "the seven tastes of food," the first five being the five basic tastes; the sixth, the taste of fermentation and aging; and the seventh, the culinary sensibility of the chef.

컨템퍼러리 •

Contemporary

02-542-3010

강남구 학동로 97길 41, 4층

4F, 41 Hakdong-ro 97-gil, Gangnam-gu

www.7thdoor.kr

■ 가 격 PRICE: ₩₩₩₩

강남구

솔밤
SOLBAM

컨템퍼러리 · *Contemporary*

070-4405-7788

강남구 학동로 231, 2층

2F, 231 Hakdong-ro, Gangnam-gu

www.restaurantsolbam.com

■ 가 격 PRICE: ₩₩₩₩

엄태준 셰프는 본인이 요리사로서 경험한 다양한 순간과 노하우를 한국적인 요소들과 접목시켜 솔밤의 요리로 만들어 발전시키고 있다. 특히 자연 존중의 철학, 계절과 절기에 입각한 한국 식재료에 대한 연구와 이해, 그리고 한국적인 요리 테크닉 등을 절묘하게 활용하여 셰프 자신의 요리 자산과 접목시킨 현대적인 요리를 선보인다. 이 같은 셰프의 지극한 관심과 노력은 코스가 진행되는 동안 순수한 미식의 즐거움을 고객에게 안겨준다. 차분하고 유연하게 흘러가는 맛과 향, 풍미의 연계성이 훌륭한 모던 퀴진을 솔밤에서 경험해 보도록 하자.

Visit Solbam to enjoy modern cuisine that offers an outstanding balance of tastes, aromas and flavors. Here, Chef Eom Tae-jun's wide range of culinary experience and expertise meet Korean elements. His study of local ingredients (guided by his respect for nature and Korea's four seasons) and his knowledge of Korean cooking techniques culminate in an uncanny synergy that gives rise to the restaurant's unique modern dishes. With each course, the chef's passion and exemplary effort delivera singularly rewarding gastronomic experience to guests.

스시 마츠모토
SUSHI MATSUMOTO

한국에서 스시 문화가 지금처럼 성장하기까지 많은 셰프들의 노력이 있었다. 특히 마츠모토 미즈호는 정통성을 로컬에서 표현하는 데 일가견이 있는 셰프로 손꼽힌다. 스시 마츠모토는 트렌디함을 추구하기보다 셰프가 일본 본토에서 익힌 스시 요리를 로컬에서 그대로 재현하는 데 많은 노력을 기울이고 있다. 샤리와 네타의 구성과 조합은 물론 손님을 접대하는 자세에서도 그러한 노력을 확인할 수 있다. 인상적인 츠마미 라인과 풍미의 강약이 자연스레 흐르는 니기리의 구성은 여전히 매력적이다.

Chef Matsumoto Mizuho is renowned for replicating authenticity in local settings. Rather than chasing after gastronomic trends, this sushiya strives to faithfully reproduce the authentic sushi of mainland Japan amidst the Korean milieu. Such efforts are unmistakable—from the composition and arrangement of shari (rice) and neta (fish topping) to the knowledgeable service provided. The impressive line of tsumami (appetizers) and the progression of nigiri sushi —reflecting the natural cadence of flavors — remain the main culinary appeal.

스시 • *Sushi*

02-543-4334
강남구 도산대로 75길 24
24 Dosan-daero 75-gil, Gangnam-gu

■ 가 격 PRICE: ₩₩₩₩

윤서울
YUN

한식 • Korean

02-336-3323

강남구 선릉로 805

805 Seolleung-ro, Gangnam-gu

■ 가 격 PRICE: ₩₩₩

윤서울의 한식은 익숙하면서도 과감한 도전이 느껴지는 독특함이 있다. 특히 자가 제면 들기름 면과 자체 숙성한 생선을 활용한 요리에서 셰프가 추구하는 한식의 방향성을 엿볼 수 있다. 기존의 고급스러운 한식의 매력과는 다른, 정교하면서도 거침없는 한식의 매력을 경험해 보기를 바란다.

YUN offers familiar Korean dishes with bold twists. Its nutty-flavored perilla oil noodles featuring housemade Korean wheat noodles, various house-aged fish dishes, and newly added umami-rich Korean beef offerings – all hint at the culinary direction the chef is headed towards. With a relocation from Mapo to Gangnam, this restaurant has expanded and renovated its dining hall, which now exudes elegant yet striking vibes. Come to Yun Seoul and experience the precision and audacity that are rarely found in ordinary Korean cuisine.

이스트
Y'EAST

다양한 해석이 가능한 레스토랑의 이름처럼 요리의 다양성을 다채롭게 표현하는 레스토랑이다. 이스트의 조영동 셰프는 기존의 요리들을 자신만의 방식으로 재해석 하여 고객에게 즐거움을 선사한다. 조 셰프는 국내에서 흔히 볼 수 없는 재료를 조합해 요리의 맛을 새롭게 표현하기 위해 정성을 쏟는다. 카야 토스트를 모티브로 한 아뮤즈 부쉬(amuse bouche)는 물론, 한국의 갈비 요리를 다양한 버전으로 소개한 갈비 스톤 역시 익숙함 속에서 새로움을 추구하는 방식으로 고객에게 즐거움을 주는 요리들이다. 이처럼 새로움이라는 컨셉을 중시하지만 요리 본연의 가치인 맛도 놓치지 않았다.

컨템퍼러리 •
Contemporary

070-8855-0470

강남구 언주로 170길 26-6, 3층

3F, 26-6 Eonju-ro 170-gil, Gangnam-gu

www.yeastseoul.co.kr

■ 가 격 PRICE: ₩₩₩

In a nod to the property's name, an appellation that invites varied interpretations, Y'east is home to expressions of unlimited culinary possibilities. Chef Cho Young-dong, its chef de cuisine, delights diners with familiar dishes reimagined via his singular aesthetics. The chef channels his passion into creating novel flavors by artfully blending ingredients that are hard to come by in Korea. From the signature amuse bouche inspired by kaya toast to Galbi Stone, braised short ribs that come in several variations, each dish embodies the novel within the familiar, presenting out-of-the-box gastronomic ecstasy that evokes fresh new tastes while still retaining the very essence of the original flavor.

이타닉 가든
EATANIC GARDEN

컨템퍼러리 •
Contemporary

02-727-7610

강남구 테헤란로 231, 조선팰리스 호텔 36층

36F Josun Palace Hotel, 231 Teheran-ro, Gangnam-gu

www.eatanicgarden.com

■ 가 격 PRICE: ₩₩₩₩

'이타닉 가든'의 '식물원'은 '심을 식(植)' 자가 아닌 '먹을 식(食)' 자를 사용한다.그 이름처럼 아름다운 도심 속 화원 같은 공간에서 새로운 한국식 음식을 창조적으로 보여주는 곳이다. 오감으로 느끼는 식물원답게 메뉴판이 없는 대신, 주재료를 일러스트로 표현한 도감이 제공되어 눈과 귀를 동시에 만족시킨다. 라망시크레의 손종원 셰프가 주방을 맡아 발효와 숙성의 미학이 담긴 또 다른 한식을 기대해 볼 만하다. 36층에서 내려다보이는 도심뷰를 즐길 수 있는 커플석도 마련되어 있으니 예약은 필수다.

Eatanic Garden is a wordplay since, amusingly, both “botanic garden” and “eatanic garden” are pronounced the same way in Korean. As the name suggests, the space evokes a beautiful urban garden that awakens the five senses. There is no menu here; instead, you'll receive an illustrated guide depicting the main ingredients. Chef Son Jong-won, who is also the head chef at L'Amant Secret, helms the kitchen, reinventing Korean food with a creative twist and reflecting the aesthetics of fermentation and aging. Eatanic Garden offers seats for couples providing a commanding view of the cityscape from the 36th floor.

익스퀴진

EXQUISINE

장경원 셰프의 익스퀴진. 최대한 한국적인 재료를 사용하고 재료 각각의 개성에 초점을 맞춰 새로운 맛을 창조하고자 하는 셰프의 실험 정신이 그의 요리에 그대로 묻어난다. 레스토랑 내에서 직접 재배한 허브와 산지 직거래로 공급받는 싱싱한 재료로 만든 음식을 합리적인 가격에 제공한다. 점심 코스 메뉴와 저녁 코스 메뉴가 한 가지씩 준비되어 있고, 식재료나 주방 사정에 따라 메뉴가 수시로 변경된다. 공간이 아담한 만큼 예약은 필수다.

Chef Jang Kyung-won at Exquisine has a knack for reinventing flavors. His creativity is driven by his knowledge of local ingredients and understanding of the balance between each component, which leads to dishes that are ultimately his own invention. The restaurant offers a single course menu for lunch and dinner that changes frequently depending on the availability of ingredients. The fresh herbs are from the restaurant's garden. The space is small so make sure you call ahead to reserve a table.

컨템퍼러리 • *Contemporary*

02-542-6921

강남구 삼성로 140길 6

6 Samseong-ro 140-gil, Gangnam-gu

■ 가 격 PRICE: ₩₩₩

GANGNAM-GU

하네
HANE

스시 • Sushi

010-9773-0887

강남구 언주로 172길 14

14 Eonju-ro 172-gil, Gangnam-gu

■ 가 격 PRICE: ₩₩₩₩

계절의 순리를 따르는 우수한 자연산 식재료를 맛본다는 건 미식의 큰 즐거움 중 하나이다. 자연산 식재료 사용을 고집하는 최주용 셰프의 스타일이 잘 구현된 '스시 하네'가 그런 즐거움을 만끽할 수 있는 레스토랑이다. 스시 하네에서는 재료의 선별부터 고객에게 스시 한 점을 건네는 일까지, 일련의 과정에서 셰프의 의도가 느껴지지만 요리 자체만으로도 특유의 매력을 즐기기에 충분하다. 전통적 소재들을 현대적으로 표현한 세련되고 고급스러운 다이닝 공간에서 즐기는 스시는 무척 즐거운 다이닝 경험이다.

When it comes to gastronomy, savoring the freshest natural ingredients that capture the essence of the season is undoubtedly one of the greatest delights. At Sushi Hane, Chef Choi Ju-yong's quest for natural ingredients is well reflected and can be fully appreciated. When making sushi, he focuses on bringing out the inherent flavor of each product and recreating authentic tastes. The fare itself exudes a unique charm during the entire culinary process – from selecting ingredients to serving sushi to patrons – and genuinely reflects the chef's gastronomic beliefs. Relishing this food in an elegant fine dining space decorated with modern interpretations of traditional materials also adds to the overall allure.

게방식당
GEBANGSIKDANG

흡사 소담한 카페테리아나 베이커리를 연상시키는 외관과는 달리 이곳은 게장 전문점이다. 패션 마케터 방건혁 대표와 25년간 게장 전문점을 운영해온 부모님의 합작으로 탄생한 게방식당에선 게장이라는 한식 메뉴를 보다 다양한 고객층에게 선보이고자 노력한다. 이곳엔 간장게장과 양념게장 세트뿐만 아니라 좀 더 먹기 수월한 게알 백반, 전복장 백반, 새우장 백반까지 다양한 메뉴가 준비되어 있다. 세트에는 기본적으로 밥과 국, 기본 반찬을 함께 제공하며, 테이크아웃도 가능하다.

Soy sauce-marinated crab and stylish décor don't always go hand in hand, but at Gebangsikdang, they do. A collaboration between fashion marketer Bang Geon-hyuk and his parents, veterans of the soy sauce marinated crab restaurant business, Gebangsikdang caters to a trend-conscious crowd with its polished interior and its wide selection of raw crab dishes. For those who find it bothersome to eat crab on the shell, there are options that come with just the crab flesh and crab roe on a mound of hot rice.

게장 • *Gejang*

010-8479-1107

강남구 선릉로 131길 17

17 Seolleung-ro 131-gil, Gangnam-gu

www.gebangsikdang.com

■ **가 격 PRICE: ₩**

강남구

곰탕랩 N
GOMTANG LAB

곰탕 • Gomtang

02-517-4656

강남구 도산대로 153

153 Dosan-daero, Gangnam-gu

■ 가 격 PRICE: ₩

곰탕랩은 그 이름처럼 곰탕을 연구하고 다양한 조리법을 개발하는 곳이다. 임정식 셰프는 평화옥 시절부터 국물 연구에 줄곧 매진해 왔다. 사골과 스지, 우족, 꼬리를 10시간 넘게 고아 걸쭉하게 만든 콜라겐 사골 곰탕이 그의 시그니처 메뉴이다. 먹고 나면 콜라겐의 점성이 입술에서 꾸덕꾸덕하게 느껴지는 게 특징이다. 식감이 쫄깃하고 부드러운 고기와 밑간이 잘 된 국물이 한 끼 식사로 제격이다. 고기만 넣은 맑은 고기곰탕과 매운 양곰탕 등 메뉴 선택의 폭도 넓다. 콜라겐 사골 곰탕은 하루 20그릇만 판매하니 개점 시간에 맞춰 방문하기를 추천한다.

True to its name, Gomtang Lab is dedicated to studying gomtang (beef bone soup) and developing diverse new recipes. Chef Yim Jung-sik has relentlessly pursued this culinary journey since the days when he helmed Pyeonghwaok. His signature dish is collagen beef bone soup, made by simmering beef leg bones, tendons, feet and oxtail for more than 10 hours until thick. Once you finish the bowl brimming with chewy, tender meat and savory broth that make a perfect meal, you'll find your lips sticky with gelatinous collagen. To cater to different tastes, the menu offers several variations of gomtang, including a clear, meat-only version and a spicy version with added beef tripe. One last note: The signature soup is limited to only 20 bowls per day, so be sure to visit when the eatery opens.

만두집

MANDUJIP

고급 레스토랑이 즐비한 청담동 근방에서 30년 동안 만두 하나로 외길을 걸어온 만두집. 소박하고 정갈한 평안도 스타일의 만둣국이 이 집의 대표 메뉴로, 레스토랑의 내부 또한 아담하고 깔끔하다. 돌아가신 어머니의 가업을 계승한 현 대표는 많은 이들의 사랑을 받았던 어머니의 손맛을 묵묵히 지켜내고 있다. 정성 들여 빚은 이곳의 만둣국은 깔끔하면서도 감칠맛 나는 양지머리를 삶은 육수에 매콤한 양념을 얹어 내므로 혹 매운맛을 선호하지 않는다면 주문 시 양념을 빼달라고 부탁하면 된다.

Located in a trendsetting part of the city dominated by state-of-the-art fashion, this restaurant has stood its ground for 30 years with a humble dish that has wooed the palates of countless people — dumpling soup. Mandujip specializes in Pyeongando-style dumplings, filled with minced beef, bean curd, mung bean sprouts, green onions and sesame oil. Each order comes with six large dumplings in a clear, flavorful beef broth made with chunks of brisket.

만두 • *Mandu*

02-544-3710

강남구 압구정로 338

338 Apgujeong-ro, Gangnam-gu

■ 가 격 PRICE: ₩

국수 • Noodles

050-71449-8878

강남구 선릉로 805

805 Seolleung-ro, Gangnam-gu

■ 가격 PRICE: ₩

면서울 N

MYEON SEOUL

김도윤 셰프가 윤서울에 이어 두 번째로 문을 연 공간이다. 윤서울에서 선보였던 자가 제면 요리를 따로 판매해 달라는 요청에 따라 오픈한 곳이다. 화학 첨가물 없이 통밀과 녹두, 백태만으로 면을 뽑는데 최적의 조합을 위해 국내산과 프랑스산, 터키산 통밀을 섞어 사용한다. 신선하고 고소한 면의 맛을 오롯이 느낄 수 있는 들기름면 외에 알싸한 양념의 비빔면, 고사리와 들깨로 맛을 낸 고사리면도 일품이다. 반주로 판매하는 전통주도 한 잔 곁들이기를 추천한다.

Myeon Seoul is Chef Kim Do-yun's second restaurant following the success of his Yun Seoul. The inspiration came from a stream of customer requests at the original spot for a separate offering of its housemade noodles, which are made exclusively with whole wheat, mung bean, dried pollack, and without chemical additives. For a perfect flavor composition, the chef blends whole wheat varieties sourced from Korea, France and Turkey. Highlights include perilla oil noodles imbued with fresh, nutty flavors; spicy noodles glazed with a piquant sauce; and bracken whole wheat noodles flavored with bracken and perilla seeds. Also recommended is a pairing of traditional Korean alcohol sold as an accompaniment.

강남구

현우동

HYUN UDON

삼전동 시절 이미 유명세를 떨쳤던 우동의 달인 박상현 셰프의 논현동 우동 전문점 겸 제면소. 통통한 우동 면발을 한입 가득 베어 물면 매끈하면서도 탄력 있는 사리의 기분 좋은 식감과 씹을수록 은은하게 퍼지는 단맛을 동시에 즐길 수 있다. '현우동'의 대표 메뉴는 '덴푸라 붓카케' 우동이다. 굵직하고 탱탱한 면발과 갓 튀겨 낸 바삭하고 폭신한 튀김이 감칠맛 가득하면서도 섬세한 쯔유와 절묘한 조화를 이룬다.

Chef Park Sang-hyeon is a well-respected master of the udon craft. At his Nonhyeon-dong location, Park continues to serve up bowls of thick, silky-smooth, home-made udon noodles with their characteristic firmness and elasticity. If you're unsure of what to order, go for his signature tempura bukkake udon. The plump bouncy noodles and the freshly fried light crispy tempura make for a delicious mouthful when dipped in the umami-rich tsuyu sauce.

우동 • *Udon*

02-515-3622

강남구 논현로 149길 53

53 Nonhyeon-ro 149-gil, Gangnam-gu

■ 가격 PRICE: ₩

GANGNAM-GU

강남구

가겐 바이 최준호 N

GAGGEN BY CHOI JUNHO

일식 • *Japanese*

02-542-0176

강남구 압구정로 80길 19-1, 2층

2F, 19-1 Apgujeong-ro 80-gil, Gangnam-gu

www.youtube.com/@gaggen_seoul

■ 가격 PRICE: ₩₩₩₩

'가겐'이라는 상호는 최현아, 원진희 부부의 이름에서 각각 '아(雅)'와 '원(元)'을 조합해 일본어로 표기한 것이다. 원진희 셰프는 '쿠로기'에서, 최현아 셰프는 '칸다'에서 경력을 쌓았다. 가겐의 요리는 일식 특유의 계절감을 뚜렷이 느낄 수 있다는 점이 특징이다. 쿠로기에서 전수한 소면, 볶은 깨를 바로 빻아 향이 풍부한 깨 무침, 고사리 전분으로 만든 와라비 모치처럼 흔치 않은 요리들이 오감을 즐겁게 한다. 셰프의 자세한 설명이 음식에 대한 이해를 돕고 따뜻한 접객 서비스는 식사의 즐거움을 더한다.

Gaggen is a portmanteau of the Chinese characters "雅" (a) and "元" (won) pronounced Japanese-style (ga, gen). Each character is a syllable from the names of the chef couple Choi Hyun-a and Won Jin-hui, who received culinary training in Japan at the noted Tokyo restaurants Kanda and Kurogi, respectively. Seasonality, a core characteristic of Japanese cuisine, is what clearly defines Gaggen's menu. Rare gems, including Kurogi-style somen noodles, aromatic dishes featuring freshly roasted and ground sesame seeds, and warabi mochi made with bracken starch, are a treat to the senses. Accompanied by detailed informative explanations by the chefs and their hospitality, dining here is a pure delight.

곰바위

GOM BA WIE

1983년, 삼성동 봉은사 인근에 소규모로 시작한 곰바위는 질 좋은 한우의 양과 대창구이를 전문으로 하는 곳이다. 현재는 본관 뒤편에 3층 규모의 신관이 자리하고 있어 레스토랑의 과거와 현재 모습을 한눈에 알 수 있다. 고소한 풍미와 쫄깃한 식감이 별미인 특양구이와 대창구이 외에도 꽃등심, 갈비, 차돌박이 등 다양한 부위의 한우를 함께 맛볼 수 있다. 수작업으로 정성스레 손질한 양과 대창은 참숯에 구워 깊은 풍미를 지니고 있다. 내부는 늘 분주하지만 깔끔하고 기능적인 것이 특징이다.

Grilled tripe and large intestines reign supreme at Gom Ba Wie, which has seen three decades of customers hooked on their buttery, pleasantly chewy goodness. The original location and the new location stand back to back, offering a glimpse of the restaurant's past and present. If beef intestines aren't your cup of tea, the restaurant also offers other cuts like ribeye, short ribs and brisket. All meats are grilled over wood charcoal.

바비큐 • *Barbecue*

02-511-0068

강남구 영동대로 115길 10

10 Yeongdong-daero 115-gil, Gangnam-gu

www.gbw.co.kr

■ **가 격 PRICE: ₩₩**

프렌치 • French

02-517-6034
강남구 도산대로 59길 16
16 Dosan-daero 59-gil,
Gangnam-gu

■ 가격 PRICE: ₩₩₩

레스쁘아 뒤 이부

L'ESPOIR DU HIBOU

정통 프렌치 비스트로인 레스쁘아 뒤 이부는 유행에 흔들리지 않는 클래식 프렌치 메뉴로 꾸준한 사랑을 받아왔다. 한결같이 진중한 음식을 선보여온 임기학 셰프는 테린과 파테 등 한국인들에겐 다소 생소한 프랑스 전통 숙성 육가공 제품도 직접 만들어 소개하고 있다. 오리 콩피와 양파 수프 역시 이곳을 대표하는 메뉴다. 프랑스에서 먹는 음식과 별다를 것 없는 프렌치 요리를 대접하고 싶다는 임 셰프. 날씨 좋은 계절엔 프랑스 분위기가 물씬 풍기는 아름다운 테라스에 앉을 것을 추천한다.

All of the elements at this bistro — from the food to the décor to the outdoor patio — fall into place to create an ambience that is immediately charming and oh so French! Consistency has been key to L'Espoir du Hibou's longevity, not least when it comes to food. Chef Lim Ki-hak makes traditional French charcuterie like terrines and pâtés from scratch. The onion soup is outstanding, as is the classic duck confit. Terrace dining is a must during the warmer months.

레스토랑 오와이

RESTAURANT OY

한적한 주거 지역 골목 한 켠에 위치한 '레스토랑 오와이'는 차분한 느낌의 외관부터가 동네의 분위기와 이질감 없이 잘 어우러진다. 프렌치 퀴진에 대한 열정과 애정으로 한국과 프랑스에서 짧지 않은 시간을 요리사로 일해 온 부부가 운영하는 레스토랑이다. 화려함보다는 진중함과 안정감이 어울리는 이곳의 셰프들은 클래식과 모던의 경계를 자유롭게 넘나드는 요리로 정통을 표현해낸다. 식재료에 대한 높은 이해에서 나오는 조리의 정확성과 뚜렷하고 깊이 있는 요리의 맛을 경험해 보기 바란다.

Nestled in a quiet residential alley, Restaurant OY has a homey façade that befits the ambience of the neighborhood. Run by a chef couple who have spent much of their time in Korea and France dedicated to pursuing their passion for French cuisine, this establishment serves up classy and comforting dishes rather than elaborate arrangements. Blurring the boundaries between the traditional and the modern, the cuisine still remains true to authentic tastes. Their sophisticated understanding of ingredients and precise cooking skills result in dishes with well-defined tastes and depth of flavor. In short, diners can expect culinary gems that consistently satisfy.

프렌치 • French

02-515-7250

강남구 선릉로 148길 48-12, 지하 1층

B1F, 48-12 Seolleung-ro 148-gil, Gangnam-gu

www.restaurantoy.co.kr

■ **가 격 PRICE: ₩₩₩₩**

류니끄
RYUNIQUE

이노베이티브 • *Innovative*

02-546-9279

강남구 도산대로 45길 8-1

8-1 Dosan-daero 45-gil, Gangnam-gu

www.ryunique.co.kr

■ 가 격 PRICE: ₩₩₩₩

류니끄는 2011년 오픈한 이후 식재료에 대한 연구와 해석에 공을 들여온 류태환 셰프의 창의적인 요리와 함께 성장해 왔다. 셰프는 절기와 계절의 변화에 맞춰 메뉴를 구성하고, 계절과 생산 지역에 따라 달라지는 식재료를 다루는 데 집중한다. 자신의 무한한 상상력을 요리에 반영할 줄 아는 셰프의 능력이 류니끄의 요리가 가진 독특한 매력의 비결이다. 단정하면서도 모던한 다이닝 공간은 1층의 셰프 연구실과 2층의 레스토랑으로 구분되어 있다. 참신함을 놓치지 않으면서도 맛에 대한 상상력을 자극하는 류니끄의 요리에는 특별한 즐거움이 있다.

Since its opening in 2011, Ryunique has been constantly reinventing the art of cuisine, driven by Chef Ryu Tae-hwan's independent research and creative interpretation of ingredients. The chef continually updates the menu to reflect the solar term and season, with an emphasis on fresh ingredients that vary by season and source. His talent for turning his unbounded gastronomic imagination into reality is the secret to Ryunique's unique fare. Remarkably, this tidy and modern space is home to both the chef's research center (first floor) and a dining area (second floor). All in all, there is something special about Ryunique's cuisine that sparks our culinary imagination while never losing its freshness or charm.

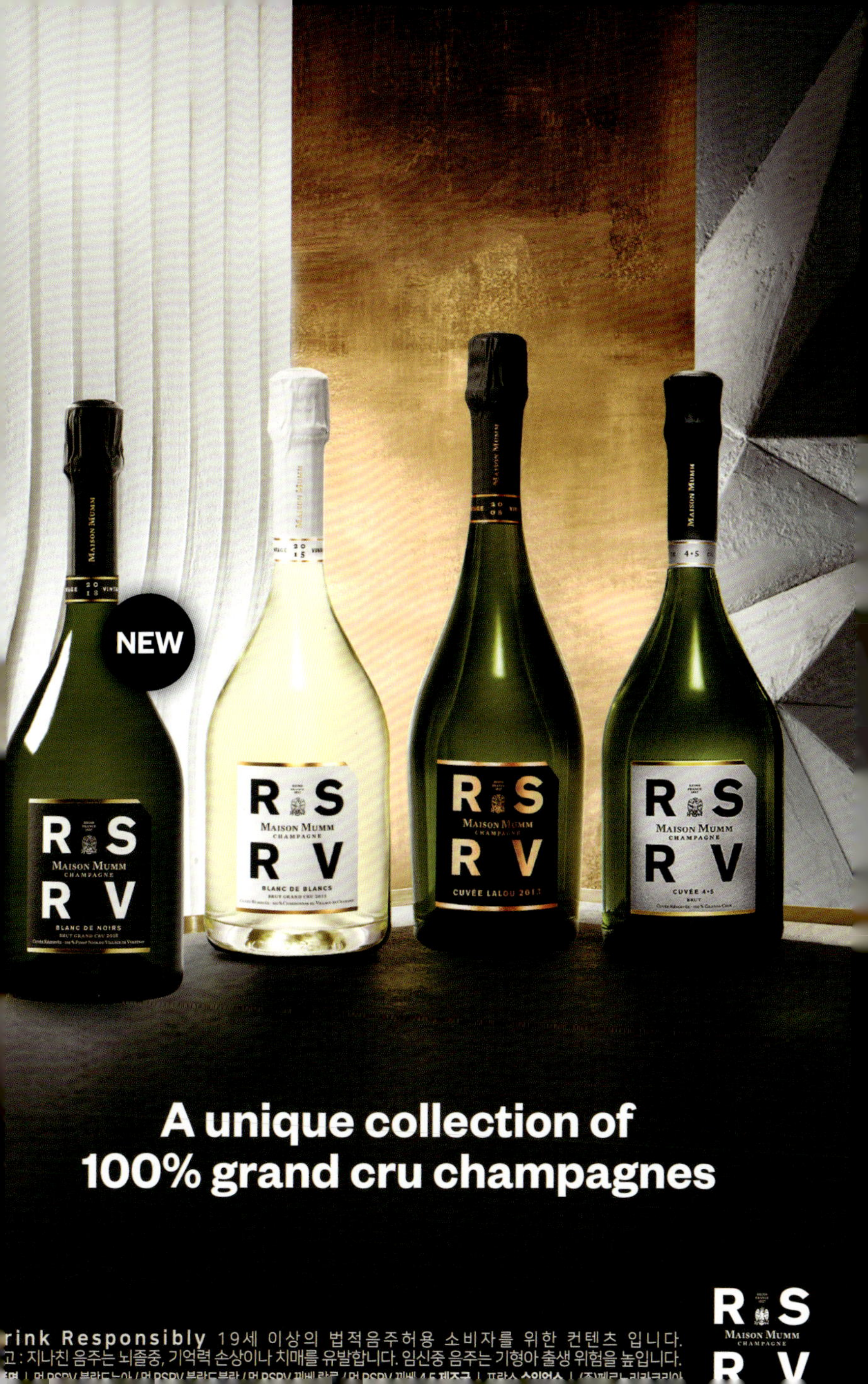
NEW
R S
MAISON MUMM
CHAMPAGNE
R V
BLANC DE NOIRS
BLANC DE BLANCS
CUVÉE LALOU 2013
CUVÉE 4·5
BRUT
A unique collection of
100% grand cru champagnes
rink Responsibly 19세 이상의 법적음주허용 소비자를 위한 컨텐츠 입니다.
고 : 지나친 음주는 뇌졸중, 기억력 손상이나 치매를 유발합니다. 임신중 음주는 기형아 출생 위험을 높입니다.

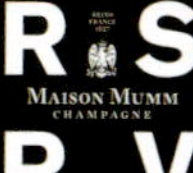

르오뇽
L'OIGNON

가로수길의 한적한 골목에 위치한 르오뇽. 프랑스어로 '양파'라는 뜻의 이곳은 프렌치 요리를 베이스로 페스코 베지테리언용 음식, 즉 육류를 빼고 생선과 난류, 유제품만 사용해 만든 음식을 선보인다. 환경과 동물 복지에 관심이 높은 셰프가 본인이 직접 실천 중인 식단을 손님들과 나누기 위해 오픈했다. 깊은 맛을 내는 육수는 버섯과 채수를 이용하고, 케이크는 밀가루 대신 콜리플라워와 페코리노 치즈로 식감을 내지만 깊은 맛과 감칠맛이 진하게 나와 육류나 밀가루를 대체하기에 모자람이 없다. 비건 또는 베지테리언 식단에 관심이 있다면 이곳에서 페스코 베지테리언 식단부터 가볍게 경험해 보면 어떨까?

프렌치 • French

010-9033-9187

강남구 압구정로 4길 13-4

13-4, Apgujoeng-ro 4-gil, Gangnam-gu

■ **가 격 PRICE: ₩₩₩**

Nestled in a quiet alley within the ultra-trendy Garosu-gil district, L'Oignon, which means "the onion" in French, is a French-based pescatarian restaurant that offers dishes made only with vegetables, fish, eggs and dairy products. With a steadfast dedication to the principles of ecological harmony and compassionate treatment of animals, the chef opened this eatery with the intention of imparting to patrons the wholesome sustenance he himself reveres. The kitchen uses vegetable broth with mushrooms as a substitute for rich meat broth and creates the texture of its cakes using cauliflower and pecorino cheese instead of flour. Yet, the umami flavors and textures produced through these novel means are as deep and as luscious as those concocted by conventional recipes. If the allure of a plant-based diet beckons, why not indulge in the captivating flavors of L'Oignon's pescatarian fare?

리알토 N

RIALTO

이탤리언 • *Italian*

02-544-4761

강남구 삼성로 149길 13, 2층

2F, 13 Samseong-ro 149-gil, Gangnam-gu

■ **가 격 PRICE: ₩₩**

안티파스티를 단출하게 제공하고 프리미에 집중하는 메뉴 구성은 최근 몇 년 새 서울의 이탈리안 다이닝을 특징짓는 트렌드이다. 이곳 역시 메뉴 구성은 간소하지만 '리알토(Rialto)'라는 상호에 담고자 한 셰프의 요리 철학에 그만의 감각과 스타일이 합쳐져 이곳만의 독특한 요리를 경험할 수 있다. 특히 버터와 치즈의 절묘한 조화가 깊은 맛을 자아내는 따야린과 카치오 에 페페가 일품이다. 다양하게 준비된 다른 파스타 메뉴들도 소스의 밸런스가 훌륭하다. 알타리무 피클 역시 추억의 맛을 소환하는 리알토만의 비장의 무기이다.

Over the past few years, a streamlined selection of antipasti, paired with a focus on primi dishes, has been an overarching trend across Seoul's Italian dining landscape. In line with the trend, this fine diner offers a simple menu while remaining true to its northern Italian roots, as highlighted by the name "Rialto," and to the chef's unique culinary philosophy, sensibilities and style. Winning dishes include tajarin and cacio e pepe, deeply flavored with a beguiling harmony of butter and cheese. The kitchen's other pastas flaunt an equally excellent balance of sauce flavors. Pickled ponytail radish is yet another standout that evokes the endearing flavors of our memories.

마테르

MATER

김영빈 셰프는 발효라는 요리 기법을 중심으로, 자신이 먹고 자란 한식 요리와 아시안 요리, 그리고 셰프로서 경험한 웨스턴 퀴진과 노르딕 퀴진을 자유롭게 재해석한 요리를 마테르에서 선보이고 있다. 그는 발효를 통해 식재료의 풍미와 식감에 독특한 변화를 입히고 이렇게 완성된 식재료를 때로는 섬세하게 때로는 강렬하게 요리에 활용함으로써 발효의 풍미를 다채롭게 표현한다. 이러한 시도에서 산미와 감칠맛을 조화시키려는 셰프의 의도와 노력을 엿볼 수 있다. 발효 식품을 일상적으로 즐기는 한국에서 발효 음식의 다양한 묘미를 표현하고 맛의 조화를 꾀하고자 하는 마테르의 여러 시도가 무척 흥미롭다.

컨템퍼러리 • *Contemporary*

02-518-5879

강남구 언주로 154길 16 지하 1층

B1F, 16 Eonju-ro 154-gil, Gangnam-gu

■ 가 격 PRICE: ₩₩

With the focus on fermentation, Chef Kim Yeong-bin brings together the Korean and Asian cuisines he grew up with and the Western and Nordic cuisines he has been exploring as a chef, creating dishes bursting with unbridled imagination. Through the process of fermentation, the chef adds a unique twist to the flavor and texture of his ingredients, which are then exploited, sometimes subtly and at other times vigorously, for resonant and diverse expressions of fermented flavors. Such attempts reveal the kitchen's intent and efforts to balance sour and umami taste profiles. Since Korea is where fermented foods are regular staples, it is all the more intriguing to witness Mater's series of gastronomic experiments aimed at balancing the tastes and expressing the varied flavors of fermented dishes.

소바 • *Soba*

070-4233-5466

강남구 강남대로 160길 29

29 Gangnam-daero 160-gil, Gangnam-gu

■ **가 격 PRICE: ₩**

미미 면가

MIMI MYEONGA

재치 있는 소바 요리로 손님들의 발길이 끊이지 않는 미미 면가. 이곳의 메밀 면은 쫄깃한 식감을 자랑하는데, 메밀 함량 3할이라는 파격적인 비율 덕분이다. 그럼에도 불구하고 메밀의 구수한 풍미가 살아 있는 것을 보면 장승우 셰프의 노력과 고민의 흔적이 엿보인다. 이곳은 기본이 탄탄한 자루소바 외에도 형식에 구애받지 않는 다양한 메뉴가 인상적이다. 국수 한 그릇의 온도, 국물과 고명에 따라 각각의 개성이 뚜렷한 소바 요리를 즐기고 싶다면 미미 면가로 향하자.

Mimi Myeonga is a local favorite, sought after by lovers of buckwheat noodles. Made in-house with an unconventional ratio of only three parts buckwheat, Chef Jang Seung-woo's noodles have an undeniably chewy texture, while still maintaining the subtle nutty fragrance of buckwheat. There is something for everyone on the menu; in addition to the basic zaru soba, customers can choose from a list of soba dishes that are served hot or cold, featuring different broths and toppings that always hit the spot.

보름쇠

BOREUMSAE

2015년 10월에 오픈한 보름쇠는 서울에선 그리 알려지지 않은 제주산 흑우를 제공하는 소고기 전문점이다. 이곳에서 운영하는 제주 농장에서 고기를 직접 공수하는데 등심과 안심, 안창살, 살치살, 생육회, 양지머리 등 취향에 따라 다양한 부위를 즐길 수 있다. 제주 농장에서 항공편으로 직배송하는 흑우인 까닭에 품질에 대한 자부심과 신뢰도가 남다르다. 한편, 식사 공간은 1층의 현대적인 다이닝 홀과 2층의 12개 개별 룸으로 구성되어 있다.

Beef restaurants are ubiquitous all over Korea, but this spot which opened in late 2015, offers something prized and uncommon: Jeju black cattle. Choose from a wide range of cuts including sirloin, tenderloin, chuck tail flap, outside skirt steak, brisket and two types of raw beef dishes: tartare and sashimi. The prime meat is flown in directly from the family-operated farm. Private rooms are available on the second floor.

바비큐 • *Barbecue*

02-569-9967

강남구 테헤란로 81길 36

36 Teheran-ro 81-gil, Gangnam-gu

■ 가격 PRICE: ₩₩

스테이크하우스 •
Steakhouse

02-544-9235

강남구 압구정로 72길 22, 2층

2F, 22 Apgujeong-ro 72-gil, Gangnam-gu

www.vaultsteakhouse.co.kr

■ 가격 PRICE: ₩₩₩₩

볼트 스테이크하우스

VAULT STEAKHOUSE

볼트 스테이크하우스는 인테리어에서부터 맛과 품질에 이르기까지 미국식 정통 스테이크 하우스를 표방한다. 미국 농무부가 인증한 프라임육 중에서도 항생제와 성장호르몬을 주입하지 않은 소고기만을 엄선해 사용하므로 품질에 대한 신뢰도가 높은 곳이기도 하다. 28일과 14일간 건조 숙성시킨 스테이크가 주메뉴로, 다양한 소고기 부위를 제공한다.

The dimly lit masculine décor and a comprehensive whiskey collection with nearly 400 bottles to choose from make Vault0one of the most sought-after whiskey bars in Seoul. Right above it is the American-style Vault Steakhouse where premium USDA-approved American beef free of antibiotics and hormones is dry-aged for 14 and 28 days. Available cuts include T-bone, L-bone, bone-in ribeye, filet mignon, New York strip and boneless ribeye.

봉밀가

BONGMILGA

2007년부터 레스토랑 운영을 해온 권희승 셰프는 본인이 가장 즐겨 먹는 메밀 면에 대한 열정으로 지금의 봉밀가를 오픈했다. 기라성같이 훌륭한 냉면집들에 '시간과 정성이 들어간 요리'로 도전하고 싶다는 권 셰프는 그 누구보다 재료 준비에 많은 시간을 투자한다. 한우 양지머리, 설깃살, 한약재 등을 이용하여 5시간 동안 끓여낸 순수한 육수만을 사용하고 타 냉면집보다 굵은 면발을 만들어 낸다. '냉면' 대신 '평양 메밀 물국수'라는 이름을 사용하는 것도 봉밀가만의 특징이다.

This restaurant is a relative newcomer to Seoul's Pyeongyang cold buckwheat noodle scene but Chef Kwon Hee-seung's passion for serving authentic bowls of cold buckwheat noodles more than makes up for its short history. Kwon begins each day by preparing the broth for the cold noodles, using cuts from local beef such as brisket, flank and round. He also throws in some medicinal herbs for good measure. Kwon's noodles are made of 80% buckwheat flour, 20% sweet potato starch and are thicker than the versions served at most of its competitors.

냉면 • *Naengmyeon*

02-546-2305

강남구 선릉로 664

664 Seolleung-ro, Gangnam-gu

www.bongmilga80.modoo.at

■ 가 격 PRICE: ₩

강남구

비스트로 드 욘트빌

BISTROT DE YOUNTVILLE

프렌치 • *French*

02-541-1550

강남구 선릉로 158길 13-7

13-7 Seolleung-ro 158-gil, Gangnam-gu

■ 가 격 PRICE: ₩₩

클래식한 프렌치 비스트로를 그대로 옮겨 놓은 듯한 비스트로 드 욘트빌. 이곳의 편안하고 아늑한 분위기는 마치 프랑스 본토에 와 있는 듯한 착각에 빠져들게 한다. 기본에 충실한 타미 리 셰프와 박재형 셰프의 프랑스 요리는 그의 세심한 배려와 끊임없는 노력을 대변한다. 레스토랑의 이름도 캘리포니아 나파 밸리의 '프렌치 런드리' 레스토랑이 있었던 욘트빌 에서 따올 만큼 그곳에서 지낸 최고의 경험을 손님들에게도 선사하고 싶었다고. 그가 선사하는 맛있는 음식과 분위기를 음미하며 잠시 도심의 소란스러움을 잊어보는 것도 좋을 듯하다.

With its classic French bistro charm, Bistro de Yountville feels like a slice of France transported into the heart of the city. The cozy and inviting atmosphere evokes the essence of the French countryside, while the cuisine by Chefs Tommy Lee and Jae-hyung Park reflects their dedication to the fundamentals of French cooking, infused with meticulous care and unwavering effort. The restaurant's name pays homage to Yountville, the home of the famed French Laundry in California's Napa Valley, where the chefs were inspired to recreate their unforgettable experiences for diners. Savoring the thoughtfully prepared dishes and warm ambiance here offers a delightful escape from the hustle and bustle of city life.

산로 N

SANRO

050-6465-6292

강남구 도산대로 518, 2층

2F, 518 Dosan-daero, Gangnam-gu

■ **가 격 PRICE: ₩₩₩₩₩**

유성엽 셰프는 일식 요리사로서 체득한 조리 기술과 전통 일본 요리의 가치를 산로에서 구현하고 있다. 입구에 걸린 '산로(三露)'라고 적힌 족자는 손님맞이가 끝나면 입구에 물을 세 번 뿌리는 일본의 문화를 표현한 것이다. 공간 이곳저곳을 채우고 있는 섬세하고 세련된 작품들은 유성엽 셰프가 이 공간과 자신의 요리를 통해 전하고자 하는 분위기와 감성이 무엇인지를 잘 보여준다. 요리를 대하는 셰프의 마음과 세심한 조리 기술은 계절의 향을 담은 식재료와 만나 요리를 통해 맛으로 구체화된다. 산로는 무엇보다 식사하는 내내 이어지는 섬세한 풍미의 흐름이 압권이다. 단정함과 정갈함에 매력적인 풍미까지 갖춘 셰프의 와쇼쿠 요리만큼이나 접객 서비스 역시 흠잡을 데 없이 뛰어나다.

Chef Yoo Sung-yup's culinary mastery and dedication to washoku, or traditional Japanese cuisine, shine through at Sanro. The entrance greets diners with a hanging scroll that reads "三露," the name of this spot that expresses the Japanese practice of sprinkling the entrance with water three times after welcoming customers into an establishment. The nuanced and chic objets d'art adorning every corner are in sync with the vibes and sensibilities the chef seeks to convey through his menu and dining space. When refreshing seasonal ingredients meet his ardor for culinary art and sophisticated skills, what's born is a smorgasbord of subtle flavors that invariably soothes the palate throughout the meal. To top it off, the service here is as impeccable as the clean and refined flavors of the chef's washoku cuisine.

삼원가든

SAMWON GARDEN

바비큐 • *Barbecue*

02-548-3030

강남구 언주로 835

835 Eonju-ro, Gangnam-gu

www.samwongarden.com

■ 가 격 PRICE: ₩₩

한국식 바비큐 문화의 대중성과 고급성의 접합점을 절묘하게 찾아낸 전통있는 레스토랑이다. 새롭게 정비된 삼원가든은 최상급 한우의 부위별 식재료와 서비스 팀의 숙련된 그릴 스킬이 만나 안정된 접객 서비스를 제공한다. 여기에다 정성껏 조성한 아름다운 야외 가든, 한국적인 여백의 미가 깃든 높은 층고와 통유리로 디자인된 개방감 있는 다이닝 공간 등 무엇하나 부족함 없는 근사한 식사 환경을 선사한다. 다양한 규모의 프라이빗 룸을 갖추고 있어 고객의 필요에 맞게 다양한 식사 모임이 가능하다. 지나온 시간 만큼 한국 전통의 맛과 고유의 바비큐 문화를 계승해 발전시키고 있는 삼원가든에서 즐거운 식사를 경험해 보자.

In the cultural landscape of Korean barbeque, Samwon Garden has long enjoyed fame based on its intricate balance between comfort and haute cuisine. It is where diverse cuts of prime Korean beef meet the seasoned grilling skills of its staff, a synergy that creates a delightful and comfortable gastronomic experience. What's more, a gorgeously landscaped outdoor garden, coupled with high ceilings and glass walls infused with the Korean aesthetics of empty space, adds a sense of openness to this gracious dining. Its various private dining rooms cater to a variety of communal dining needs. For several decades, Samwon Garden has transformed Korean barbeque culture while carrying on the country's culinary tradition. Visit this culinary landmark and enjoy a meal loaded with great traditional flavors.

시오

SIIO

시오의 요리에는 틀과 규격에서 벗어난 자유분방함이 있다. 한 가지 요리에서 다양한 요리 문화와 기법들이 엿보이고 그것들이 서로 어우러져 새로움을 표현하기 때문이다. 그럼에도 그 자유분방함과 새로움 속에는 한국의 사계절과 다양한 절기를 반영한 식재료 선정과 맛의 조화를 염두에 둔 셰프만의 꼼꼼한 규칙들이 존재한다. 주방을 이끄는 셰프의 경험이 온전히 녹아 있는 시오의 창의적인 요리는, 계절감이 담긴 한국의 제철 식재료와 어우러져 매력적인 맛을 고객들에게 선사한다.

At SIIO, the head chef's experience is seen in imaginative dishes featuring seasonal Korean ingredients, ready to delight diners with sumptuous flavors. SIIO's fare breaks free from the mold and embraces freedom of expression. At this fine diner, novel dishes represent a melting pot of culinary cultures and techniques. Yet, under the veneer of this freewheeling, fresh take on food lies the careful selection of ingredients that reflect Korea's four distinct seasons. Meticulous rules dictate the perfect balance of subtle flavors.

컨템퍼러리 •
Contemporary

02-6013-5110

강남구 도산대로 54길 33
33 Dosan-daero 54-gil, Gangnam-gu

■ 가격 PRICE: ₩₩₩

컨템퍼러리 • *Contemporary*

010-3015-3869

강남구 도산대로 49길 8, 2층

2F, 8 Dosan-daero 49-gil, Gangnam-gu

■ 가 격 PRICE: ₩₩₩

알고리즘

AELGERIZM

양민우 셰프는 요리와 함께한 일본에서의 다양한 경험과 삶을 알고리즘의 요리에 반영하여, 일식을 기반으로 하지만 그 문턱을 낮춰 양식과의 다양한 조합을 시도함으로써 완성도 높고 균형 잡힌 요리를 추구한다. 한국의 사계절을 반영한 연중 4번의 메뉴 변경은 앞선 계절과의 유기적인 연결성을 고려하고, 식재료 본연의 풍미가 돋보이면서 소스와의 균형 있는 맛의 조화를 고려한 메뉴를 만들어내고 있다. 계절별로 변화하는 알고리즘의 모던 퀴진에서 일식과 양식이 조합된 요리의 다양한 변주를 즐겨 보기 바란다.

Aelgerizm's Japan-meets-West modern cuisine will delight your palate with delicate seasonable variations on a theme. The food is inspired by Chef Yang Min-woo's rich culinary and life experience in Japan. He blurs the boundaries of his brand of Japanese cuisine through the inventive use of Western ingredients, always seeking to maintain the right balance to achieve culinary perfection. The menu changes four times a year, reflecting Korea's four distinct seasons, with each seasonal menu organically related to the preceding one. Each dish brings out the genuine flavors of the ingredients, then delicately balanced with the sauces.

에빠뉘

EPANOUI

프렌치 • *French*

02-548-2020

강남구 선릉로 146길 33, 3층

3F, 33 Seolleung-ro 146-gil, Gangnam-gu

■ **가 격 PRICE: ₩₩₩**

프랑스어로 '만개하다', '꽃이 피어오르다'를 뜻하는 '에빠뉘'. 청담동 뒷골목에 위치한 이곳은 3개월 주기로 새로운 작가들의 작품을 벽에 전시한다. 그 덕분에 마치 갤러리 같은 느낌의 공간에서 섬세하고 아름다운 맛의 프렌치 요리를 경험할 수 있다. 특히, 부드러운 샴페인 바닐라 소스와의 조합이 인상적인 랍스터와 라비올리, 바삭한 크런치에 둘러싸인 푸아그라 마브레는 이곳의 대표 메뉴. 플레이팅도 그림을 보는 것같이 섬세하고 인상적이다. 조화로운 맛과 플레이팅을 중요시한다는 권지훈 셰프가 세심하게 준비한 음식이 눈과 입을 만족시킬 것이다.

As if to prove its etymological origin, Épanoui (which means "Flourished" in French) adorns its walls with novel artists' paintings every three months, thereby imbuing this nice little back alley establishment in Cheongdam-dong with a gallery-like ambience befitting its sensitive, beautifully crafted French cuisine. The kitchen team's signature dishes include lobster ravioli in a mellow champagne-vanilla sauce; and foie gras marbré surrounded by crunchy bread crumbs. Perhaps as a nod to the restaurant's artwork, the presentations are also delicate and vibrant. Chef Kwon Ji-hun's pursuit of balanced flavors and elevated plating will delight your eyes and your palate.

엘픽

ELPIC

스테이크하우스 • *Steakhouse*

010-6556-9757

강남구 도산대로 78길 25

25 Dosan-daero 78-gil, Gangnam-gu

■ 가 격 PRICE: ₩₩₩

제주에서 그릴 하우스로 유명했던 엘픽이 서울로 자리를 옮겼다. 드라이 에이징, 웻 에이징 및 밀랍을 이용한 숙성 스테이크를 선보이는 스테이크 하우스이지만 제주에서 올라오는 신선한 제철 오징어 구이나 세비체 요리도 맛볼 수 있다. 고기를 굽는 방식이 독특한데 저온의 숯불에서 구웠다 식히는 과정을 30분 이상 반복하여 질감의 부드러움과 육즙의 풍부함을 극대화한다. 고기 색이 붉어 보이지만 아주 잘 익은 상태다. 와인과 함께 곁들여 드시는 걸 추천한다.

El Pic, once a famed grill house on Jeju Island, has found its new home in Seoul. Although dry-aged, wet-aged and beeswax-aged beef steaks are signature dishes at this steakhouse, its grilled fresh seasonal squid, caught in the waters off Jeju Island, and ceviche are pleasant surprises as well. The way the steaks are grilled is extraordinary: They are cooked over charcoal at low temperature and cooled, with the process repeating for more than 30 minutes to maximize tenderness and juiciness. The sliced meat looks red, but is indeed cooked to perfection. Pair the meat with wine for additional gastronomic indulgence.

오프닝

OPNNG

'미식과 와인의 경험을 통해 새로운 취향을 연다'는 뜻의 오프닝. 와인바 혹은 레스토랑이라기보다 갤러리의 느낌이 강한 이곳은 아치 문양의 입구를 비롯해 유명한 작가들의 미술 작품, 넓은 공간에 펼쳐진 500여 종 이상의 와인셀러가 시선을 압도한다. 주요 디너 식사 시간인 1부에는 코스 요리를, 2부 시간부터는 단품 요리를 와인과 함께 즐길 수 있다. 다른 곳에서는 쉽게 찾을 수 없는 와인과 더불어 전체적인 분위기도 함께 즐겨 보시기를 바란다.

At OPNNG, delight your taste buds with hard-to-find rare wines while relishing the overall vibe. The name symbolizes "the opening up of new taste vistas through gastronomy and wine." Resembling more of a gallery than a wine bar or restaurant, this fine dining venue impresses patrons with an arch-shaped entrance, paintings by renowned artists, and a vast wine cellar that plays host to more than 500 different types of wine. It offers handmade pasta dishes and refined à la carte items.

컨템퍼러리 •
Contemporary

02-2088-5844

강남구 도산대로 34길 22, 지하 1층

B1, 22 Dosan-daero 34-gil, Gangnam-gu

www.baropnng.com

■ 가 격 PRICE: ₩₩₩

GANGNAM-GU

강남구

온

ON

프렌치 • *French*

02-547-0467

강남구 도산대로 92길 42, 지하 1층

B1F, 42 Dosan-daero 92-gil, Gangnam-gu

■ 가 격 PRICE: ₩₩₩

레스토랑 '온'. 이름에 담긴 뜻처럼 따뜻하고 편안한 음식을 대접하려는 셰프의 마음을 느낄 수 있는 곳이다. 다이닝 공간은 손님들의 프라이버시를 완벽히 보장할 수 있게 설계되었고, 테이블 두세 개가 전부이기 때문에 철저히 예약제로만 운영된다. 제철 프렌치 요리의 진수를 경험하기에 안성맞춤인 곳으로, 찰 토마토와 송이 토마토를 오븐에 건조하여 당도와 산미를 최대로 끌어올린 토마토와 루비 자몽이 '온'을 대표하는 채소 요리다.

The name may have changed from the previous Siot to the current On, but the food at this refined French restaurant retains its integrity. The elegant space is simple and intimate with just two or three tables, with the layout designed to guarantee the privacy of diners. Because there is limited seating, prior reservations are mandatory. On focuses on seasonal produce to prepare its signature offerings, including a vegetable dish that consists of ruby red grapefruit and two types of oven-dried tomatoes that highlight their exquisite sweetness and acidity.

옳음

OLH EUM

옳음은 '옳다' 혹은 '바르다'를 의미하는 우리말에서 따온 이름으로 '한결같이 정직한 음식을 만들겠다'는 서호영 셰프의 다짐이 반영되어 있는 곳이다. 식당을 운영하셨던 할머니와 부모님의 영향으로 요리를 시작한 그는 남도에서 부모님이 직접 농사지어 보내주시는 신선한 재료와 해외에서 익힌 경험을 바탕으로 장르의 경계를 넘나드는 창의적인 요리를 선보인다. 그중에서도 민물새우와 액젓, 된장으로 깊은 맛을 낸 '새우 성게장 비빔면'은 익숙한 재료에 본인만의 색깔을 입혀 새로운 맛을 끌어내는 서 셰프의 요리 스타일을 단적으로 보여주는 예라 할 수 있다.

Cooking honest food that respects the integrity of ingredients is the motto of Chef Seo Ho-young, who cooks with the freshest produce sent to him by his farmer parents. Transporting familiar flavors to new territories is his game. Take, for example, his shrimp and sea urchin capellini in a silky smooth bisque-like sauce made with freshwater shrimp heads, fermented fish sauce and doenjang, or his smoked striploin carpaccio served with a mushroom and soy sauce consommé.

컨템퍼러리 •
Contemporary

02-549-2016

강남구 선릉로 152길 37, 3층

3F, 37 Seolleung-ro 152-gil, Gangnam-gu

www.olheum.co.kr

■ 가 격 PRICE: ₩₩₩₩

GANGNAM-GU

설렁탕 • Seolleongtang

02-567-5225

강남구 삼성로 555

555 Samseong-ro, Gangnam-gu

www.naver.me/xQeHF5Lt

■ 가 격 PRICE: ₩

외고집 설렁탕

OEGOJIP SEOLLEONGTANG

2005년 장모님에게 전수받은 설렁탕 조리법을 개선하여 시작했다는 외고집 설렁탕의 현 대표는 단출하지만 정성 가득한 설렁탕 맛을 이어가고 있다. 설렁탕과 수육, 그리고 육개장에 사용하는 소고기를 직접 선별할 만큼 좋은 식재료만을 고집하는 그의 마음이 기본에 충실한 이곳 음식에 고스란히 드러난다. 편안한 한국식 밥집 분위기를 온전히 느낄 수 있는 곳이다.

What this restaurant lacks in variety, it makes up for it in quality. Since 2005, the establishment has been serving up hearty bowls of ox bone soup, the ultimate Korean comfort food. The recipe, handed down to the current proprietor by his mother-in-law, has been tweaked over the years, but one thing remains constant — the love and care put into each and every bowl of soup. It is highly-recommended for those seeking a truly local experience.

우가
WOOGA

한우의 본고장인 횡성을 시작으로 2015년 서울에 둥지를 튼 우가는 최상급 건조 숙성 한우를 완전히 익혀 제공하는 독특한 콘셉트로 주목받아왔다. 이 방법은 허세병 셰프가 'Meat Science(고기 과학)' 라는 슬로건 아래 오랫동안 고민하고 연구한 끝에 얻은 결과로 소고기의 풍미를 최대한 살려주는 것이 특징이다. 우가의 대표 메뉴인 숙성 꽃등심과 차돌박이 외에도 당뇨를 앓던 가족을 위해 셰프의 어머니가 오랜시간 발효시킨 장으로 끓인 토장찌개 또한 많은 사랑을 받고 있다.

Wooga was originally born in Hoengseong, the beef capital of Korea. The restaurant is known for preparing the choicest quality local beef in its unique style: dry aged and well done. Chef Heo Se-byeong has been experimenting tirelessly with beef under the slogan meat science to maximize the characteristics of this meat such as tenderness, juiciness and flavor. Don't miss out on another perennial favorite: a stew made with soybean paste fermented over long stages by the chef's own mom.

바비큐 • *Barbecue*

02-6272-2223

강남구 도산대로 49길 22, 지하 1층

B1F, 22 Dosan-daero 49-gil, Gangnam-gu

■ 가 격 PRICE: ₩₩₩

GANGNAM-GU

강남구

아시안 • *Asian*

070-4333-8884

강남구 학동로 43길 8

8 Hakdong-ro 43-gil, Gangnam-gu

■ **가 격 PRICE: ₩**

원 디그리 노스

ONE DEGREE NORTH

싱가포르의 좌표를 표현한 레스토랑 이름에서 느껴지듯이 이곳은 대중적인 싱가포르 현지의 요리와 아시안 바비큐 메뉴를 선보이고 있다. 전통 조리법을 기반으로 젊은 셰프의 정교하고 기술적인 감각이 더해진 싱가포르 치킨 라이스, '광동 크리스피 로스트 포크'는 대표 메뉴답게 현지의 대중적인 맛과 풍미를 온전히 제공한다. 서울에서 즐길 수 있는 현지의 맛은 언제나 즐거운 미식 경험이다.

As suggested by its name, which denotes Singapore's geographical coordinate (one degree north in latitude), this establishment is dedicated to popular Singaporean dishes and Asian barbeque specialties. Singapore chicken rice and Cantonese crispy roast pork, are two traditional recipes enhanced by the young chef's meticulous technical skills. These signature dishes bring popular Singaporean flavors alive in an authentic way, and exploring other cuisines in Seoul is always a fascinating gastronomic experience.

일드청담

ILE DE CHEONGDAM

'도심속의 섬(ile)'이란 뜻의 일드 청담. 일식과 한우 오마카세의 장점만을 모아 코스로 제공한다. 셰프의 부모님이 경작하고 키우는 식재료를 공급받아 사용함으로서, 일드 청담의 요리는 더욱 그 개성을 달리하고, 셰프의 의도가 담긴 요리를 선보인다. 그날그날 달라지는 재료를 식전에 선보여 재료를 직접 확인하게 하는 일부터 세 번에 걸쳐 우려내는 마지막 티 세리모니(tea ceremony)까지 레스토랑의 섬세함을 느낄 수 있다.

Meaning "an island within the heart of the city," Ile de Cheongdam brings together the best of Japanese omakase with Korean beef omakase. Formerly a membership-only venue, it has opened its doors to the public to share its gastronomic delights with a wider audience. From the chef's pre-dining explanation of ingredients that change daily to the final tea ceremony, where the tea is steeped three times, every course of the omakase showcases the nuanced service of this establishment. Dining at Ile de Cheongdam is by reservation only.

컨템퍼러리 •
Contemporary

02-545-4015

강남구 도산대로 59길 13, 2층

2F, 13 Dosan-daero 59-gil, Gangnam-gu

www.iledecd.com

■ **가격 PRICE: ₩₩₩₩**

냉면 • *Naengmyeon*

02-515-3469

강남구 학동로 305-3

305-3 Hakdong-ro, Gangnam-gu

■ 가 격 PRICE: ₩

진미 평양냉면

JINMI PYEONGYANG NAENGMYEON

"유명 평양냉면 식당에서 쌓은 20년의 경험과 노력의 결과물이 바로 진미 평양냉면"이라 말하는 임세권 셰프. 고객이 만족할 만큼 맛있는 냉면을 만드는 것이 그의 첫 번째 목표이고, 언제 찾아도 한결같은 맛을 즐길 수 있게 일관성을 유지하는 것이 두 번째 목표라고 한다. 다른 어떠한 요소 없이 오직 맛으로만 승부하고 싶다는 그의 마음가짐에서 냉면 장인의 고집스러움이 느껴진다. 냉면 외에도 편육, 제육, 불고기 같은 냉면집 단골 메뉴를 비롯해 접시 만두와 어복쟁반, 온면도 맛볼 수 있다.

According to owner and chef Yim Se-kwon, long time experience in the kitchens of one of the most iconic Pyeongyang cold buckwheat noodle restaurants is the secret to the success of this place. The menu here is what you would expect to see in a typical cold buckwheat noodle restaurant. Other than the noodles, it offers staples such as boiled pork and beef slices, bulgogi, dumplings and Pyeongyang-style beef hot pot.

코자차

KOJACHA

아시안 • Asian

010-9023-7771

강남구 학동로 97길 17

17 Hakdong-ro 97-gil, Gangnam-gu

■ **가 격 PRICE: ₩₩₩₩**

한국인 셰프가 (KO) 만드는 일식과(JA) 중식의(CHA) 만남이라는 의미의 코자차. 신라호텔 출신의 최유강, 조영두 셰프가 의기투합하여 색다른 장르의 음식을 선보인다. 1950-1960년대 빈티지 조명과 가구로 꾸민, 독특한 분위기의 장소에서부터 중식과 일식이 번갈아 나오는 코스 요리까지, 코자차에서는 고정관념을 깨는 경험이 가능하다. 황후가 쓰던 비눗갑에 담아낸 전복 냉채와 진한 상탕 육수로 끓인 샥스핀 찜이 이곳의 시그니처 메뉴다. 셰프들이 음식 이야기와 함께 직접 테이블 앞에서 서빙하는 퍼포먼스도 볼 만하다. 코자차는 모두 단독실로만 이뤄져 있다.

Kojacha — Korean ("Ko") chefs' Japanese ("ja") and Chinese ("cha") cuisine. The shared culinary ambition of Chefs Choi Yu-gang and Jo Yeong-du, who previously cooked at The Shilla Hotel, has given rise to a distinct culinary genre. From its vintage lighting and furniture from the 50s and 60s that creates a singular vibe to a course meal that alternately features Chinese and Japanese dishes, this is a true icon. Signature dishes include chilled abalone salad, served in a replica of the peacock-shaped soap dish used by an empress of the Qing Dynasty, and shark fin braised in thick Chinese Superior Stock. The chefs' performance-inspired table is a veritable display of their culinary narratives and enriches the eatery's appeal. All dining spaces are in the form of private rooms.

쿠시아게 • *Kushiage*

02-579-0538

강남구 논현로 24길 37

37 Nonhyeon-ro 24-gil, Gangnam-gu

■ 가 격 PRICE: ₩₩

쿠시카와

KUSHI KAWA

일본 유학 시절 섭렵했던 일본의 대중 요리를 밑거름 삼아 '쿠시카와'를 오픈한 윤석현 대표. '쿠시카와'는 일본의 대표적인 대중 음식 중 하나인 꼬치 튀김(쿠시카츠)을 전문으로 하는 곳이다. 그날의 재료에 따라 제공되는 주방장 특선 요리 '오마카세' 코스는 약 14종의 꼬치 튀김으로 구성되며, 해산물과 육류, 채소 등 다양한 식재료를 곁들여 먹는 즐거움이 쏠쏠하다. 고객들의 만족스러운 표정을 볼 때마다 보람을 느낀다는 대표는 어린 시절을 보낸 동네에서 가게를 운영할 만큼 지역 주민의 입맛을 사로잡기 위해 노력한다고 한다.

Owner Yoon Seok-hyeon's inspiration to open Kushikawa stems from his sojourn in Japan where he became a connoisseur of popular Japanese dishes including kushikatsu (deep-fried skewered meat and vegetables). The omakase course at Kushikawa consists of 12 to 14 different types of deep-fried skewers prepared with seafood, meat and vegetables. Running a restaurant on his home turf where he grew up, Yoon tries to appeal to the local palate, and nothing brings him greater joy than the joyful expressions on his customers' beaming faces.

키라메키 N

KIRAMEKI

일식 • *Japanese*

010-3894-2356

강남구 도산대로 28길 18

18 Dosan-daero 28-gil, Gangnam-gu

■ 가 격 PRICE: ₩₩₩₩

밥을 메인으로 코스 요리를 선보이는 일식당이다. 원래 밥이 메인 아닌가 했지만 여러 가지 코스를 직접 먹어 보니 요리로서 당당히 코스의 한 자리를 차지하고 있다. 키라메키는 일본식 와쇼쿠를 바탕으로, 따뜻한 가이세키 요리를 제철 재료를 사용해 다양하게 선보인다. 솥밥이 나온 뒤에는 흰 쌀밥 위에 올린 작은 요리들이 다채롭게 제공되는데 쌀의 향미와 함께 입안을 맴도는 감칠맛을 느낄 수 있다.

Kirameki is a Japanese restaurant that serves a tasting menu centered on rice. I expected rice to be the primary focus of the meal, but after experiencing the meal, but it consisted as a wide array of dishes. The menu is designed around the Japanese washoku, and showcases kaiseki cuisine prepared with seasonal ingredients. Once the ceramic pot rice is served, small morsels of food were served over scoops of aromatic white rice. Each savory bite lingered pleasantly on the palate.

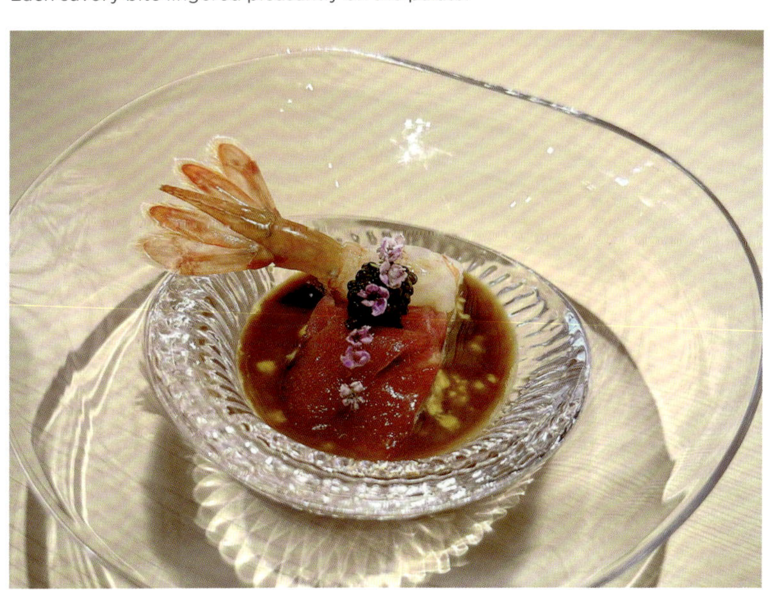

텐지몽

TENJIMON

일식 • *Japanese*

02-542-3010

강남구 학동로 97길 41, 4층

4F, 41 Hakdong-ro 97-gil, Gangnam-gu

www.dccreative.kr/tenjimon

■ 가 격 PRICE: ₩₩

'톡톡'의 김대천 셰프와 일본 '덴'의 하세가와 셰프의 협업으로 탄생한 텐지몽. 한자로 '천지문'을 뜻하는 텐지몽은 '하늘과 땅의 재료로 미식 세계의 문을 연다'는 의미를 담고 있다. 협업 체계인 까닭에 일본에서 메뉴 감수를 받지만 오마카세는 한국의 신선한 재료를 이용해 만든다. 특히, 시그니처 메뉴인 솥밥은 부지깽이, 취나물 같은 한국의 제철 재료를 넣어 독특한 풍미를 더했다. 좌석이 많지 않아 개성있는 요리를 맛보려면 예약은 필수다.

A collaboration between Chef Kim Dae-chun—owner of TOC TOC—and Chef Zaiyu Hasegawa—owner of Den in Tokyo—"Tenjimon' is the Japanese pronunciation of a Chinese/Korean word that means "To open the door to the gastronomic world via ingredients from heaven and earth." Although this partnership requires that the menu be confirmed from Japan, Tenjimon's omakase features fresh Korean ingredients. Of particular note, the signature hot pot rice is a uniquely flavored delicacy made with seasonal and local ingredients, such as amur wallflower and aster leaf. Since seating is limited for this unique culinary discovery, reservations are a must.

톡톡

TOC TOC

요리에 대한 김대천 셰프의 꾸준한 향상심과 좋은 재료에 대한 고집은 '톡톡'의 요리에서 뚜렷이 나타난다. '톡톡(Toctoc)'과 '요리학(Gastronomy)'을 합성한 'Toconomy'에는 김대천 셰프의 요리 철학이 담겨 있다. 김대천 셰프는 정확한 조리법으로 식재료 본연의 맛을 고스란히 전달하는 데 중점을 둔다. 그만큼 재료의 가치를 중요하게 생각하는 것이다. 개성 넘치는 요리들은 셰프의 정성과 창의성이 어떻게 톡톡의 요리에 반영되어 있는지를 잘 보여준다. 코스 요리 외에도 완성도 높은 다양한 단품 요리로 구성된 메뉴를 통해 톡톡이 제공하는 다양한 요리의 풍미를 즐길 수 있다.

For Chef Kim Dae-cheon, the ingredients and precise techniques that summarize his cooking philosophy are summed up in one word: toconomy (Toc Toc + gastronomy). Signature dishes at Toc Toc and pasta with Chef Kim's original flair. In addition to the course meals, the restaurant also offers a wide range of well-executed à la carte dishes.

컨템퍼러리 • *Contemporary*

02-542-3030

강남구 학동로 97길 41, 3층

3F, 41 Hakdong-ro 97-gil, Gangnam-gu

www.restauranttoctoc.com

■ **가격 PRICE: ₩₩**

GANGNAM-GU

강남구

트리드

TRID

컨템퍼러리 •

Contemporary

02-512-8312

강남구 선릉로 162길 16, 2층

2F, 16 Seolleung-ro 162-gil, Gangnam-gu

■ 가 격 PRICE: ₩₩₩

다양성, 좋은 맛, 즐거움. 이 세 가지는 모던 퀴진에 있어 셰프와 고객의 공통 관심사이다. 모던 퀴진 레스토랑 '트리드'는 이런 관심사를 충족시키고자 하는 요리사들의 노력이 느껴지는 곳이다. 트리드의 셰프가 여러 문화권에서 경험한 다양한 다이닝 환경은, 식재료와 풍미의 조합을 통한 새로운 맛을 발견하기 위해 과감하고 흥미로운 선택을 할 수 있게 해 주었다. 공간의 안락함과 차분한 서비스, 세련된 디자인의 개방형 주방이 이곳의 근사한 요리와 어우러져 일체감을 제공한다.

Diversity, deliciousness, and delight are the three D's that serve as the basis for this restaurant's name. They are also the points of interest to chefs and patrons when it comes to the modern cuisine. Trid is a contemporary haunt that focuses on these elements; in fact, it's here where that perpetual culinary struggle to meet such standards is most strongly felt. The head chef has experienced diverse dining environments in a multitude of cultural milieus, which has allowed him to make bold and interesting choices while pursuing new tastes and combinations of ingredients. The spatial coziness, refined services, and elegantly designed open kitchen blend in with the restaurant's fare, exemplifying a sense of unity.

팀호완

TIM HO WAN

홍콩식 딤섬이 홍콩을 넘어 다양한 나라의 고객들이 즐기는 메뉴로 성장하는 데 크게 기여한 팀호완. 홍콩의 전통 딤섬 스타일을 지키면서 맛있고 합리적인 가격의 딤섬을 제공하고자 한 팀호완의 정책이 그러한 성장의 가장 큰 원동력이었다. 서울에 진출한 팀호완 역시 그 정책을 반영하듯 본연의 모습에 충실하다. 팀호완의 서울 본점인 삼성점은 110명의 고객을 모실 수 있는 넓은 규모와 넉넉한 주차 공간을 제공한다. 다양한 스타일의 홍콩식 딤섬을 즐기기에 더없이 좋은 레스토랑이다.

Tim Ho Wan has played a major role in making Hong Kong-style dim sum popular in many countries worldwide. The main force behind such growing popularity has been its policy of maintaining the traditional form of Hong Kong dim sum dishes and making them available at affordable prices. This management philosophy has been upheld in its branches in Seoul, making them as authentic as the original. The franchise's capacious Samseong outpost, which is also the main location in Seoul, can serve up to 110 customers at one time and offers ample parking spaces. It is the perfect place to indulge in a wide variety of traditional dim sum.

딤섬 • *Dim Sum*

02-6207-3082

강남구 봉은사로 86길 30

30 Bongeunsa-ro 86-gil, Gangnam-gu

■ **가 격 PRICE: ₩**

GANGNAM-GU

컨템퍼러리 • *Contemporary*

010-6550-8912

강남구 봉은사로 68길 6-5

6-5 Bongeunsa-ro 68-gil, Gangnam-gu

■ 가 격 PRICE: ₩₩

페리지 N

PERIGEE

'페리지'는 '지구와 위성의 근지점'이란 뜻이다. 요리와 와인을 좀 더 친밀하게 느낄 수 있었으면 하는 바람에서 상호를 이렇게 정했다. 신가영, 임홍근 셰프 부부가 운영하는 페리지는 직접 제면한 파스타를 제공한다는 원칙을 고수한다. 카바텔리, 안다리노스, 피치 등 국내에서 쉽게 접하기 힘든 식감과 모양을 다양하게 즐길 수 있다는 점이 특징이다. 피치를 이용한 봉골레를 비롯해 안다리노스와 랍스터 파스타 등 익숙하면서도 색다른 조합을 경험해 볼 수 있다.

Perigee means the point in the orbit of a satellite at which it is closest to the Earth. The restaurant was named in the hope of bringing diners closer to food and wine. The restaurant, which is run by chef couple Shin Ga-young and Lim Hong-keun, serves pasta that is all made fresh in-house. Diners can enjoy different types of pastas with textures and shapes rarely found in Korea, such as cavatelli, andarinos, and pici. Experience familiar yet unique combinations like vongole with pici, and lobster pasta with andarinos.

Jon Arnold Images/hemis.fr

마포구
서대문구
영등포구
MAPO-GU
SEODAEMUN-GU
YEONGDEUNGPO-GU

교다이야
KYODAIYA

우동 • *Udon*

02-2654-2645

마포구 성지길 39

39 Seongji-gil, Mapo-gu

■ 가 격 PRICE: ₩

합정역 근처의 조용한 주택가에 들어서면 나무 도마에 탁탁탁 작두날 튕기는 소리가 경쾌하게 들려온다. '형제의 집'을 뜻하는 교다이야는 두 형제가 운영하는 우동 전문점이다. 이곳에선 주문이 들어오는 대로 면을 써는 것을 원칙으로 한다. 면을 만들어놓으면 수분이 증발해 사누키 우동 특유의 매력을 느낄 수 없기 때문이다. 탱글탱글한 동시에 쫄깃하며 매끄러운 사누키 우동 면발, 정어리 훈제 포와 연간장으로 맛을 낸 시원한 감칠맛의 국물. 늘 한결같은 이곳의 우동 맛은 두 사장의 뚝심 있는 모습과 닮아 있다.

When one can hear the dull tap of a blade against a wooden board every time a customer places an order, it's a telltale sign that the chefs are serious about their craft. At Kyodaiya, that craft is Sanuki udon. The thick noodles are always cut to order to preserve their characteristic elasticity and smoothness until the very last minute. In addition to the classic kake udon, flavored with dried and smoked sardines and seasoned with light soy sauce, the chef brothers also offer classics like tempura udon and chilled bukkake udon.

니시무라멘 N

NISHIMURAMEN

라멘 • Ramen

010-9596-1122

서울 마포구 동교로 265, 4층

4F, 265 Donggyo-ro, Mapo-gu

■ 가격 PRICE: ₩

후쿠오카의 흥미로운 프렌치 레스토랑을 운영하는 니시무라 타카히토 셰프의 라멘 식당이 서울에 문을 열었다. 니시무라멘 서울은 니시무라 타카히토 셰프의 남다른 라멘 사랑의 결과물이다. 토핑과 소스, 오일 등을 곁들여 완성한 풍성하고 입체적인 라멘 맛에서 셰프의 독특한 스타일을 엿볼 수 있다. 라멘 고유의 스타일을 유지하면서도 김 오일과 청양고추, 백김치 스타일의 쯔께모노를 활용하는 등 현지화에도 신경을 많이 썼다. 갓 지은 솥밥에 치즈와 라멘 국물을 함께 즐길 수 있는 밥 요리도 니시무라멘의 개성이 느껴지는 메뉴이다.

Nishimuramen, a famed restaurant in Fukuoka known for its unique marriage of Japanese ramen and French cooking, has finally opened its doors in Seoul. The culinary offspring of Chef Takahito Nishimura born out of his unparalleled enthusiasm for ramen, this noodle joint flaunts his distinctive style by bringing out the rich, multifaceted flavors of ramen through an intriguing union of toppings, sauces and oils. While maintaining the authenticity of ramen, the kitchen has successfully localized its fare, for instance, by using laver oil, Cheongyang chili pepper, and tsukemono (Japanese pickles) in the style of white kimchi. Freshly cooked pot rice mixed with cheese and ramen broth (like risotto) is another standout dish that asserts this eatery's unique role in the gastronomic universe.

담택

DAMTAEK

라멘 • *Ramen*

02-336-0974

마포구 월드컵로 8길 34

34 World Cup-ro 8-gil, Mapo-gu

■ 가격 PRICE: ₩

합정역 인근의 한적한 골목길 한 켠에 위치한 소박한 라멘집이다. 이미 세월의 흔적이 묻어 있는 공간이지만 조원현 셰프는 담택의 공간을 의도적으로 빈티지 소품으로 꾸몄다. 소박한 공간과는 달리 이곳의 시오 라멘을 비롯해 시오 라멘 베이스에 맛의 변주를 가한 각종 라멘 메뉴는 소박함과는 거리가 멀다. 세련되면서도 깔끔한 수프의 맛이 꽤나 개성 있고 중독성 있는 여운을 준다. 틀에 얽매이지 않는 맛을 개발하기 위해 우직하게 시오 라멘에 집중한 셰프의 라멘에는 누구나 즐길 수 있는 맛이 담겨 있다.

Damtaek is a cozy little ramen haven nestled in a quiet alley near Hapjeong Station. Chef Jo Won-hyeon has purposefully adorned this quaint space with vintage artifacts. The restaurant's shio ramen, and associated variations that use the same soup base, are in stark contrast to its homey, down-to-earth vibe. The refined and clean flavors of the soups are singular and inspire lingering addiction. With a passion for creating tastes unbound by culinary convention, the chef has persistently dedicated his craft toward perfecting the art of shio ramen, creating ramen that can delight any palate.

마포옥
MAPO OK

고기와 국물을 선호하는 한국인에게 설렁탕만 한 음식이 또 있을까? 서울 설렁탕 중에서도 마포식 설렁탕은 국물이 뽀얗지 않고 맑은 편이다. 1949년에 개업한 마포옥은 양지와 차돌박이, 사골로 곤 진한 국물에 두툼하게 썬 양지머리를 푸짐하게 올려 제공한다. 국물에 밥을 토렴해 내는 것도 이 집의 특징인데, 무엇보다 소고기 국물의 고소한 감칠맛과 달달한 밥의 조화가 일품이다. 여기에 배추 겉절이, 파김치, 깍두기 등 다양한 김치를 제공한다. 이 외에도 차돌 수육을 넉넉하게 얹어주는 차돌탕도 추천한다.

In the realm of Korean comfort food, there is little else more quintessential than seolleongtang — a hearty bowl of soup made by boiling ox bones and beef for hours until the broth turns almost milky white. Mapo Ok, which opened its doors in 1949, makes its signature dish by boiling brisket and ox bones until slightly opaque. The ox bone soup is served with thick slices of tender brisket and rice already mixed into the piping hot broth. Ask for a side of kimchi juice to season your soup for that extra dimension of flavor.

설렁탕 • *Seolleongtang*

02-716-6661

마포구 토정로 312

312 Tojeong-ro, Mapo-gu

■ **가 격 PRICE: ₩**

미필담 N

MIPILDAM

만두 • Mandu

010-5455-5041

마포구 성지 3길 22

22 Seongji 3-gil, Mapo-gu

■ 가격 PRICE: ₩

한적하지만 동시에 젊음의 생기가 느껴지는 합정동의 어느 골목에 자그마한 이북식 손만둣국집 미필담이 있다. 이곳의 주인인 젊은 부부는 황해도 출신 외할머니의 조리법을 바탕으로 이북식 만둣국의 담백한 맛을 손님상에 올린다. 두툼하고 속이 꽉 찬 손만두에 별다른 가미 없이도 담백한 육향을 자랑하는 국물의 조합은 거부하기 쉽지 않은 맛이다. 담백하고 슴슴한 만둣국 외에 계절에 맞춰 정성껏 선보이는 한식 메뉴에서 주인 부부의 노력이 느껴진다. 좌석 구조상 혼자 식사하기에도 적합하고 친구나 연인과 함께 찾기에도 부족함이 없는 공간이다.

Tucked in a quiet yet youthfully vibrant alley in Hapjeong-dong, Mipildam is an unpretentious little spot specializing in handmade mandutguk (dumpling soup) in northern Korean style. The recipe for this lightly flavored dish is based on the home recipe of the young owner couple's grandmother, who was born and raised in Hwanghae Province, now in North Korea. The perfect combination of plump dumplings packed with juicy filling and the broth infused with subtle flavors (and without any additional artificial flavors) is not something a diner can easily resist. In addition to the signature soup, the menu offers seasonally updated traditional dishes that reflect the couple's passion for serving good food. The seating layout accommodates solo diners as well as couples and friend groups.

베이스 이즈 나이스

BASE IS NICE

채소 친화적 레스토랑인 베이스 이즈 나이스. 이곳의 주인장인 장진아 대표는 레스토랑 컨설턴트와 푸드스타일리스트, 식음 기획자로 꽤 긴 시간을 해외에서 활동하였다. 이곳의 내추럴한 분위기와 채소를 중심으로 풀어낸 균형 잡힌 요리에는 그녀의 이런 경험이 오롯이 담겨 있다. 채소를 이용한 덮밥 스타일의 메뉴와 정갈하게 차려낸 국과 반찬은 깔끔하면서도 맛이 일품이다. 주인장의 표현처럼 이곳은 채식에 대한 의식적 접근이 아닌 자연스러운 채소 식생활과 일상 속의 미식을 경험할 수 있는 메뉴를 지향한다. 1인 운영 레스토랑이라 예약 손님만 받고 있으니 방문 전 예약은 필수다.

Base is Nice is a vegetarian-friendly restaurant. Chef/owner Jang Jin-a had a fairly long career overseas as a restaurant consultant, food stylist, and food & beverage planner. The diner's natural ambience and well-balanced, vegetable-centered dishes are proud manifestations of her lifelong culinary endeavors. Creations of rice and vegetables, accompanied by soup and side dishes, are refined and tasty. As Jang puts it, the restaurant's menu is a way to experience everyday food through a natural, veggie-centered diet, and not thanks to a conscious approach to vegetarianism. Reservation required.

베지테리안 •
Vegetarian

050-71306-6724
마포구 도화 2길 20
20 Dohwa 2-gil, Mapo-gu

■ 가 격 PRICE: ₩

MAPO-GU SEODAEMUN-GU YEONGDEUNGPO-GU

라멘 • *Ramen*

마포구 연남로 15

15 Yeonnam-ro, Mapo-gu

■ **가 격 PRICE: ₩**

사루카메
SARUKAME

사루카메는 현재 2대째 혼마 히로토 오너 셰프가 운영을 하고 있다. 그는 단순히 식당 이름만을 이은 것이 아닌, 1대 셰프와의 교감으로 기존 레시피도 보존하여 레스토랑의 발자취를 이어 간다. 이렇게 레스토랑의 역사를 지키며 세계 각국의 도시에서 쌓은 자신의 외식업 경험과 감각을 살려 사루카메만의 새로운 이야기를 만들어 가고 있다. 사루카메는 일본에서 유행하는 라멘의 맛에 전통의 맛과 창작의 맛을 더한 한정 메뉴를 꾸준히 개발해 소개하면서 레스토랑 고유의 라멘 브랜드를 만들어 고객과 소통하고 있다.

Sarukame is currently run by its second-generation owner-chef Hiroto Honma. Going beyond merely retaining the title of the restaurant, the current chef is carrying on its culinary legacy by staying in contact with its founder and preserving its original recipes. Such effort, coupled with Chef Honma's vast experience in the restaurant business and gastronomic sensibility, garnered and developed over the years working in cities around the world, are adding new narrative layers to this establishment. Sarukame continues to create exclusive menus that combine the flavors of trendy ramen in Japan, classic flavors and new original flavors, thereby shaping its brand identity and serving the ever-changing needs of Seoul's ramen aficionados.

서교난면방 N

SEOKYONANMYUNBANG

이탈리안 퀴진 전문 셰프로서 견실한 시간을 보내 온 김낙영 셰프의 개성 있는 면 요리 레스토랑 서교난면방. 파스타와 라자냐를 전문적으로 다루던 셰프의 손에서 나온 난면은 그의 경험과 아이디어가 녹아든 한국적이면서도 이탤리언 퀴진의 감성과 터치가 가미된 독창적인 맛의 즐거움을 준다. 셰프는 이 독특한 경계 사이에서 균형을 유지하면서 난면의 매력을 제대로 전달하고 있다. 구엄닭 난면, 그리고 닭 육수와 한우 육수를 섞어 만든 서교 난면 등 매력적인 국물 맛과 난면의 식감을 즐길 수 있는 면 요리가 대표 메뉴다. 이 외에도 계절에 따라 달라지는 면 요리도 있어 철마다 방문해 색다른 맛을 즐기기에 좋다.

국수 • *Noodles*

010-9516-0934

마포구 동교로 12길 16

16 Donggyo-ro 12-gil, Mapo-gu

■ 가 격 PRICE: ₩

Chef Kim Nak-young, an expert on Italian cuisine, offers his unique take on noodle dishes at Seokyonanmyunbang. The nanmyeon, or egg noodles, crafted by a chef specializing in pasta and lasagna, are a unique, creative fusion of Korean and Italian culinary traditions. The chef delicately balances these two distinctive traditions, showcasing the unique appeal of nanmyeon. Signature dishes include Gueomdak nanmyeon made from a Jeju breed of chicken and Seokyo nanmyeon that features a broth made from a mix of chicken and hanwoo beef, which highlight the delectable flavors of the broth and the texture of the noodles. The chef creates seasonal noodle dishes, making it worthwhile to make multiple visits for new experiences.

역전회관
YUKJEON HOEKWAN

불고기 • *Bulgogi*

02-703-0019

마포구 토정로 37길 47

47 Tojeong-ro 37-gil, Mapo-gu

www.yukjeon.com

■ 가 격 PRICE: ₩₩

1962년에 '역전식당'으로 시작해 90년대에 '역전회관'으로 상호를 변경한 50년 전통의 한식 레스토랑. 이곳의 명물은 국물 없이 바삭하게 즐기는 바싹 불고기로, 메뉴명을 특허청에 등록한 바싹 불고기의 원조라 할 수 있다. 활활 타오르는 센 불에 구웠지만 촉촉한 육즙과 부드러운 식감이 그대로 살아 있는 고기에 달지 않은 양념 맛이 일품으로 보통 맛과 매운맛 중 선택이 가능하다. 이곳은 4층 건물 전체를 사용하므로 넓은 공간에서 편안한 식사를 즐길 수 있지만 그래도 저녁 시간에는 예약하고 올 것을 추천한다.

Three generations spanning five decades have kept this restaurant in business since its opening in 1962. At the time, their iconic crispy thin-sliced bulgogi, grilled over open flames, was all that was offered on the menu. The dish became so popular that the name bassak bulgogi was patented. Today, the restaurant stands four stories high, still serving the same dish that has fed generations. Their coagulated beef blood soup with a clear broth is another stunner.

오레노 라멘
ORENO RAMEN

국내에서 외국 음식의 대중화는 곧 현지화의 성공을 의미한다. 진입 장벽이 낮은 대중음식의 경우 더욱더 그러하다. 신동우 셰프는 오랜 시간에 걸쳐 축적한 라멘 비즈니스 노하우로 정통성과 대중성이라는 두 마리 토끼를 모두 잡았다. 진한 닭 육수가 매력적인 토리파이탄과 깔끔하면서도 깊은 맛을 자랑하는 쇼유 라멘에서 그가 추구하는 색깔이 뚜렷이 드러난다. 신 셰프는 라멘의 생명인 육수와 면을 매일매일 만들어내며 끊임없는 테스팅으로 품질 유지에 심혈을 기울인다 "스스로에게 떳떳한 라멘을 만들고 싶다"는 그의 말에서 자부심이 엿보인다.

Foreign foods are not always embraced by local diners. In fact, authenticity is often shunned by many due to its sheer "foreignness. " But for chef Shin Dong-woo, years of experience in the ramen business has led him to success, and he did it by introducing the authentic flavors of Japanese ramen to local consumers. The restaurant's tori paitan ramen, with its rich, velvety-smooth chicken stock, and the shoyu ramen, clean yet deeply flavorful, are good examples of Shin's ramen know-how. The fresh noodles and stocks are prepared in the kitchen, daily.

라멘 • *Ramen*

02-322-3539

마포구 독막로 6길 14

14 Dongmak-ro 6-gil, Mapo-gu

■ **가 격 PRICE: ₩**

옥동식

OKDONGSIK

마포구 서대문구 영등포구

돼지국밥 • *Dwaeji-gukbap*

010-5571-9915

마포구 양화로 7길 44-10

44-10 Yanghwa-ro 7-gil, Mapo-gu

■ 가 격 PRICE: ₩

돼지국밥에 대한 선입견을 완전히 뒤엎어버린 옥동식. 이곳의 돼지국밥 또는 돼지 곰탕은 지리산 버크셔 K 흑돼지의 앞다리와 뒷다리 살만을 고아 육수가 유난히 맑은 것이 특징이다. 한소끔 김을 뺀 밥과 80%만 익혀 얇게 썬 고기를 방짜유기에 담은 후 뜨거운 육수를 부으면 고기는 마저 익고, 육수는 더 깊게 우러나 담백하면서도 진한 감칠맛을 낸다. 특곰탕은 고기 양이 두 배다. 10석밖에 없는 작은 공간에 1일 100그릇만 한정 판매하고 있으니 방문을 서두르기 바란다.

With his take on dwaeji-gukbap, Chef Ok Dong-sik has managed to singlehandedly change any preconceptions the local diners previously had about the hearty pork and rice soup dish Koreans hold near and dear to their hearts. Think bacon-thin slices of silky tender pork meat piled on a bed of rice, all submerged in his trademark consommé-like clear broth. The 'extra large' portion comes with double the amount of meat. The space is limited and only 100 bowls of gukbap are sold daily so get here early.

정육면체
TASTY CUBE

'정육면체(情肉麵體)'는 각각 '마음'과 '고기', '국수', '식당'을 뜻하는 한자를 조합해 만든 이름이다. 오로지 다양한 면 요리를 선보이고 싶어 친구들끼리 의기투합하여 만든 작은 공간이다. 사골과 소고기를 장시간 고아 만든 육수가 베이스인 우육면, 땅콩과 깨를 갈아 넣은 고소한 즈마장을 곁들인 깨부수면이 이곳의 간판 메뉴다. 현재는 동남아식 면 요리와 중식 위주의 메뉴를 제공하고 있지만, 점차 다른 문화권의 면 요리도 선보일 예정이라고 한다. 식당에서 직접 뽑은 생면의 쫄깃한 식감이 돋보이는 재기 발랄한 면 요리를 즐길 수 있는 곳이다. 전 좌석이 오픈형 주방을 에워싸고 있는 카운터석이다.

A combination of Chinese characters for heart, meat, noodles and restaurant make up the four-syllable name Jeongyukmyeonche. The cozy space, which only offers bar seating facing the open kitchen, is the brainchild of a group of friends who wanted to launch an eatery that focuses on a wide array of noodle dishes. Although Chinese and Southeast Asian flavors dominate the menu at present, the owners say the plan is to eventually introduce noodle dishes from other cultures as well. Signature dishes include beef noodle soup and noodles dressed with zhi ma jiang, a savory paste made with crushed sesame seeds.

국수 • *Noodles*

070-4179-3819
서대문구 연세로 5다길 22-8
22-8 Yeonsei-ro 5da-gil, Seodaemun-gu

■ 가격 PRICE: ₩

MAPO-GU SEODAEMUN-GU YEONGDEUNGPO-GU

정인면옥
JUNGIN MYEONOK

냉면 • *Naengmyeon*

02-2683-2615

영등포구 국회대로 76길 10

10 Gukhoe-daero 76-gil, Yeongdeungpo-gu

www.junginmyunok.modoo.at

■ 가 격 PRICE: ₩

좋은 품질의 식재료와 변함없는 맛에 대한 정인면옥 대표의 고집이 냉면 한 그릇에 고스란히 담겨 있다. 북한 출신 부모님의 존함에서 한 자씩 따온 식당 이름도 전통을 계승하고자 하는 그의 의지의 반영이다. 2014년, 서울 여의도로 이전 오픈한 이곳은 현재 광명시에 있는 정인면옥과는 별개로 운영되고 있다. 직장인들이 많은 여의도에 위치한 까닭에 점심시간에는 어느 정도 대기 시간을 감안해야 한다. 아롱사태 수육, 암퇘지 편육과 접시 만두는 반 접시만도 주문이 가능하다.

When a restaurant continues to attract large crowds of hungry diners, then it is doing something right. The proprietor of Jungin Myeonok has had just one goal since day one — to continue the legacy of his parents for as long as he can, using only the best ingredients. The establishment's legendary Pyeongyang cold buckwheat noodles are based on a tightly guarded family recipe handed down to him by his parents, who both hail from North Korea. The room gets packed quickly during lunch service, especially during the warmer months.

진진

JIN JIN

중식의 대중화를 위해 40년 동안 힘써온 왕육성 셰프의 차이니즈 레스토랑. 방대한 메뉴가 일반적인 중식당의 패러다임에서 벗어나 10가지의 단출한 메뉴를 선보이는 이유는 맛과 품질을 일관되게 유지하기 위해서라고 한다. 고품격 요리를 합리적인 가격에 맛볼 수 있는 진진의 대표 메뉴로는 멘보샤, 대게살 볶음, 마파두부, 카이란 소고기 볶음 등을 꼽을 수 있다.

For over 40 years, Chef Wang Yuk-sung has been committed to popularizing Chinese cuisine in Korea. Unlike most generic Korean-style Chinese restaurants ubiquitous to Seoul, Chef Wang offers a limited menu of just ten dishes to ensure that the quality of the food he serves is consistently high. Some of the most requested dishes include shrimp toast, stir-fried crab meat with egg white, mapo tofu and stir-fried beef with gai lan.

중식 • *Chinese*

070-5035-8878

마포구 월드컵북로 1길 60

60 World Cup buk-ro 1-gil, Mapo-gu

www.jinjinseoul.modoo.at

■ **가 격 PRICE: ₩₩**

타이 • *Thai*

070-4407-5130

마포구 성미산로 161-8

161-8 Seongmisan-ro, Mapo-gu

■ 가 격 PRICE: ₩

툭툭 누들 타이

TUK TUK NOODLE THAI

현지에서 경험할 수 있는 정통의 맛을 국내에서도 즐길 수 있다는 것은 참으로 반가운 일이다. 임동혁 사장과 태국인 셰프가 의기투합해 오픈한 툭툭 누들 타이는 바로 이러한 취지로 탄생한 태국 음식 전문점이다. 이곳에선 레몬 그라스와 고수, 라임과 코코넛 밀크 등 태국 음식에서 빠질 수 없는 재료를 이용해 특유의 시큼 달달한 맛의 음식을 선보인다. 셰프의 넉넉한 인심과 태국 현지의 분위기를 느낄 수 있어 더욱 매력적인 이곳에서 파란색 툭툭(Tuk Tuk)과 함께 이국의 정취를 느껴보길 바란다.

Authenticity is the name of the game at Tuk Tuk Noodle Thai, a collaborative effort between a local Korean owner and a native Thai chef to bring the real flavors of Thailand to Korea. The components that make up a typically Thai meal — the colors, textures, scents, flavors and the ambience — are present from start to end. If you want to feel the authentic taste and aroma of Thailand, try Thai sausages, or spicy and sour 'larb moo' - stir-fried minced pork. While you are tasting the dishes, the joy of your daily life will increase by a span.

합정옥
HAPJEONGOK

곰탕 • *Gomtang*

02-322-4822
마포구 양화로 1길 21, 2층
2F, 21 Yanghwa-ro 1-gil, Mapo-gu

■ 가 격 PRICE: ₩

합정옥의 시작은 시아버지께서 손수 끓여 드시던 곰탕과 수육 맛에서 비롯됐다. 시아버지가 훗날 대표가 된 며느리에게 "곰탕집 한번 차려볼까?"라고 말한 것이 계기가 되어 오늘에까지 이르게 된 것. 진한 국물과 은은한 육 향, 토렴해 내오는 달달한 밥과 야들야들한 소고기, 그리고 내포까지, 이곳 음식은 푸짐함을 미덕으로 삼고 있다. 또한 구수한 된장국에 달큰한 배추속대를 넣어 끓인 속댓국의 시원한 맛도 일품이다. 하루에 탕 100인분 정도만 준비하며, 재료 소진 시엔 영업을 종료한다.

Hapjeongok is a restaurant born of nostalgia. As they were reminiscing one day on the father-in-law's beef bone soup and boiled beef slices, the latter suggested to his daughter-in-law that they should open a beef bone soup restaurant. The establishment stays true to the inspiration — deeply flavorful beef broth, rice rendered soft and sweet in the piping hot soup, tender slices of beef, and a generous serving of boiled offal. The restaurant's cabbage soybean paste soup is also a must try. Only around 100 portions of soup are served daily, so go early.

화해당
HWA HAE DANG

게장 • Gejang

02-785-4422

영등포구 국회대로 62길 15

15 Gukhoe-daero 62-gil, Yeongdeungpo-gu

www.hwahaedang.com

■ 가 격 PRICE: ₩₩

한자어로 '꽃게집'을 뜻하는 화해당은 태안에서 유명한 간장게장 집의 첫 번째 서울 분점이다. 매년 봄, 통통하게 살이 오른 꽃게를 급랭 시켜 1 년 내내 사용한다. 채소 육수와 양조간장을 혼합하여 만든 이 집만의 특제 간장은 인공 조미를 첨가하지 않은 깊은 맛을 자랑하고, 단맛 나는 게살의 식감 또한 탱탱한 것이 일품이다. 모든 게장은 이틀에 한 번꼴로 태안에서 공급받으며, 탱글탱글한 어리굴젓 역시 태안에서 올라온다. 갓 지어 나오는 솥 밥에 게장을 얹어 향긋한 감태에 싸 먹으면 어느새 밥 한 그릇이 뚝딱 없어진다.

This is the first Seoul branch of the acclaimed Taean County restaurant, located on the west coast of Korea. The name of the restaurant, which translates into "Flower crab house" specializes in soy sauce marinated blue crab, prized for its sweet flesh. Each spring, when local crabs are in season, they are caught and flash frozen to be used throughout the year. The crabs are prepared in Taean and sent to Seoul. The seafood side dishes are also good.

황금콩밭
HWANGGEUM KONGBAT

100% 국내산 콩과 소금으로 매일 새벽 당일 판매할 두부를 만드는 두부 전문점. 황금콩밭의 두부는 진한 두유와 소량의 간수를 사용해 콩 특유의 고소하면서도 달달한 맛과 우유처럼 부드러운 식감을 자랑한다. 출판사를 운영하는 작가 출신의 윤태현 대표는 본인이 즐기는 건강한 음식을 주변 사람들과 나누고픈 마음에 손수 담근 청국장과 쌀과 누룩, 물 이외에는 아무것도 넣지 않은 전통 탁주도 함께 판매한다. 두부 전문점이지만 제주 무항생제 돼지고기 보쌈과 자연산 우럭찜도 이곳의 별미다.

Tucked away in Ahyeon-dong, this hidden gem specializes in rustic homemade bean curd. The unctuously creamy bean curd is made from scratch, daily, at the crack of dawn. The secret to the elevated nuttiness of local soybeans that shine through in Hwanggeum Kongbat's bean curd is the extra thick soymilk and reduced levels of the coagulant. With a desire to share healthy food with other people, the proprietor also makes and sells homemade rich soybean paste stew and unrefined rice wine.

두부 • *Dubu*

02-313-2952

마포구 마포대로 16길 9

9 Mapo-daero 16-gil, Mapo-gu

■ 가 격 PRICE: ₩

프렌치 • French

070-7779-8181

마포구 동교로 30길 17-1

17-1 Donggyo-ro 30-gil, Mapo-gu

■ 가 격 PRICE: ₩₩

랑빠스 81

L'IMPASSE 81

연남동의 한적한 골목길에 위치한 랑빠스 81은 Nose to tail, 즉 머리부터 꼬리까지 모든 부위를 이용하여 샤르퀴트리를 만들어 내는 다이닝바 이다. 샤르퀴트리는 프랑스인들이 즐겨 먹는 육가공 제품을 일컫는 말로, 다양한 종류의 햄과 소시지를 포함한다. 염장해 건조시켜야 하는 일부 제품은 6개월에서 1년 정도 숙성시키는데, 특유의 진한 감칠맛을 자랑한다. 한편, 제주도에서 직접 공수한 빈티지 가구가 레스토랑에 멋스러움을 더해준다.

Nestled in a quiet alley of Yeonnam-dong, L'Impasse 81 is a dining bar dedicated to the art of charcuterie, embracing the 'nose-to-tail' philosophy to utilize every part of the animal. Charcuterie, a staple of French cuisine, encompasses a variety of cured meats and sausages. Some products, such as those requiring salting and drying, undergo a meticulous aging process of six months to a year, resulting in an intense, umami-rich flavor. Adding to its charm, the restaurant is adorned with vintage furniture sourced directly from Jeju Island, enhancing its unique and sophisticated ambiance.

리북방

LEE BUK BANG

한식 • Korean

02-720-2345
마포구 마포대로 1길 16, 2층
2F, 16 Mapo-daero 1-gil, Mapo-gu

■ 가격 PRICE: ₩₩

레스토랑의 이름처럼 이북 음식을 즐길 수 있는 공간이다. 리북방이 전하는 이북 음식의 핵심은 셰프 가족의 내리 음식인 순대에 있다. 전통적인 조합의 순대부터 창의적으로 식재료가 어우러진 순대까지 다양한 순대 요리를 코스에 포함시킨 셰프의 참신한 아이디어가 돋보인다. 단순히 익숙한 것을 새롭게 포장하는 보여주기 식이 아닌 집안에서 내려오는 맛의 전통을 계승하고 자신의 경험을 더해 익숙한 요리를 완성도 높은 요리로 승화시킨 점이 매력적이다. 100년이 넘은 한옥의 대들보와 문을 이용해 만든 고재 바 테이블과 공간이 주는 전통적인 분위기, 순대를 중심으로 전개되는 다양한 이북 음식을 시대에 맞게 표현한 요리가 가치 있는 경험을 제공한다.

As the name suggests, Lee Buk Bang is where one can enjoy meals from the leebuk, or North Korean, region. In this setting, blood sausage and other diverse North Korean dishes with a modern flair offer a valuable dining experience to patrons. However, this spot's signature is blood sausage dishes made from the chef's family recipes. His creativity shines in an array of dishes, from traditional to those featuring ingenious new ingredients. Also noteworthy is his effort to create familiar yet refined cuisine that combines family culinary traditions with his culinary experience. The countertops, made from old crossbeams and doors once used in century-old traditional Korean houses, add to the venue's traditional vibe.

MAPO-GU SEODAEMUN-GU YEONGDEUNGPO-GU

소바쥬 N

SOBAJUU

일식 • *Japanese*

070-8676-0218

마포구 큰우물로 75, 지하 1층 22호

B1 #22, 75 Keunumul-ro, Mapo-gu

■ **가 격 PRICE: ₩₩**

소바쥬는 메밀을 주재료로 창의적인 일식을 선보이는 곳이다. 형제가 같이 운영을 시작하여 현재는 동생이 혼자 담당하고 있다. 조리법을 다양하게 활용하여 코스로 제공되는 요리마다 각기 다른 메밀의 식감과 풍미를 구현한다. 참치와 생김 소스를 활용한 자가 제면 소바마키에 프랑스식 메밀 부침인 갈레트와 생선 구이를 제공하는 식이다. 모던하면서도 아늑한 공간, 정갈한 느낌의 접시에서 셰프의 정성이 느껴진다.

Sobajuu is a place that offers creative Japanese dishes using buckwheat as the main ingredient. It was initially run by two brothers, but now the younger sibling is in charge. By employing various cooking techniques, each course showcases different textures and flavors of buckwheat. For example, they offer self-made soba rolls with tuna and seaweed sauce, along with French-style buckwheat pancakes called galettes and grilled fish. The modern yet cozy space, combined with the clean presentation of the dishes, reflects the chef's dedication and attention to detail.

쉐시몽

CHEZ SIMON

프렌치 레스토랑 쉐시몽은 삼청동 시절부터 서교동으로 자리를 옮긴 지금까지 십수 년간 꾸준히 성장해 왔다. 이 식당을 운영하는 부부는 매년 일정 기간 동안 가게 문을 닫고 여행을 다니면서 식재료를 맛보고 연구한다. 여행에서 얻은 영감은 메뉴 개발로 이어진다. 요리 전공자가 아님에도 이들이 쉐시몽을 이만큼 성장시킬 수 있었던 데에는 이러한 끊임없는 노력과 겸손한 자세가 숨어 있다. 쉐시몽만의 단정하고 차분한 프렌치 요리는, 기본에 충실한 조리법과 좋은 식재료를 선별하는 과정을 통해 완성된다. 쉐시몽에서는 한 가지 코스 요리만 제공되며, 예약 인원에 따라 휴무일이 달라지는 독특한 시스템이라 예약은 필수이다.

Chez Simon, This French bistro has been growing at a steady pace. The couple who runs this eatery closes its doors every year for a certain period, so that they can travel around the world to discover new ingredients. It is this unrelenting dedication to cuisine and humility that has marked the success, even though the chefs have had no professional culinary training. This French kitchen offers only course meals, featuring plain, simple dishes that are the culmination of authentic recipes and fresh, carefully curated ingredients.

프렌치 • French

02-730-1045

마포구 월드컵로 10길 48

48 World Cup-ro 10-gil, Mapo-gu

■ **가 격 PRICE: ₩₩**

야키토리 묵

YAKITORI MOOK

야키토리 • *Yakitori*

070-8835-3433

마포구 성미산로 165-1

165-1 Seongmisan-ro, Mapo-gu

■ **가 격 PRICE: ₩₩**

고즈넉한 연남동에 위치한 야키토리 전문점. 실내에 들어서면 길게 펼쳐진 카운터 테이블과 오픈형 주방, 그리고 그 중심에 있는 화로 앞에서 연신 숯불과 짚불을 이용해 구이에 집중하는 김병묵 셰프를 볼 수 있다. 화로를 비추는 밝은 조명 아래의 셰프는 마치 무대에서 독백을 하는 배우처럼 강렬한 시각적 흡입력을 보여준다. 그는, "신선한 토종닭을 매일 손질하며, 최고급 비장탄에 구워 즉시 손님에게 제공한다."는 본질에 집중한다. 셰프가 추구하는 그 본질이야말로 야키토리 묵의 가장 큰 매력이다. 1부와 2부로 나누어 오마카세만을 제공하기 때문에 예약은 꼭 필요하다.

This yakitori specialist is nestled in a quiet corner in Yeonnam-dong. Make your way inside to discover an elongated counter, open kitchen and, at its center, Chef Kim Byoung-mook busy concentrating on grilling yakitori skewers over a charcoal as well as a straw fire. This visually arresting image of the chef, standing under the intense lights that also illuminate the grill, is reminiscent of an actor delivering a monologue on stage. The restaurant's motto is plain and simple, "We prepare fresh purebred Korean chicken every day and grill our skewers over the highest-grade Japanese Binchotan charcoal and serve them immediately to our patrons."

야키토리 키유 (N)

YAKITORI KIYU

닭을 굽는 셰프들의 분주한 손놀림과 은은하게 익어 가는 토종닭 야키토리의 향이 그윽하게 공간을 채우는 곳. 토종닭의 다양한 부위를 그 특성에 맞게 구워 내는 셰프들의 능숙한 솜씨가 음식의 또다른 매력을 느끼게 한다. 한약재를 먹여 자연 친화적으로 키운 닭을 사용하기 때문에 건강하고 질 좋은 부위를 맛볼 수 있다. 특히 뱃속에서 계란이 만들어지고 있는 암탉을 잡아야만 얻을 수 있는 미숙란 쵸친(일본어로 '호롱불'을 뜻한다)에서 재료의 신선함을 확신하게 된다. 토종닭의 특성을 연구해 야키토리의 맛을 발전시키고자 하는 키유는 야키토리를 즐기기에 더없이 훌륭한 선택지가 될 것이다.

The chefs' busy hands deftly grill the chicken as the enticing aroma of Korean tojongdak chicken yakitori fills the entire space. The experienced chefs who grill each cut of tojongdak to perfection add extra charm to each dish. The restaurant uses chickens that are naturally raised on various medicinal herbs so diners can experience healthy, quality cuts of chicken. The menu features unlaid chicken eggs, or chochin, (which means lantern in Japanese), that can only be obtained when an egg-laying hen is slaughtered, highlighting the freshness of the ingredients. Kiyu's goal is to study the attributes of tojongdak to take the flavors of yakitori to the next level, is the place to enjoy delicious yakitori.

야키토리 • *Yakitori*

02-702-1120

서울 마포구 도화4길 31

31 Dohwa 4-gil, Mapo-gu

■ 가 격 PRICE: ₩₩

바비큐 • *Barbecue*

02-3144-1312
마포구 잔다리로 3안길 44
44 Jandari-ro 3 an-gil, Mapo-gu
www.ichiryu.kr

■ **가 격 PRICE: ₩₩**

이치류

ICHIRYU

'일류'를 의미하는 일본어 이치류. 국내 최초의 삿포로식 양구이 전문점으로, 1년 미만의 호주산 생 양고기만을 취급하며, 삿포로에서 직접 공수한 칭기즈칸 불판과 인체에 무해한 비장탄을 사용해 고기를 굽는다. 숙련된 직원들이 돌아가면서 빠른 손놀림으로 고기를 직접 구워주기 때문에 양고기에 익숙지 않은 고객도 편안하게 즐길 수 있다. 바 형식의 그릴 테이블은 즐거운 식사 분위기에 한몫하는 이치류 본점만의 개성으로, 양고기를 즐기기에 더없이 훌륭하다.

Meaning "first class" in Japanese, Ichiryu offers an authentic taste of a Sapporo-style grilled lamb dish prepared on a convex metal skillet. The restaurant, the first of its kind in Korea, only handles young Australian lamb under a year old, and uses skillets imported from Sapporo. The efficient chefs behind the counter make sure the meat is grilled to perfection. Counter seating makes for a casual and interactive dining experience.

일 베키오

IL VECCHIO

이탈리언 • *Italian*

02-302-0944

마포구 월드컵북로 332-12

332-12 World Cup buk-ro, Mapo-gu

■ 가 격 PRICE: ₩₩

일 베키오는 김민균, 김빈나 부부 셰프가 운영하는 소박하고 따뜻한 분위기의 리스토란테로, 뚜렷하면서도 집중된 풍미의 이탈리안 요리를 맛볼 수 있는 곳이다. 또, 한국의 제철 채소와 해산물을 적극 활용한 요리에서 계절의 맛을 물씬 느낄 수 있다. 특히 셰프는 빈틈없이 정확한 쿠킹을 바탕으로 식재료의 익힘 정도를 조절하여 수분 변화에 따른 맛과 향, 질감을 요리에 반영한다. 이러한 특징이 잘 드러나는 요리가 바로 반건조 생면 파스타이다. 셰프는 고객들이 다양한 맛의 변화를 음미할 수 있도록 요리의 변화를 모색하면서도 기복 없이 일관된 풍미를 선사하기 위해 노력한다. 레스토랑이 좁은 골목에 위치해 있어 주차가 쉽지 않으니 참고하기 바란다.

Il Vecchio is a down-to-earth, homey ristorante run by the chef couple Kim Min-gyun and Kim Bin-na. The eatery's Italian fare brims with well-defined and focused flavors, and its signature dishes made with fresh local produce and seafood capture perfectly the tastes of the season. With meticulous execution, the chef duo cooks each and every ingredient to a precise degree with optimal juiciness, bringing out a range of nuanced flavors, aromas, and textures. Indeed, its semi-dried fresh pasta sets the standard for such extraordinary attention to culinary detail. At Il Vecchio, unrelenting gastronomic innovation that aims to delight diners with diverse yet consistent epicurean experiences is the norm. Just one caveat: The establishment is nestled in an alley, so parking may prove a challenge.

중화복춘 살롱

ZHONGHUAFUCHUN SALON

중식 • *Chinese*

010-5124-2207

마포구 연남로 10

10 Yeonnam-ro, Mapo-gu

■ 가 격 PRICE: ₩₩

시대의 흐름에 맞춰 능동적인 변화를 꾀하는 요리는 그 변화 못지않게 전통에 대한 정확하고 바른 이해가 있어야 대중에게 진정성을 전달할 수 있다. 중화복춘 살롱의 남복춘 셰프는 중화요리의 발전적인 변화를 고민하고, 그러한 고민과 연구를 자신의 요리에 담고자 노력한다. 특히 좋은 요리의 근간인 식재료 선별에 각별히 노력을 기울이고 있고, 중국 현지 요리사들과 활발히 교류하면서 중화복춘 살롱의 요리에 점진적인 변화를 도모하고 있다. 중국의 전통 조리법을 바탕으로 현지인의 기호를 고려한 조리법을 적용하여 다양한 풍미의 요리를 선보이는 매력적인 중화요리 레스토랑이다.

To convey its authenticity to diners, a cuisine that transforms and responds to changing times must be founded on a clear and accurate understanding of culinary tradition. At Zhonghuafuchun Salon, Chef Nam Bok-chun's concern for and dedication to bringing positive change to Chinese cuisine is unmistakable in its culinary creations. The chef pays particular attention to selecting quality ingredients, the basic building blocks of good food, while engaging in active exchanges with chefs in mainland China, to promote a gradual evolution in his native cuisine, one dish at a time. Zhonghuafuchun Salon is a fascinating Chinese establishment, where traditional Chinese recipes combined with local twists translate into a feast of richly flavorful dishes.

진미식당

JINMI SIKDANG

간장게장 한 가지만을 자신 있게 선보이는 게장 전문점으로, 이곳에선 최상급의 서해안 꽃게만을 사용한다. 진미식당이 오랫동안 꾸준한 사랑을 받을 수 있었던 비법은 바로 재료의 품질과 변함없는 맛에 대한 고집이다. 그간 정치인과 연예인을 비롯해 이곳을 다녀간 수많은 유명 인사들의 자취와 세월의 흔적이 소박한 식당 곳곳에 남아 있다. 이곳은 당일 판매할 양만큼만 그때그때 준비하기 때문에 혹여 늦은 시간에 가면 동날 수도 있으니 가급적이면 예약 후 방문하기를 권한다.

This humble yet busy restaurant has been serving raw soy-marinated crabs and nothing else for the past decade. Only the freshest local blue swimmer crabs, sourced from the west coast, are prepared daily with the kitchen's special recipe soy sauce marinade. Keep in mind that just enough crab for consumption is prepared each day, so if you drop by at a late hour, they may be completely sold out. A prior reservation is highly recommended.

게장 • *Gejang*

02-3211-4468

마포구 마포대로 186-6

186-6 Mapo-daero, Mapo-gu

■ **가 격 PRICE: ₩₩**

Ovnigraphic/Shutterstock

서초구
송파구
SEOCHO-GU
SONGPA-GU

비채나
BICENA

한식 • *Korean*

02-3213-1261

송파구 올림픽로 300, 롯데월드 타워 81층

81F Lotte World Tower, 300 Olympic-ro, Songpa-gu

www.bicena.com

■ **가 격 PRICE: ₩₩₩₩**

단아한 한식 다이닝을 선보이는 비채나. 이곳의 차별화된 맛은 시간과 정성이 깃든 장과 김치 등 가장 기본적인 것에서부터 시작된다. 현대적 이면서도 전통에 충실하며 고급스러운 메뉴에선 한식에 대한 셰프의 철학을 엿볼 수 있다. 여기에 전 세계에서 가장 높은 층에 위치한 한식 레스토랑에서 바라보는 서울 전경은 또 다른 즐거움이다.

Towering above Seoul on the 81st floor of the Signiel Seoul Hotel, Bicena is trying to stay true to the spirit of traditional Korean fine dining. Bicena continues to respect the most fundamental details of slow Korean cuisine such as Jang (fermented sauces) and kimchi, the outcome of time and nature doing their work. The views from the restaurant - officially the tallest traditional restaurant in the world - are unrivaled.

꿉당
GGUPDANG

돼지 목살 전문점 '꿉당'. 신사역 바로 앞에 위치한 꿉당은 15일간 숙성한 목살이 주 메뉴다. 직접 제작한 알루미늄 불판과 비장탄 위에서 빠르게 구워 낸 고기는 풍부한 육즙과 부드러운 지방이 일품이다. 일식 셰프의 컨설팅을 받았다는 쌀밥에 고추냉이를 곁들여 스시처럼 만들어 먹으면 육즙이 밴 부드러운 밥맛을 맛볼 수 있으니 꼭 함께 주문할 것.

Situated right near Sinsa station, this restaurant specializes in grilled pork butt cured for 15 days before being quickly grilled on a specially made aluminum grate over Binchotan charcoal. Thanks to this method of cooking, the meat is fatty, tender, and juicy. As in the case of sushi, when it is eaten with rice (prepared with a recipe conceived by a Japanese consultant chef) and Korean horseradish, the meat juice is absorbed by the rice, making it even softer. The side orders are not to be missed.

바비큐 • *Barbecue*

02-545-9600

서초구 강남대로 615

615 Gangnam-daero, Seocho-gu

■ **가 격 PRICE: ₩**

스바루
SUBARU

소바 • Soba

02-596-4882

서초구 방배중앙로 21길 7

7 Bangbae-jungangno 21-gil, Seocho-gu

■ 가 격 PRICE: ₩

"소바의 본고장과 다름없는 맛을 구현하여 고객에게 최고의 소바를 제공하겠다."는 철학으로 끊임없는 연구와 개발을 지속해온 강영철 셰프. 오랜 일본 생활에서 경험한 소바의 순수한 맛에 매료되어 지금까지 소바를 위한 한길을 걷고 있다. 강영철 셰프는 별도의 제면실을 두고 전통 방식으로 그날그날 소바 면을 뽑는데, 밀과 메밀의 비율을 2:8로 맞춘 니하치 스타일의 소바를 고수한다. 소바의 순수한 맛이 강점인 자루 소바를 비롯해 깊은 감칠맛의 오리 메밀과 들기름 메밀이 스바루에서 가장 인기 있는 대표 메뉴이다.

Chef Kang Yeong-cheol has for long studied and developed the soba-making craft, with the sole aspiration to serve the same outstanding soba as can be tasted in the birthplace of the dish, The chef spent many years in Japan, where he became enamored with the pure taste of soba; and it is this love that propelled him on his culinary journey. In Subaru, soba for the day's meals are freshly made in the traditional way. He sticks to the classic ni-hachi-style version, which consists of two parts wheat and eight parts buckwheat. The signature dishes include zaru soba, which boasts a clean and pure taste; soba with umami-rich duck meat and green onion; as well as soba with perilla oil.

양양 메밀 막국수
YANGYANG MEMIL MAKGUKSU

100% 순수 메밀만을 사용하고 주문을 받은 후에 제면 작업을 시작하는 것을 원칙으로 하는 것이 양양 메밀 막국수의 비결이라면 비결이다. 십 수년간 메밀 막국수 식당을 운영해온 이유도 대표 자신이 막국수를 너무 좋아해서라고. 메밀 막국수가 대표 메뉴지만 직접 담근 김치를 이용한 김치 비빔국수 또한 이곳의 별미다. 기본 상차림은 단출하지만 정성이 가득하고, 무엇보다 주력 메뉴인 막국수 맛이 변함없이 훌륭하다. 11월 김장철에는 열흘간 영업을 하지 않으니 참고하기 바란다.

The not-so-secret secret to the longevity and success of Yangyang Memil Makguksu is that its noodles are made with 100% buckwheat and that they are made to order every time. The proprietor of the restaurant began his business many years ago for one reason only - buckwheat noodles were his favorite food. Although the restaurant specializes in the Gangwon-do Province-style cold buckwheat noodles, it also makes a fine bowl of spicy noodles composed with homemade kimchi. The basic spread is simple, but it's rustic food at its best, made with love.

메밀국수 • *Memil-guksu*

02-3482-3738

서초구 동광로 15길 10

10 Donggwang-ro 15-gil, Seocho-gu

■ 가 격 PRICE: ₩

옥돌현옥 N

OKDOL HEYONOK

냉면 • *Naengmyeon*

02-404-4824
송파구 오금로 36길 26-1
26-1 Ogeum-ro 36-gil, Songpa-gu

■ 가 격 PRICE: ₩

오로지 메밀만을 사용해 씹을수록 메밀의 구수함이 느껴지는 순면에 고소하고 진한 육수와 풍부한 메밀향을 느낄 수 있는 옥돌현옥. 생긴 지는 그리 오래 되지 않았지만 평양냉면 마니아들 사이에서는 호평을 받는 곳이다. 두부가 많이 들어가 구수한 만두를 비롯해 어복쟁반과 가자미식해도 인기 메뉴이다. 콜키지를 지불하면 와인과 함께 즐길 수도 있다. 슴슴하지만 깊은 맛을 즐겨보시길.

Taste the deeply savory broth and the nutty flavor of the noodles made from 100% buckwheat that intensifies the more you chew at Okdol Hyeonok. The restaurant is fairly new, but it has gained a solid following among Pyongyang naengmyeon connoisseurs. Some of their most popular dishes are mandu with a nuttiness that comes from plenty of tofu in the filling, eobok jaengban, and gajami shikhye. You can also have your favorite wine with your meal for a corkage fee. Enjoy the mild flavors with incredible depth.

임병주 산동 칼국수
LIMBYUNGJOO SANDONG KALGUKSU

1988년에 문을 열어 30년 이상의 긴 역사를 자랑하는 임병주 산동 칼국수. 매일 신선한 재료로 직접 만들어내는 수제 칼국수를 찾는 사람들은 여전하다. 기분 좋은 쫄깃한 식감과 푸짐하게 들어간 조개에서 우러나온 시원한 국물 맛이 일품이다. 더불어 평양식 왕만두, 고소한 콩국수, 물고추를 갈아 만든 겉절이까지 여전히 맛있는 음식을 즐길 수 있다.

Since 1988, this restaurant has been proving that a humble bowl of noodle soup can be truly memorable when done right. The pleasant texture of their hand-cut noodles, prepared daily from scratch, and immensely comforting broth, served piping hot and packed with flavor from the clams in all their naturally sweet glory, are stellar. Other favorites include Pyeongyang jumbo sized dumplings and noodles in cold soybean soup. Simple but warm service.

칼국수 • *Kalguksu*

02-3473-7972

서초구 강남대로 37길 65

65 Gangnam-daero 37-gil, Seocho-gu

■ **가 격 PRICE: ₩**

도우룸

DOUGHROOM

이탤리언 • *Italian*

02-535-9386

서초구 동광로 99, 2층

2F, 99 Donggwang-ro, Seocho-gu

www.soignerestaurantgroup.com

■ 가 격 PRICE: ₩₩

100% 수제 파스타 면을 전문으로 하는 이탤리언 레스토랑. 영어로 '반죽'이라는 의미의 '도우'에서 이름을 딴 이곳에서 가장 주목해야 하는 곳은 파스타를 만드는 도우룸이다. 10가지 종류의 파스타를 제공하며, 포장 판매도 겸하고 있다. 레스토랑의 반 이상을 차지하고 있는 오픈 키친은 주방과 손님과의 거리를 최소화하고 음식의 맛에 대한 손님들의 반응을 실시간으로 확인하고 싶은 셰프의 마음을 반영했다. 정통 이탤리언 파스타 외에도 메밀과 곰취를 이용한 한국적인 파스타도 맛볼 수 있다.

Dedicated to making artisanal pasta from scratch, Doughroom is a keeper for all Italian food lovers. The dough room itself, where all the pastas are made fresh daily, is undoubtedly the heart of the restaurant. While offering authentic flavors of Italy, it also serves fusion dishes using ingredients familiar to the local palate — for example, their buckwheat cannelloni. Asking for the action-packed dough room table when making a reservation is highly recommended.

미나미
MINAMI

일식 분야에서 다양한 경험을 쌓은 남창수 셰프의 소바 전문점 미나미. 무궁무진한 일식 요리 중 굳이 소바를 선택한 이유는 부지불식간에 메밀 면 특유의 은은한 매력에 빠졌기 때문이라고 한다. 그는 일식 소바의 오랜 역사와 전통을 존중하는 동시에 자신만의 개성이 묻어나는 다양한 소바 요리를 선보이고 있다. 그윽한 불 향의 간장조림 붕장어를 올린 아나고난방과 교토에서 직접 공수한 간장조림 청어를 올린 니신난방이 이곳의 대표 메뉴다. 소바 외에 생선구이와 튀김 요리 같은 단품 요리도 제공한다.

The star of the show at Minami is Japanese-style soba noodles. Trained at the prestigious Tsuji Culinary Institute in Osaka, Japan, Chef Nam Chang-soo is no stranger to the world of Japanese cuisine, but he professes that soba is his one true love. While respecting the time-honored traditions of Japanese-style buckwheat noodles, Nam adds his own spin to the soba dishes he serves. Customer favorites include soba noodle soup topped with soy sauce-braised and grilled conger eel as well as another variety with soy sauce-braised herring imported from Kyoto.

소바 • *Soba*

02-522-0373

서초구 서초대로 58길 31-2

31-2 Seocho-daero 58-gil, Seocho-gu

■ **가 격 PRICE: ₩**

백년옥

BAEK NYUN OK

두부 • Dubu

02-523-2860

서초구 남부순환로 2407

2407 Nambusunhwan-ro, Seocho-gu

■ **가 격 PRICE: ₩**

예술의전당 맞은편 도로변에 위치한 백년옥은 1992년 영업을 개시한 이래 많은 이들의 사랑을 받는 두부 요리 전문점이다. 세월이 고스란히 묻어나는 소박한 실내는 테이블석과 방석 자리로 나뉘어 있다. 두부 전문점답게 콩비지, 되비지, 신선한 순두부 등 여러 가지 수제 두부 요리를 선보인다. 손님들이 붐비는 식사 시간에 본관이 만석일 경우, 신관의 식사 공간을 이용하기 바란다.

Located across the main road from Seoul Arts Center, Baek Nyun Ok has been attracting loyal patrons, including local performers and musicians in droves, since 1992. This humble institution specializes in fresh homemade bean curd, which is the central ingredient in a variety of dishes offered. These include plain soft bean curd and soft bean curd stew with nutty perilla seeds. The interior is simply decorated and offers both table and floor seating.

버드나무집

BUDNAMUJIP

버드나무집은 1977년부터 명맥을 이어온 한우 구이 전문점이다. 초창기엔 주물럭만을 판매했지만, 지금은 소갈비와 특수 부위도 제공한다. 오랜 세월 한자리를 지켜온 동네 터줏대감답게 한 집안의 3대가 단골인 경우도 많다고 한다. 간장을 전혀 사용하지 않고 천일염으로만 간한 암소 갈비는 특유의 부드러운 육질과 고소한 풍미를 자랑한다. 조미료를 넣지 않은 깔끔하고 삼삼한 반찬 역시 이곳만의 매력이다.

Since 1977, this family-style restaurant has garnered an appreciative following of barbecue lovers, often seeing three generations of loyal patrons from one family frequenting the shop. A popular locality for residents south of the river, it specializes in various cuts of meat exclusively from the cow including ribs, sirloin and tripe. The rich flavors of the exceptionally tender meat is enhanced simply with quality bay salt.

바비큐 • *Barbecue*

02-3473-4167

서초구 효령로 434

434 Hyoryeong-ro, Seocho-gu

www.budnamujip.com

■ 가 격 PRICE: ₩₩

서초구 송파구

벽제갈비

BYEOKJE GALBI

바비큐 • *Barbecue*

02-415-5522

송파구 양재대로 71길 1-4

1-4 Yangjae-daero 71-gil, Songpa-gu

www.bjgalbi.com

■ **가 격 PRICE: ₩₩₩**

양념 소갈비의 대명사로 불리는 벽제갈비에선 매일 마리째 경매하는 최상위 1% 한우(BMS No9)를 사용한다. 이곳이 오랜 시간 바비큐, 냉면, 탕류 등 다양한 한식 요리에서 한결같은 맛을 유지할 수 있었던 비결은 바로 분야별 장인들로 구성된 팀의 지식과 전문성에 기반을 두고 있다. 이곳에선 대표 메뉴인 설화생갈비와 설화꽃등심을 비롯해 다양한 탕 요리와 식사 메뉴를 제공해 가벼운 한 끼 식사를 선호하는 손님은 물론, 푸짐한 소고기 바비큐를 원하는 단체 모임까지 가능해 매 끼니때마다 인산인해를 이룬다.

Byeokje Galbi is a local institution that has been serving legendary barbecued beef short ribs since 1986. The restaurant's attention to quality begins from the breeding of the cows at a local farm in Pocheon. Only the top 1% (BMS No9) are purchased, whole, at a daily auction, after which they are handled by an artisan butcher. The signature dishes are the beautifully marbled short ribs and ribeye grilled over charcoal. From a simple meal of cold buckwheat noodles and soup to an elaborate barbecue feast, Byeokje Galbi caters to all occasions.

봉산옥
BONGSANOK

서민들의 일상에 깊숙이 자리매김한 한국의 대표적인 대중음식 중의 하나가 바로 만둣국이다. 이곳의 윤영숙 대표는 황해도 사리원 출신의 시어머니를 통해 자연스럽게 황해도식 만둣국을 접하게 되었으며, 오랜 경험을 통해 터득한 깊은 맛을 고객들에게 전하고 있다. 그녀는 삼삼하고 깔끔한 맛의 만두소를 만들기 위해 오랫동안 시어머니의 비법을 고수하고 있다. 무엇보다 '고향의 맛 혹은 어린 시절 할머니가 만들어주셨던 만둣국 맛'이라는 평을 들을 때 뿌듯함을 느낀다는 윤 대표의 말에서 자부심이 느껴진다.

Mandutguk, or Korean dumpling soup, is a dish that is deeply rooted in the day-to-day lives of Koreans. Owner Yoon Young-sook became acquainted with Hwanghaedo-style dumpling soup through her mother-in-law, a native of Sariwon, which is north of the border. To emulate the pure taste of the original dumpling filling, Yoon says she follows her recipe to the tee and feels very proud when she hears customers say her dumplings remind them of their own grandmother's.

만두 • *Mandu*

02-525-2282

서초구 반포대로 8길 5-6

5-6 Banpo-daero 8-gil, Seocho-gu

■ 가 격 PRICE: ₩

SEOCHO-GU SONGPA-GU

프렌치 • French

02-3213-1231

송파구 올림픽로 300, 롯데월드 타워 81층

81F Lotteworld Tower, 300 Olympic-ro, Songpa-gu

www.lottehotel.com/seoul-signiel/ko/dining/restaurant-stay-modern.html

■ 가 격 PRICE: ₩₩₩₩

스테이

STAY

옐로와 골드 컬러로 포인트를 준 경쾌하고 모던한 인테리어, 전 좌석에서 감상할 수 있는 서울의 화려한 스카이라인. 시그니엘 81층에 위치한 STAY는 프렌치 파인 다이닝의 진수를 보여주는 세계적인 명성의 셰프, 야닉 알레노의 모던 프렌치 레스토랑이다. 이곳에선 수준 높은 요리를 편안한 분위기에서 즐길 수 있는데, 매주 새로운 요리를 하나씩 소개하며 계절마다 새로운 메뉴를 선보인다. 또한 레스토랑 중앙에 자리한 페이스트리 라이브러리에선 프렌치 요리의 피날레를 장식하는 디저트를 다양하게 즐길 수 있다.

Perched on the 81st floor of Signiel Seoul Hotel, STAY takes 'dining with a view' to a whole new level with its sweeping vistas of the metropolis. STAY is celebrated Chef Yannick Alléno's modern casual French restaurant, a youthful and vibrant space accented with yellow and gold. The live Pastry Library is its signature feature that offers a tantalizing assortment of sweets and confections that guests can help themselves to.

에쌍스

ESSENCE

클래식한 프렌치 요리로 유명한 쏠레이의 김영선 셰프가 우여곡절 끝에 쏠레이에서의 여정을 정리하고 에쌍스에서 자신만의 프렌치 퀴진을 선보이고 있다. 에쌍스에서는 전보다 편안하고 가벼운 비스트로 스타일의 프렌치 요리를 제공함으로써 요리에 대한 접근성을 높였다. 레스토랑에도 변화의 바람이 불고 있지만 김영선 셰프는 클래식한 퀴진 스타일을 변함없이 고수하면서, 정확한 방식으로 굽고 익힌 식재료와 정성이 깃든 소스를 통해 깊이 있는 맛을 전하고 있다. 다양한 스타일의 매력적인 현대식 요리가 대세로 자리잡은 시대이지만 진정성이 느껴지는 에쌍스의 차분한 요리는 프렌치 퀴진의 기본을 다시 한번 생각하게 해준다.

프렌치 • *French*

010-8010-5099

서울시 서초구 반포대로 4길 12

12 Banpo-daero 4-gil, Seocho-gu

■ **가 격 PRICE: ₩₩**

After a series of twists and turns, Chef Kim Yeong-seon wrapped up his famed career as a classic French chef at Restaurant Soleil and opened Essence to offer his very own version of French cuisine. Here, the chef provides bistro-style French fare that is cozier and lighter, and therefore more accessible, than the fare at his previous restaurant. Although the winds of change are sweeping through the dining industry, he is steadfastly committed to the classic style, delivering deep flavors through precisely baked and cooked ingredients and carefully crafted sauces. In this era of contemporary cuisine that appeals to diners with a wide range of novel culinary styles, Essence's unpretentious meals highlighting genuine authenticity remind us, once again, of the core of French cuisine.

컨템퍼러리 •

Contemporary

02-534-9544

서초구 동광로 164

164 Donggwang-ro, Seocho-gu

■ 가 격 PRICE: ₩₩₩

줄라이

JULY

고즈넉한 서래마을에서 오랜 시간 동안 우직하고 충실한 음식을 만들어온 줄라이. 정통 프렌치 요리에 기반을 두고 있지만, 국내 식재료를 최대한 활용해 셰프의 개성대로 전통을 재해석한 노력이 돋보인다. 한국 고유의 발효 식품인 간장과 된장 등을 요리에 이용하는 것이 그러한 예다. 이곳에선 화려하진 않지만 재료 본연의 맛이 살아 있는 정직한 음식을 선보이며, 작지만 아늑한 다이닝 홀은 특별한 식사 분위기를 제공한다

This restaurant's creativity is apparent in the food it creates — inherently French, but with an unexpected spin on flavors from using distinctly local ingredients. For example, the chef incorporates traditional fermented condiments such as gochujang and doenjang into his sauces and uses indigenous grains like godaemi — organic ancient colored rice. It's located in Seoraemaeul, also known as 'Little France', and the restaurant's vibe is cozy and intimate.

해남천일관

HAENAM CHEONILGWAN

다채로운 한식 문화의 한 축을 담당하는 남도 한식. 해남천일관은 세대를 거듭해 남도 한식을 지켜왔다는 점에서 그 의미가 남다른 곳이다. 해남천일관은 해남에서 오랜 역사를 자랑하는 천일식당의 한 뿌리로, 창업자의 가족 중 하나인 이화영 대표가 운영 중이다. 일반적인 요리사들과 달리 이화영 대표가 오롯이 가족과의 일상 속에서 축적한 맛과 레시피는 해남천일관만의 자산이다. 시대 흐름에 맞춰 한식도 현대화되었지만 해남천일관은 식재료가 풍부하던 시절의 메뉴와 조리법, 식재료를 보존하기 위해 애쓰고 있다. 푸짐하게 차린 남도 한식 한 상에는 많은 요리가 올라가지만 특히 반지김치, 토하젓을 넣은 고추김치, 떡갈비에서 남도의 풍미를 물씬 느낄 수 있다. 다이닝 공간이 모두 개별 룸으로 구성되어 있어 목적에 맞게 이용이 가능하다.

한식 • *Korean*

02-568-7775

서초구 반포대로 39길 36-1

36-1 Banpo-daero 39-gil, Seocho-gu

www.haenamcheonilgwan.kr

■ **가 격 PRICE: ₩₩₩**

Namdo cuisine, the cuisine of South Jeolla Province, occupies an eminent position in the diverse Korean culinary landscape. Haenam Cheonilgwan is a singular undertaking as it has steadfastly safeguarded Namdo cuisine through the generations. It branched out from Cheonil Sikdang, a Haenam-based diner with a proud history, and is headed by CEO Lee Hwa-young, a relative of the original founder. The asset that distinguishes Lee's establishment from typical diners run by chefs is its tried-and-true flavors and recipes evolved and accumulated through the everyday vignettes she shares with her family. Korean cuisine has modernized to meet changing times, yet this food haven still strives to preserve the menus, recipes, and ingredients used when traditional ingredients were aplenty. Among the mélange of dishes that sumptuously fill your table, standouts bursting with Namdo flavors include banji kimchi (Namdo-style white kimchi), chili pepper kimchi with salted freshwater shrimp, and grilled short rib patties. The dining space consists entirely of private rooms suitable for a diverse range of occasions.

TwilightShow/Getty Images Plus

성동구
광진구
SEONGDONG-GU
GWANGJIN-GU

뛰뚜아멍 N

TUTOIEMENT

프렌치 • French

02-499-9056

성동구 광나루로 11길 20

20 Gwangnaru-ro 11-gil, Seongdong-gu

■ 가 격 PRICE: ₩₩₩₩

'뛰뚜아멍(Tutoiement)'은 '말 놓기', '반말'이라는 뜻이다. 격식을 차리기보다 요리를 매개로 편안하게 고객과 소통하겠다는 김도현 셰프의 의도가 담긴 공간이다. 그래서인지 이곳에서는 식사하는 내내 차분한 분위기와 따뜻한 서비스를 경험하며 편안하게 다이닝을 즐길 수 있다. 흥미로운 사실은, 소탈함을 지향하는 셰프의 바람과 달리 디테일의 완성도가 뛰어난 세련된 프렌치 퀴진이 후각과 미각을 자극해 요리에 집중하게 만든다는 점이다. 요리를 통해 표현하고자 하는 식재료의 세밀한 맛과 질감, 풍미를 살리면서 소스와의 어우러짐을 감안한 배치와 조합이 매력적이다. 셰프는 자신이 쌓아온 요리 경력이 누군가를 오마주하거나 흉내 내기 위한 것이 아니라는 점을 뛰뚜아멍에서 증명하면서 오래 기억되는 맛의 여운을 제공하고 있다.

The name Tutoiement means to speak in a friendly, informal way, reflecting Chef Kim Do-hyeon's desire to connect casually with his diners through food. Diners can enjoy their meal in a calm, welcoming setting with attentive, friendly service. Interestingly, contrary to the chef's preference for a casual dining experience, the precisely cooked, sophisticated French cuisine stimulates the olfactory and gustatory senses, drawing focus to the food. The chef skillfully expresses the subtle flavors, textures, and nuances of each ingredient, and plates the food in ways that best showcases the harmony between the food and accompanying sauces. At Tutoiement, Chef Kim shows his diners that his culinary journey is not about paying homage to or imitating others but instead about creating a memorable dining experience.

계월곰탕

KYEWOL GOMTANG

성수동 계월 곰탕. 이름에서 알 수 있듯이 닭곰탕을 맛볼 수 있는 곳으로 메뉴도 닭으로 만든 요리 세 가지가 전부다. 이곳의 곰탕은 따뜻한 밥 위에 저온으로 부드럽게 조리한 닭 가슴살과 아삭하게 데친 얼갈이 배추, 기름을 걷어낸 깔끔한 육수를 더해 심심하면서도 풍부한 맛을 자랑한다. 점심에는 김부각과 함께 내는 매콤한 닭무침, 된장을 발라 토치로 구운 닭 수육을 저렴한 가격에 곁들임 메뉴로 즐길 수 있다. 여름에는 차가운 국수도 판매하니 참고하시길.

Kyewol Gomtang in Seongsu-dong specializes in Korean chicken soup or gomtang, as the name of the eatery plainly suggests, with the menu consisting of a mere three chicken-based offerings. Warm rice, chicken breast slices tenderly cooked at low temperatures, winter cabbage blanched to crunchy perfection, and clear broth skimmed of fat - all culminate in clean yet rich flavors in the soup. For lunch, spicy seasoned chicken with laver chips; and boiled chicken, which is then marinated with soybean paste and torch-grilled, are available as wallet-friendly side orders. The joint's cold noodle soup, a summer special, is another not-to-be-missed treat.

곰탕 • *Gomtang*

070-8703-0310

성동구 성덕정 3길 8

8 Seongdeokjeong 3-gil, Seongdong-gu

■ 가 격 PRICE: ₩

SEONGDONG-GU GWANGJIN-GU

맷돌
MATTDOL

멕시칸 • *Mexican*

010-4886-2928

성동구 성덕정길 63

63 Seongdeokjeong-gil, Seongdong-gu

■ **가 격 PRICE: ₩**

레스토랑 맷돌은 남다른 도전 의식을 가지고 요리사로서 실력을 키워온 이창윤 셰프의 멕시칸 퀴진 레스토랑이다. 그가 가장 공을 들이는 건 멕시코 요리에 두루 쓰이는 토르티야다. 맷돌에 가면 그가 멕시코에서 배운 대로 마사를 손으로 눌러 가며 토르티야를 만드는 모습을 종종 볼 수 있다. 이렇게 셰프가 직접 만든 토르티야가 들어간 맷돌의 토스타다와 타코를 먹어 보면, 식감과 풍미가 천편일률적인 기존의 토르티야 요리와는 차원이 다르다는 것을 느끼게 된다. 셰프가 배우고 익힌 여러 요리 스타일을 한국의 제철 식재료에 접목시켜 완성한 맷돌의 멕시칸 퀴진은 직관적인 맛으로 미식가의 입을 즐겁게 한다.

Mattdol is a Mexican restaurant run by Chef Lee Chang-yun, who has been steadfastly honing his culinary skills with an exceptional adventurous spirit. He has a particular passion for tortilla. At Mattdol, customers can often see the chef kneading masa to make tortilla, just as he learned in Mexico. Anyone who tries its tostada and taco dishes, featuring his housemade tortilla, will instinctively realize that, compared with common tortilla-based dishes with run-of-the-mill flavors and textures, his creations are on a whole other level. Mattdol is where the chef's training in diverse culinary styles meets Korean seasonal ingredients. And the result is a unique Mexican cuisine with intuitive flavors that can captivate the palates of gourmets.

정면
JEONGMYEON

7석 남짓의 스테인리스 테이블과 오픈형 주방이 전부인 이곳. '뜻이 담긴 국수'라는 뜻의 정면은 셰프가 홀로 운영하는 고기 국수 집이다. 메뉴는 백면과 홍면, 딱 두가지가 전부이지만 깊은 맛 하나는 일품이다. 해물과 돼지고기, 닭고기를 이용해 만든 육수에서 깊은 맛을 느낄 수 있으며 얇게 저민 쫄깃한 돼지고기와 양파, 홍고추가 올라간 쌀국수는 보기만 해도 풍성하다. 홍면은 맵기 조절이 가능하며 작은 공깃밥이 함께 나와 배부른 한 끼를 즐길 수 있다.

A seven-seat stainless steel table and an open kitchen are all there is to Jeongmyeon, which means "noodles infused with meaning." This one-chef operation serves noodle soups with meat. White noodle soup and red noodle soup are the only two dishes on the menu, but both offer deep flavor profiles. The broth, made with seafood, pork, and chicken, reveals a rich set of tastes. Garnishes topping the rice noodles, including thin slices of pleasantly chewy pork, onion, and red pepper, are truly a sight to behold. The red noodle soup, which can be made with varying levels of spiciness, is served with a bowl of rice for a filling meal.

국수 • *Noodles*

010-9974-3592

광진구 능동로 13길 88

88 Neungdong-ro 13-gil, Gwangjin-gu

■ **가 격 PRICE: ₩**

팩피
FAGP

이탤리언 • *Italian*

02-6052-7595
성동구 왕십리로 136
136 Wangsimni-ro, Seongdong-gu

■ 가 격 PRICE: ₩₩

가족의 영향으로 어린 시절부터 자연스럽게 요리 인생을 꿈꿔온 이종혁 셰프. 국내외에서 다양한 경험을 쌓은 그는 팩피에서 대중적인 파스타 장르를 자신만의 창의적인 감성으로 풀어낸 간결하면서도 개성 넘치는 메뉴를 선보인다. 오픈 주방에서 고객과 소통하며 요리하는 순간이 무척이나 행복하다는 이 셰프. 팩피를 찾는 모든 고객이 편안하고 행복하게 식사를 즐길 수만 있다면 그걸로 만족한다는 그의 바람이 잘 투영된 공간이다.

In a city where a plate of pasta is as ubiquitous as a bowl of kalguksu, it takes a good dose of creativity and knowledge of the genre to be recognized for one's craft. Chef Lee Jong-hyuk is armed with both. FAGP is a casual restaurant that offers a simple yet inventive menu with a focus on the relatively humble pasta. There is a genuine sense of conviviality here, which comes as no surprise, as the chef says he revels in engaging with his customers while cooking in the open kitchen.

본 앤 브레드

BORN AND BRED

자타 공인 최상급 한우를 즐길 수 있는 '본 앤 브레드'는 정상원 대표의 남다른 한우 사랑에서 시작됐다. 한우 전문 유통업체를 운영하는 아버지 밑에서 쌓은 경험과 본인의 미식 취미가 합쳐져 탄생한 이곳은 다양한 콘셉트의 한우 다이닝을 제공하는 독특한 공간이다. 2층 캐주얼 레스토랑은 '마장동'하면 떠오르는 정육식당에서 콘셉트를 따왔지만, 현대적 인테리어와 고급 메뉴로 기존의 식당들과 차별화를 뒀다. 1층의 정육점 라운지를 비롯해 3층에는 코스 요리 전문 공간도 준비되어 있고, 지하에서는 본 앤 브레드의 정체성을 제대로 경험할 수 있는 한우 맡김 코스도 제공한다.

Born and Bred is the brainchild of Jeong Sang-won, whose obsession with top-quality Korean beef started young, thanks to his beef purveyor father. Jeong created a one-of-a-kind space that offers three different dining concepts. The casual eatery on the second floor has been inspired by the butcher restaurants that populate the vicinity of the Majang Meat Market, but it is decidedly more modern and refined. The butcher lounge occupies the first floor while the third floor offers a multi-course beef experience. However, for a taste of what the restaurant is truly all about, head down to the basement for the chef's specialty beef course.

바비큐 • *Barbecue*

02-2294-5005

성동구 마장로 42길 1, 2층

2F, 1 Majang-ro 42-gil, Seongdong-gu

www.bandb.co.kr

■ 가 격 PRICE: ₩₩₩

SEONGDONG-GU GWANGJIN-GU

오부이용

AU BOUILLON

프렌치 • French

02-6401-1048

성동구 독서당로 51길 29-1

29-1 Dokseodang-ro 51-gil, Seongdong-gu

■ 가 격 PRICE: ₩₩

아파트 단지로 둘러싸인, 예스러움이 묻어 있는 금호동의 작은 골목에 숨겨진 프렌치 레스토랑. 레스토랑에 들어서면 외관과는 너무나 다른 분위기의 프렌치 소품과 장식들로 꾸며진 공간과 마주하게 된다. 이 분위기와 절묘하게 어우러지는 클래식 프렌치 요리들이 미감에 즐거움을 선사한다. 기본에 충실한 클래식 프렌치 요리를 합리적인 가격으로 제공한다는 셰프의 원칙이 잘 반영된 이곳에서는 요리와 공간의 절묘한 조화와 설득력이 느껴진다.

Hidden in a quaint, tiny alley that's surrounded by apartment complexes in Geumho-dong, this French restaurant greets patrons with classic objets d'art and other fixings. However, the vibe here is different from the surrounding neighborhood, and thanks to an equally striking carte of familiar French fare, diners can expect nothing less than exceptional culinary enjoyment. The menu closely reflects the chef's desire to offer well-crafted French cuisine at reasonable prices.

주052 N

SOOL052

'주052'라는 상호는 술 '주(酒)'에 셰프들의 출신지 지역번호 '052'를 조합해 만들었다. 한식 요리 주점 주052는 범상치 않은 상호만큼이나 재미 있는 아이디어가 돋보이는 요리를 선보인다. 두 명의 셰프는 한식의 밑바탕을 이루는 '장'과 '발효 기법'을 활용하여 개성 넘치는 한식 요리를 제공한다. 이름만 들으면 익숙한 요리들이지만 직접 맛을 보면 메뉴 하나하나에서 남다른 정성과 맛이 느껴진다. 또한 요리들 간에 맛의 궁합도 좋아 여러 메뉴를 함께 즐기기에도 안성맞춤이다. 한식과 한국 술의 절묘한 조화를 경험하기에 더없이 좋은 곳이다.

Sool052 is a portmanteau of "sool" (alcohol) and "052," the area code of the region the chefs live in. It's a Korean gastropub brimming with culinary ideas as playful as the restaurant's name. Employing diverse fermented pastes and fermentation techniques, the basis of most Korean cuisine, the chef duo offers unique dishes that are household names yet prepared with exceptional care and attention to detail to draw out unforgettable flavors. On top of this, the varied menu selections tend to go well together, making it easy to enjoy multiple items at once. These allures make Sool052 a perfect place to experience the exquisite harmony between Korean food and Korean alcohol.

한식 • *Korean*

02-2281-0343

성동구 고산자로 14길 26

26 Gosanja-ro 14-gil, Seongdong-gu

www.sool052.com

■ 가 격 PRICE: ₩₩

SEONGDONG-GU GWANGJIN-GU

Mirko Kuzmanovic/Getty Images Plus

용산구
YONGSAN-GU

소설한남

SOSEOUL HANNAM

한식 • *Korean*

02-797-5995

용산구 한남대로 20길 21-18, 지하 1층

B1F, 21-18 Hannam-daero 20-gil, Yongsan-gu

■ 가 격 PRICE: ₩₩₩

한 편의 소설(小說) 같은 한식. '서울의 현 시대를 반영한 한식(SO SEOUL)'이라는 중의적 의미를 갖고 있는 '소설한남'은 소박하고 정갈한 한식을 현대적으로 재해석하는 곳이다. 맛의 조화가 곧 한식의 매력이라고 생각한다는 셰프는 한국인에게 너무 익숙하기 때문에 감동적인 식사를 제공하기 어려울 수 있는 무침, 지짐, 찜 등의 요리를 친숙한 재료를 활용해 만들어 낸다. 다시마 부각과 청국장, 곰취와 묵은지를 곁들여 먹는 생선회를 비롯해 숯불구이 주꾸미와 닭 요리도 별미이다.

Inspired by local culinary traditions but dedicated to expressing the modern-day sensibilities of Seoul cuisine, Soseoul Hannam serves up contemporary Korean food using ingredients that are most familiar to the local palate. The chef's creations are an homage to some of the more typical dishes and preparation techniques, including seasoned salads, pan-fried and braised dishes. Kelp chips, rich soybean paste stew, sliced raw fish with gomchwi (Fischer's ragwort) and aged kimchi, and chargrilled webfoot octopus are some of its signature offerings. The restaurant also offers traditional liquor pairings.

소울
SOUL

근대 서울의 흔적이 아직 남아 있는 해방촌에서 감각적인 파인 다이닝에 도전한 윤대현 셰프와 김희은 셰프의 소울. 이곳은 현대 한국에서 접할 수 있는 여러 식문화와 재료, 그리고 일상에서 접할 수 있는 익숙한 맛을 감각적으로 풀어낸 요리를 선보인다. 레스토랑 이름에는 여러 의미가 함축되어 있지만 그 이름처럼 소울이 담긴 요리를 전하고자 하는 셰프의 마음이 모든 음식에서 느껴진다. 윤 셰프는 자신의 반려자이자 동료인 김희은 셰프와 함께 건물 내부에 다양한 공간을 구성함으로써 여러 스타일의 다이닝을 즐길 수 있게 했다.

Located in a quaint part of Seoul, this operation is Chef Yun Dae-hyun's bold experiment in stylish fine dining. Here, the diverse culinary traditions and ingredients one may encounter in modern-day Korea converge with the familiar tastes found in everyday life to form unique fusion creations. Among the many connotations of the establishment's name is the chef's desire to serve soul-filled food, and this is palpable in every dish. Along with his wife, Chef Kim Hee-eun, this husband-and-wife duo have partitioned their establishment into several distinct sections, creating impeccable dining spaces for disparate cuisines.

컨템퍼러리 •
Contemporary

02-318-7685

용산구 신흥로 26길 35, 지하 1층

B1F, 35 Sinheung-ro 26-gil, Yongsan-gu

■ 가 격 PRICE: ₩₩₩

에스콘디도 N

ESCONDIDO

용산구

멕시칸 • *Mexican*

02-2038-8994

용산구 한남대로 20길 61-7, 지하 1층

B1F, 61-7 Hannam-daero 20-gil, Yongsan-gu

■ 가 격 PRICE: ₩₩₩

진우범 셰프의 에스콘디도는 멕시칸 퀴진에 대한 셰프의 열정을 제대로 느낄 수 있는 곳이다. 진 셰프는 멕시칸 요리에 매료되어 멕시코로 건너갔고 요리와 문화를 배우며 차곡차곡 실력을 쌓았다. 그는 에스콘디도에서 정통 멕시칸 요리를 바탕으로 자신만의 스타일을 추구한다. 또한 어떤 요리이든 기본이 되는 토르티야와 몰레의 특성을 잘 살림으로써 미묘한 맛의 차이를 느끼게 한다. 에스콘디도의 요리와 함께 테킬라와 메즈칼 페어링이나 칵테일 페어링을 곁들이면 더욱 깊이 있는 맛을 느낄 수 있으니 꼭 경험해 보시기를 추천한다.

Escondido is a space replete with Chef Jin Woo-bum's passion for Mexican food. His infatuation with the cuisine led him to Mexico, where he steadily learned and improved his culinary skills while engrossed in Mexican culture. The restaurant offers bona fide Mexican cuisine with the chef's unique twists. He conjures up finely nuanced flavors by making particularly nuanced use of tortilla and mole, the staples of Mexican cuisine. One last tip: pairing your dish with tequila, mezcal or a cocktail will take your gourmet experience at Escondido to a whole new level.

제로 컴플렉스
ZERO COMPLEX

오픈 이후 줄곧 식재료에 대한 독창적인 해석을 보여준 이충후 셰프. 두 번의 이사로 공간은 달라졌지만 요리의 맛과 독창성은 한결같다. 새로 자리를 옮기면서 공간이 더 넓어졌지만 좌석 수를 줄여 음식에 대한 집중도를 높였다. 왕우럭조개와 보리, 미역은 스모키한 향에 쫄깃한 보리와 꼬시래기, 미역 무스를 넣어 부드럽고 쫄깃한 식감과 미역의 진한 맛을 잘 표현했다. 서빙고동의 조용한 주택가에 위치해 찾기는 조금 힘들 수 있지만 조용한 정원을 내려다보며 즐기는 그의 요리는 방문해 먹어볼 가치가 있다.

이노베이티브 • *Innovative*

02-532-0876

용산구 서빙고로 59길 11-8

11-8 Seobinggo-ro 59-gil, Yongsan-gu

■ **가 격 PRICE: ₩₩₩₩**

Chef Lee Chung-hu has been consistently presenting innovative interpretations of the ingredients since he first opened his restaurant. The restaurant was relocated twice, but the flavors and creativity of the dishes never wavered. After moving to a larger venue, the number of tables was reduced to focus more on the quality of the food. The restaurant showcases the delightfully bouncy texture and rich, smoky flavor of sea mustard through one of their signature dishes, which is Pacific geoduck served with sides of chewy barley, sea spaghetti, and sea mustard mouse. The restaurant, located in a quiet residential area in Seobinggo-dong, might be a challenge to find but tasting the dishes overlooking the quiet garden will make it worth your while.

구복만두
GOOBOK MANDU

딤섬 • *Dim Sum*

02-797-8656
용산구 두텁바위로 7
7 Duteopbawi-ro, Yongsan-gu

■ **가 격 PRICE: ₩**

한국인 남편과 중국인 아내가 운영하는 구복만두는 좋은 재료로 정성껏 빚은 맛있는 만두를 저렴한 가격에 즐길 수 있는, 가격 만족도가 훌륭한 식당이다. 이곳의 대표 메뉴는 뜨거운 기름에 노릇하게 구운 후 자작하게 물을 부어 수분이 모두 증발할 때까지 찌는 일명 '물에 튀긴 만두'다. 스테디셀러인 샤오롱바오와 통새우 만두에 김치 만두도 별미. 테이크아웃도 가능하며, 주류는 판매하지 않는다.

Run by a Korean husband and Chinese wife, Goobok Mandu is a no-frills establishment that specializes in Chinese-style dumplings. The couple prepare the dumplings from scratch based on an old family recipe passed down to them by her grandmother. The dumplings are freshly made to order each time. Try the restaurant's signature pot stickers with their glorious wafer-thin web of crispy golden crust as well as the steamed xiao long bao.

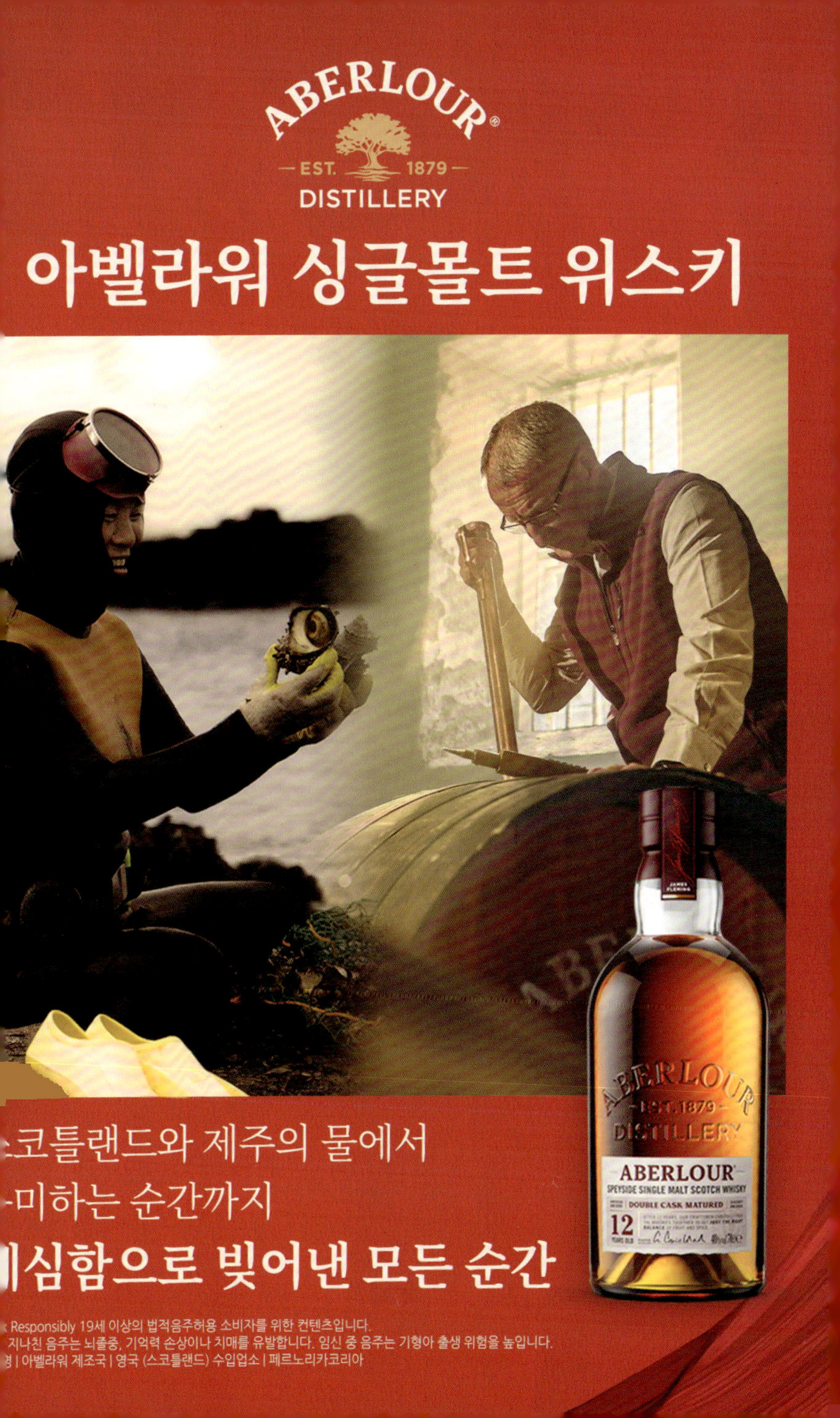

ABERLOUR®
EST. 1879
DISTILLERY
아벨라워 싱글몰트 위스키
ABERLOUR
SPEYSIDE SINGLE MALT SCOTCH WHISKY
DOUBLE CASK MATURED
12
코틀랜드와 제주의 물에서
미하는 순간까지
심함으로 빚어낸 모든 순간
Responsibly 19세 이상의 법적음주허용 소비자를 위한 컨텐츠입니다.
지나친 음주는 뇌졸중, 기억력 손상이나 치매를 유발합니다. 임신 중 음주는 기형아 출생 위험을 높입니다.
| 아벨라워 제조국 | 영국 (스코틀랜드) 수입업소 | 페르노리카코리아

능동미나리 N

NEUNGDONG MINARI

능동미나리의 곰탕은 초록색 미나리가 수북하게 쌓여 있어 얼핏 보면 이게 탕인지 분간이 가지 않는다. 맑고 깔끔한 국물에 미나리의 알싸한 맛이 시원함을 배가시키는 이 곰탕은 그날그날 도축한 신선한 한우와 맑은 물에서 키운 미나리를 사용하여 담백하고 잡내가 없다. 입장하려면 늘 대기를 해야 하지만 한입 맛보면 기다림이 아깝지 않을 맛이다.

The gomtang at Neungdong Minari is topped with a pile of minari so tall that at a glance, it doesn't look like a tang at all. The clear, clean broth is made from fresh hanwoo beef that was slaughtered on the day, which is topped with piquant minari that was grown in clear freshwater for added freshness. You should expect a wait, but you will think it is well worth it once you take your first bite.

곰탕 • *Gomtang*

050-71388-1035

용산구 한강대로 40길 28

28 Hangang-daero 40-gil, Yongsan-gu

■ **가격 PRICE: ₩**

용산구

알트에이 N

ALT.A

비건 • Vegan

02-790-8688

용산구 보광로 109

109 Bogwang-ro, Yongsan-gu

■ 가 격 PRICE: ₩

100% 식물성 재료와 대체육을 사용해 중식을 만드는 곳이다. 중식인데 비건식이라니? 고기를 넣지 않은 중식은 대체 어떤 맛일까 궁금했는데 낯선 사람도 즐길 수 있는 맛은 기본이고 기름기가 적어 소화도 잘되는 음식이 준비되어 있다. 탕수육과 유린육 등 대체육을 사용했다고 말하지 않으면 모를 쫄깃한 튀김 요리는 물론 비건 짬뽕까지 맛볼 수 있다. 비건식으로서도, 중식으로서도 훌륭한 식당이다.

This is a Korean-Chinese restaurant that uses all plant-based ingredients including plant-based alternative meats. That's right. It's a vegan Chinese restaurant. Chinese food made without any meat piqued my curiosity. They create incredible flavors that are sure to entice even diners who aren't familiar with vegan food. The food is also low-fat so it's easy on the stomach. They serve vegan jjamppong and fried dishes like tangsuyuk and yurinyuk that are so delightfully bouncy and chewy that no one will notice that they aren't made from real meat. It is both a great vegan and a great Chinese restaurant.

에그 앤 플라워
EGG & FLOUR

'에그 앤 플라워'는 그 이름처럼 계란과 밀가루만을 이용해 직접 만드는 생면 파스타 전문점이다. 입구에 들어서면 밀가루 포대와 제면기가 제일 먼저 눈에 들어온다. 해방촌의 복잡한 골목 안에 위치해 있지만 내부의 테라스와 탁 트인 통창으로 보이는 이태원의 뷰가 아름다운 곳. 당일 만드는 생면과 함께 고추장과 액젓 등을 사용해 만든 흑돼지 라구를 비롯해 부라타 치즈와 구운 감태 등 한국적 색채를 가미한 이탈리안 파스타를 경험할 수 있다.

As implied by its name, Egg & Flour is an Italian restaurant specializing in fresh, handmade pasta composed only with egg and flour. Even the entrance to the establishment greets us with sacks of flour and pasta rolling machines. The space is located along a winding alley in Haebangchon, yet the Itaewon skyline seen from the terrace and through the glass wall evokes majesty. The establishment's signature offering is freshly made Italian pasta with a Korean twist - be it Jeju black pork ragù featuring red chili paste and fish sauce, burrata cheese, or roasted Ecklonia cava.

이탈리언 • *Italian*

02-3789-7681

용산구 신흥로 26길 35, 3층

2F, 35 Shinheung-ro 26-gil, Yongsan-gu

■ 가격 PRICE: ₩₩

YONGSAN-GU

유한 N
YOUHAN

타이 • Thai

070-8691-1509
용산구 대사관로 5길 10-5
10-5, Daesagwan-ro 5-gil, Yongsna-gu

■ 가격 PRICE: ₩

유한은 작지만 세련된 타이 비스트로다. 한남동 골목 안 깊숙이 숨어 있어 초행길이면 찾기가 쉽지 않다. 태국에서 요리를 공부하고 돌아온 김유한 셰프의 공간으로, 이름은 익숙하지만 처음 접하는 메뉴를 선보인다. 태국식 소시지와 직접 만든 육포, 구운 오리 가슴살과 제철 사시미, 여기에 태국식 그린 소스를 올린 요리까지 다양한 맛을 경험해 볼 수 있다. 요리와 궁합이 좋은 내추럴 와인과 사케도 추천받을 수 있으니 함께 즐기기를 추천한다.

Yuhan is a small, chic Thai bistro. It can be difficult to find for first-time visitors, as it is hidden deep in the alleys of Hannam-dong. Established by Chef Kim Yu-han, who attended culinary school in Thailand, the restaurant offers familiar dishes with a creative twist. Diners can experience diverse flavors, including Thai sausages, jerky made in-house, grilled duck breast, seasonal sashimi, and dishes topped with Thai green sauce. The restaurant also offers natural wines and sake recommendations that perfectly pair with the dishes.

RMW CARNE N

개조한 구옥의 2층에 위치한 RMW Carne는 장소가 넓지는 않지만 아늑하고 아담한 장소에서 음식을 즐길 수 있는 곳이다. 스테이크의 굽기 정도를 표시하는 레어(Rare), 미디움(Medium), 웰던(Well-done)에서 머릿글자를 딴 RMW는 다양한 소고기 품종과 부위를 건조 숙성하여 손님상에 올린다. 직접 만든 살라미, 쵸리조, 파스트라미, 소시지 같은 샤퀴테리도 매장에서 구매가 가능하다. 고기 외에도 가볍게 먹을 수 있는 야채 구이, 파스타 요리가 준비되어 있어 부담없이 즐길 수 있다.

RMW Carne, which is located on the second floor of a renovated old house, isn't particularly spacious, but you can enjoy your food in a comfortably petite, cozy venue. The restaurant which is named after the first letters of steak doneness - rare, medium, and well-done - dry ages various cuts of beef of a variety of different cattle breeds. Salami, chorizo, pastrami, sausages and other charcuterie, all cured in-house, are available for purchase at the store inside the restaurant. They also serve simpler dishes like grilled vegetables and pasta that can be enjoyed as a light meal or refreshment.

스테이크하우스 • *Steakhouse*

010-5068-4133

용산구 대사관로 5길 12, 2층

2F, 12 Daesagwan-ro 5-gil, Yongsan-gu

www.rmw.kr

■ **가 격 PRICE: ₩₩**

YONGSAN-GU

용산구

바비큐 • *Barbecue*

010-7601-4041
용산구 이태원로 238
238 Itaewon-ro, Yongsan-gu

■ 가 격 PRICE: ₩

교양식사

KYOYANG SIKSA

상호에서부터 궁금증을 유발하는 이곳은 이태원에 자리하고 있는 삿포로식 양갈비 전문점이다. 호주에서 10개월 미만의 양고기를 공수받아 어린 양 특유의 고소한 풍미와 부드러운 식감이 살아 있다. 기름기가 적고 고소한 프렌치 랙, 쫄깃한 갈빗살, 그리고 부드러운 알등심의 세 가지 부위를 맛볼 수 있다. 닭 육수를 베이스로 다양한 채소를 구워 곁들인 수프 카레와 향긋한 마늘밥 또한 꼭 먹어봐야 하는 메뉴다. 세련된 인테리어가 돋보이는 이곳은 다이닝 룸을 제외하면 10석 남짓의 바 좌석밖에 없기 때문에 예약은 필수다.

Sapporo-style lamb barbecue is the name of the game at Kyoyang Siksa, which specializes in tender young lamb less than 10 months old. Flown in from Australia, this meat is juicy and tender and the menu offers three cuts: French rack, ribs, and loin steak. These may be grilled tableside by the staff. Other solid dishes include soup curry with grilled vegetables and aromatic garlic rice served with small sheets of laver to wrap it in. Seating is limited, so be sure to book ahead.

구찌 오스테리아 다 마시모 보투라

GUCCI OSTERIA DA MASSIMO BOTTURA

피렌체의 1호점을 시작으로 LA와 도쿄에 이어 전 세계 4호점을 서울에 선보이는 구찌 오스테리아. 이탈리아 셰프 마시모 보투라와 구찌의 협업으로 탄생한 레스토랑을 이제 서울에서도 경험할 수 있게 되었다. 한국의 계절에서 영감을 얻은 서울 가든 샐러드와 24개월 숙성한 레지아노 크림이 들어가 맛이 진하고 풍부한 토르텔리니, 작은 핑크색 상자에 담겨 나오는 에밀리아 버거가 이곳의 시그니처 메뉴다. 화려한 정원을 연상시키는 구찌 특유의 초록색 인테리어, 독창적이고 고풍스러운 식기와 가구 또한 강렬한 멋과 맛을 자아낸다. 서울의 경관이 한눈에 들어오는 테라스도 운영하니 이탈리안 와인과 함께 즐겨 보기를 권한다.

이탤리언 • *Italian*

02-795-1119

용산구 이태원로 223, 6층

6F, 223 Itaewon-ro, Yongsan-gu

www.gucciosteria.com/ko/seoul

■ 가 격 PRICE: ₩₩₩

Gucci Osteria was launched in Florence, Italy through a partnership between the chef Massimo Bottura and Gucci. The establishment's third global branch after ones in Los Angeles and Tokyo has opened in Seoul. Its signature dishes include Seoul Garden Salad, inspired by Korea's four distinct seasons; tortellini with rich-flavored, 24-month-aged Parmigiano Reggiano cream; and an Emilia Burger served in a petite pink box. The interior spaces colored in Gucci's signature green evoke a splendid verdant garden. Coupled with an assortment of cutlery and furniture that is both unique and classy, this fine diner's authentic vibes bring out the indelible tastes of its cuisine to the fullest. A visit to the terrace is highly recommended as it offers a gorgeous view of Seoul's cityscape accompanied by Italian wine.

프렌치 • French

02-6217-5252

용산구 신흥로 56

56 Sinheung-ro, Yongsan-gu

■ 가 격 PRICE: ₩₩

꼼 모아

COMME MOA

해방촌 끝자락의 가파른 언덕을 지나면 밝은 버건디 컬러 외관의 꼼 모아가 눈에 들어온다. 소담한 공간에서 프랑스 현지의 맛과 분위기를 만끽할 수 있는 이곳은 김모아 셰프의 레스토랑으로, 정감 있는 서비스가 돋보이는 곳이다. 단순한 재료로 맛있는 음식을 대접하고 싶다는 것이 그녀의 바람. 이곳의 베스트셀러는 푸아그라 크렘 브륄레와 파테 앙 크루트. 하루 전에 예약해야만 맛볼 수 있는 비프 웰링턴과 셰프의 특선 디저트 수플레는 꼭 한번 맛보길 바란다.

This cozy charmer, located towards the tail end of Haebangchon's main street, is Chef Kim Moa's cheery French bistro that serves up authentic fare. The menu is composed of classic dishes that clearly demonstrate her philosophy that good ingredients and care for the guests should be the foundation of a tasty dish. Some of the restaurant's best sellers include foie gras crème brûlée, pâté en croute and beef Wellington, which diners have to call ahead and order a day in advance. For dessert, the chef's special soufflé is a must.

디 템포레

DE TEMPORE

'디템포레'는 그 이름처럼 철마다 달라지는 제철 식재료 요리를 지향하는 모던 프렌치 레스토랑이다. 프렌치 퀴진의 큰 틀 안에서 요리에 계절감과 균형감을 담아내려는 셰프의 감각이 세련되게 반영되었다. 오리 가슴살 구이에 덕쥬 소스, 제철 생선에 비스크 소스처럼 프렌치 퀴진에 기반한 여러 특색 있는 소스는 이곳의 요리를 즐기는 또 하나의 재미 요소이다.

'De tempore,' true to its name, is a modern French restaurant that embraces the essence of seasonal ingredients in its dishes. Within the broad framework of French cuisine, the chef's refined touch brings a sense of seasonality and harmony to each plate. Signature creations like duck breast with duck jus sauce or seasonal fish paired with bisque sauce showcase the restaurant's culinary artistry, with its diverse and distinctive sauces adding an extra layer of enjoyment to the dining experience.

프렌치 • *French*

070-4848-6359

용산구 한남대로 37

37 Hannam-daero, Yongsan-gu

■ 가 격 PRICE: ₩₩

용산구

마나오 N

MANAO

타이 • Thai

050-71368-0346

용산구 한남대로 21길 18, 2층

2F, 18 Hannam-daero 21-gil, Yongsan-gu

■ 가 격 PRICE: ₩₩

마나오에 처음 들어서면 태국에서 직접 가져온 갖가지 소품과 세련된 인테리어가 이국적인 분위기를 자아낸다. 코스에 들어가는 메뉴를 작은 포션으로 구성해 다양한 요리를 한꺼번에 맛보는 재미가 있다. 태국 본토의 맛과 특유의 매운맛을 잘 살렸다. 고기와 해산물을 숯불 그릴에서 바로바로 구워 내는 것도 특징이다. '마나오(Manao)'는 태국어로 '라임'을 뜻하는데 그 이름처럼 깔끔한 태국 음식을 맛볼 수 있다.

Enter Manao, and you will be greeted with exotic vibes bolstered by seek décor and an array of art objects brought directly from Thailand. Its prix-fixe menus consist of multiple dishes in small portions, allowing guests to enjoy a variety of plates in one meal. The kitchen does an excellent job of presenting authentic Thai cuisine with its characteristic spiciness. Another appeal of this spot is that the meat and seafood are grilled to order over charcoal. Manao means “lime” in Thai, and its fare is as refreshing as its name.

보르고 한남

BORGO HANNAM

이탈리언 • *Italian*

02-6082-2727
용산구 이태원로 54길 31, 3층
3F, 31 Itaewon-ro 54-gil, Yongsan-gu

■ 가격 PRICE: ₩₩₩

이탈리아어로 '동네'를 뜻하는 '보르고 한남'. 스테파노 디 살보 셰프가 운영하는 이곳은, 작은 계단을 올라가면 아늑한 공간과 어울리는 홈메이드 음식과 리큐어들이 손님을 반긴다. 오랜 경력의 셰프가 직접 요리하는 이탈리안 다이닝을 맛볼 수 있는 곳으로, 아침에 직접 만든 빵과 파스타부터 디저트까지 그의 손을 거치지 않는 음식이 없다. 시그니처 메뉴인 칼다로 수프는 토스카나 지방에서 어부들이 먹는 수프에서 영감을 받아 만든 것으로 매콤하고 풍부한 맛이 일품이다. 각 "동네"의 다양한 이탈리안 음식을 만나볼 수 있다. 디저트 트레이에 놓인 각종 디저트도 꼭 맛보시길.

"Borgo" in Italian means "village," helmed by Chef Stefano Di Salvo. Once up the tiny set of stairs, you are greeted with homemade dishes and liqueurs befitting the cozy space. From the bread freshly baked in the morning to pastas and desserts, everything is handmade by the chef himself. The kitchen's signature Caldaro soup was inspired by the fisherman's soup in Tuscany, which has good rich spicy flavor in it with chef's own twist. Recreating the ambience of a friendly diner, this is a great spot for heartwarming Italian food from various regions. Don't miss the diverse range of desserts served on a tiered stand.

프렌치 • French

070-8624-8907

용산구 녹사평대로 210-6, 3층

3F, 210-6 Noksapyeong-Daero, Yongsan-gu

■ 가격 PRICE: ₩₩

셰누 프라이빗 키친

CHEZ NOUS PRIVATE KITCHEN

프랑스어로 '우리집'을 뜻하는 셰누. 부부가 운영하는 공간으로, 따뜻한 음식이 차려진 집 같은 공간에서 맛있는 시간을 보내길 바라는 의미가 담겨 있다. 프랑스인 셰프와 한국인 아내가 준비하는 프랑스 가정식이 대표 메뉴이지만 프랑스 유수의 스타 레스토랑과 호텔의 이그제큐티브 셰프를 역임한 마티유 셰프가 준비하는 음식은 가정식의 수준을 훨씬 뛰어넘는다. 신선한 가리비를 넣은 카르파치오 요리나 트러플 에멀젼을 사용한 비프 타르타르 등 기본에 충실한 정통 프랑스 요리를 맛볼 수 있다. 저녁에만 운영하니 예약은 필수이다. 집처럼 따뜻한 공간에서 프랑스를 느껴보는 것은 어떨까?

Meaning "our home" in French, the name Chez Nous represents the chef-owner couple's ardent desire for guests to enjoy warm, hearty food in a home-like setting. Although the French chef and his Korean wife offer mainly homestyle meals, they are anything but ordinary, reflecting Chef Mathieu Moles's culinary experience as an executive chef at major restaurants and hotels in France. At Chez Nous, you can enjoy authentic French dishes, including carpaccio made with fresh scallops, steak tartare featuring truffle emulsion. Chez Nous opens only for dinner, and reservations are a must. Come and discover your very own French joie de vivre in this cozy dining space that recreates the warmth of a home.

안씨 막걸리

MR. AHN'S CRAFT MAKGEOLLI

식사에 술을 곁들이는 '반주'라는 한국적 표현이 잘 어울리는 안씨 막걸리. 이곳의 매력은 획일적인 한국식 주점에서 탈피하여 전통적이지만 모던하고 세련된 감각의 한식이 부상하는 시대에 발맞추어 '한국 술집'의 방향성을 잘 표현하고 있다는 점이다. 계절 변화에 맞춰 제공되는 맛깔스러운 한국 요리와 안줏거리들, 여기에 시간과 함께 익어가는 한국의 술까지 편하게 즐길 수 있는 매력적인 곳이다. 가벼운 식사는 물론이고 흥겨운 술자리를 위한 장소로도 손색이 없다. 고객의 다양한 목적에 맞게 즐길 수 있는 레스토랑이다.

Mr. Ahn's Craft Makgeolli is a most befitting venue for the Korean term banju, or alcohol accompanying a meal. What distinguishes this gastropub is its avoidance of the stereotypical Korean pubs and expression of the direction they should take—in this age of new Korean cuisine that is traditional yet imbued with a modern touch. At this charming spot, patrons can enjoy seasonally changing menus of savory Korean anju (snacks paired with alcohol), main dishes, as well as a wide selection of traditional liquors that simply get better with time. It's a perfect place for both light meals and friendly social drinking—a versatile venue that appeals to distinct audiences.

한식 • *Korean*

010-9965-5112

용산구 회나무로 3

3 Hoenamu-ro, Yongsan-gu

■ 가 격 PRICE: ₩₩

YONGSAN-GU

알레즈

AL'AISE

프렌치 • French

070-8868-1686

용산구 독서당로 89

89 Dokseodang-ro, Yongsan-gu

■ **가 격 PRICE: ₩₩₩**

알레즈는 이병곤 셰프가 운영하는 프렌치 레스토랑이다. 그는 프렌치 퀴진을 경험하고 학습하기 위해 오랜 시간 성실히 노력해 왔다. 그런 성실한 시간의 힘이 담긴 그의 요리에는 기본에 대한 충실함과 식재료 고유의 맛을 살리려는 정직함이 녹아 있다. 모든 코스 요리에서 식재료와 소스의 어우러짐이 좋아 안정적이고 일관성 있는 프렌치 요리의 풍미를 즐길 수 있다. 이병곤 셰프가 클래식한 프렌치 소스 레시피에 자신만의 포인트를 입힌 소스가 특히 맛깔난다. 한국의 제철 식재료를 적극 활용한 잔잔한 풍미의 프렌치 요리를 차분하고 안락한 다이닝 공간에서 즐길 수 있다는 점이 이곳의 매력이다.

Al'aise is a French restaurant headed by Chef Lee Byeong-gon, who has dedicated extensive efforts to experience and immerse himself in authentic French cuisine. The power of such conscientious dedication is instilled in his dishes that remain faithful to the basics and are brimming with honest passion to convey the innate flavors of the ingredients. The course meals feature an exceptional balance of ingredients and sauces, bringing out the long-standing and dependable flavors expected from fine French cuisine. Another distinct culinary delight is to be found in the kitchen's classic French sauces adorned with the chef's singular twists. Treat yourself in this homey and cozy bistro that offers delicately flavored French fare crafted with imaginative seasonal Korean ingredients.

오스테리아 오르조
OSTERIA ORZO

이탈리아어 '오스테리아'는 간단한 음식과 와인을 함께 즐길 수 있는 '선술집'을 의미하는데, '오스테리아 오르조'는 이름 그대로 이탈리아의 맛과 멋을 느낄 수 있는 아늑한 공간이다. 이곳의 대표 메뉴는 소고기 다짐육과 마스카르포네 치즈, 트러플 페이스트가 들어간 진한 소스에, 레스토랑에서 직접 뽑은 생면을 곁들인 화이트 라구 파스타이다. 매콤한 소스를 듬뿍 머금은 탈리아텔레와 해산물 타르타르도 빼놓을 수 없는 별미이다. 주방 앞 테이블에 앉아 파스타가 완성되는 모습을 지켜보는 재미도 쏠쏠하다.

Osteria Orzo continues to offer an authentic taste of a casual and cozy Italian osteria at its Hannam-dong location. Signature offerings on the menu include the white ragù pasta which features home-made fresh pasta drenched in rich meat sauce with mascarpone cheese and truffles. The spicy tagliatelle and the seafood tartare are also among the restaurant's all-time favorites. Reserve a table across from the open kitchen and watch the chefs in action.

이탤리언 • *Italian*

02-322-0801

용산구 한남대로 20길 47, 2층

2F, 47 Hannam-daero 20-gil, Yongsan-gu

■ **가 격 PRICE: ₩₩**

중식 • *Chinese*

02-798-9700

용산구 독서당로 124-7

124-7 Dokseodang-ro, Yongsan-gu

■ 가 격 PRICE: ₩₩₩₩

쥬에
JUE

'쥬에'는 중국 귀족에게 부여하던 작위를 뜻하는 말을 중국식으로 발음한 것이다. 정통 광둥식 요리를 선보이는 '쥬에'는 코스 메뉴 역시 '공작', '후작', '백작', '자작', '남작'처럼 작위의 이름을 따서 구성했다. 이곳의 대표 메뉴인 돼지 바비큐는 특제 양념에 잰 통고기를 고온에서 구워 껍질의 바삭함과 촉촉한 살코기의 풍부한 육즙을 동시에 느낄 수 있다. 또한 13가지가 넘는 딤섬 중 하나인 라창펀과 전복을 올린 시우마이, 그리고 춘권은 꼭 맛봐야 할 메뉴다. 각종 요리에 곁들일 수 있는 중국 차도 준비되어 있다.

Resembling the Chinese pronunciation of a word which refers to a title of nobility, Jue is a restaurant that specializes in Cantonese cuisine. The set menu is also named after the different noble titles in China. One of Jue's signature dishes is its barbecued pork which, after being marinated, is roasted in a high-temperature oven to ensure a supremely crispy skin and juicy, flavorful meat. Of the 13 different varieties of dim sum on offer, the cheung fan (rice noodle roll), shumai topped with abalone, and the spring rolls are not to be missed.

텅 앤 그루브 조인트

TONGUE & GROOVE JOINT

21세기 감성이 잘 녹아 있어 고깃집이라기보다는 펍이나 카페를 연상시키는 텅 앤 그루브 조인트는 숙성시킨 소고기와 양고기, 돼지고기 바비큐를 전문으로 하는 레스토랑이다. 최소 21일간 숙성시킨 소고기와 12개월 미만의 부드러운 양갈비, 그리고 소 한 마리에서 2~4kg밖에 나오지 않는 꽃새우살이 이 집의 대표 메뉴다. 여기에 직접 만든 고추기름과 고수 페스토를 함께 내는 것이 특징이다. 참신한 점심 메뉴 역시 인상적이며, 다양한 종류의 크래프트 맥주와 와인도 마련되어 있다.

Don't expect to walk into a typical Korean barbecue restaurant when you visit Tongue and Groove Joint, a casually cool and modern space that feels more like a café or a beer hall. The restaurant specializes in quality Korean beef aged for at least three weeks as well as tender lamb chops and beef ribeye. These cuts are grilled at the table by the staff and come with a side of house-made chili oil and cilantro pesto which help cut the richness. The restaurant also has a good variety of lunch offerings and a wide selection of craft beers.

바비큐 • *Barbecue*

02-790-7036

용산구 보광로 60길 7

7 Bogwang-ro 60-gil, Yongsan-gu

www.tngj.modoo.at

■ 가 격 PRICE: ₩₩

컨템퍼러리 •
Contemporary

02-797-3655
용산구 대사관로 31길 25-12, 5층
5F, 25-12 Daesagwan-ro 31-gil, Yongsan-gu
http://tablefor4.fordining.kr

■ 가 격 PRICE: ₩₩₩

테이블 포 포

TABLE FOR FOUR

테이블 포포는 충남 태안의 풍광을 맞고 자란 농산물과 계절에 따라 맛의 절정을 보여 주는 각종 해산물이 특징이다. 셰프는 고향에 대한 애정은 물론, 좋은 식재료를 고객에게 전하고자 하는 순수한 마음으로 태안의 우수한 식재료를 자신의 식탁에 옮겨 놓았다. 특히 태안에서 직접 농사를 짓는 셰프 가족의 노력이 셰프와 테이블 포포가 지향하는 로컬 푸드의 토대라 할 수 있다. 셰프는 자신의 노련한 솜씨를 가미하기도 하고 때로는 개입을 최소화하기도 하면서 태안의 식재료를 근사한 요리로 탈바꿈시킨다. 테이블 포포에서 태안의 풍미가 담긴 유러피안 퀴진의 매력에 빠져 보기 바란다.

This 'Table' uses a wide range of seasonal ingredients infused with optimal flavors from Taean, South Chungcheong Province—the chef's hometown. His affection for the region and genuine passion to serve the freshest and healthiest food to patrons are the reasons behind his use of such choice. The chef, sometimes aided by the seasoned master, is able to skillfully transform his hometown ingredients into exciting dishes, and at other times there is minimal culinary intervention. Diners who visit are bound to relish the allure of this European cuisine, imbued with the flair of Taean.

테판
TEPPAN

전 세계 철판 요리를 경험할 수 있는 테판은 애피타이저부터 디저트까지 모든 음식을 철판 위에서 조리하는 신개념의 레스토랑이다. 이곳에선 바 테이블에 앉아 요리가 완성되는 과정을 직접 볼 수 있고, 널찍한 통창을 통해 남산의 아름다운 풍경도 감상할 수 있다. 신선한 해산물과 스테이크, 그리고 화려한 불 쇼와 함께 완성하는 플랑베 등 맛있는 요리뿐만 아니라 즐거운 볼거리까지 선사하는 테판은 그랜드 하얏트 서울의 미식 거리 콘셉트의 '332 소월로'에 자리하고 있다.

Located along Grand Hyatt Seoul's gourmet alley 322 Sowol-ro, Teppan is a restaurant where everything on the menu is cooked on an iron griddle — even appetizers and desserts. Food is prepared by chefs in front of the guests on flat-surface grills behind the bar counter. Diners can also gaze out at the scenic view of Namsan Mountain through the restaurant's wide windows while enjoying their meal. The menu offers plenty of fresh seafood and meats as well as spectacular fire shows.

테판야키 • *Teppanyaki*

02-799-8272

용산구 소월로 322, 그랜드 하얏트 호텔 지하 1층

B1F, Grand Hyatt Hotel, 322 Sowol-ro, Yongsan-gu

www.hyatt.com/grand-hyatt/en-US/selrs-grand-hyatt-seoul

■ **가격 PRICE: ₩₩₩**

하쿠시

HAKUSI

일식 • *Japanese*

02-792-0811

용산구 독서당로 29길 6, 2층

2F, 6 Dokseodang-ro 29-gil, Yongsan-gu

■ 가 격 PRICE: ₩₩₩

숯과 불 그리고 도화지, 최성훈 셰프가 하쿠시를 통해 표현하고자 하는 세 가지 주제를 멋지게 공간에 담아 냈다. 강렬한 블랙 앤 레드 컬러의 시각적 강렬함이 입구에서부터 다이닝 공간까지 이어지는데, 공간 곳곳에 포인트로 활용된 화이트 컬러가 조화로움과 안정감을 준다. 공간이 가진 이런 시각적 강렬함처럼, 하쿠시의 요리에도 셰프의 다양한 요리 경험이 반영된 독창성이 선명하게 드러난다. 제철 식재료의 매력이 그대로 살아 있는 하쿠시의 요리에는 모던과 클래식의 경계를 넘나드는 뚜렷한 맛과 향이 담겨 있다.

Charcoal, fire and paper – these are the three themes Chef Choi Seong-hun seeks to convey in Hakusi's captivating culinary narrative. The triumphant result is a testament to his masterful storytelling. Beginning at the entrance and extending all the way to the dining area, an arresting visual tableau of black and red imbues the space with personality, punctuated by white elements that exude a sense of harmony and stability. This vivid vitality is also manifest in the establishment's distinctive cuisine that reflects the chef's vast culinary experience. In every dish, the allure of seasonal ingredients is brought to life in vivid detail, with distinct flavors and aromas, which transcend the boundaries between modern and classic cuisine, figuring prominently.

F. Guiziou/hemis.fr

종로구
성북구
JONGNO-GU
SEONGBUK-GU

온지음
ONJIUM

종로구 성북구

한식 • *Korean*

02-6952-0024

종로구 효자로 49, 4층

4F, 49 Hyoja-ro, Jongno-gu

www.onjium.org

■ 가 격 PRICE: ₩₩₩₩

경복궁 돌담길이 가진 전통미와 '온지음 맛공방'이 위치한 주택가의 현대미가 길 하나를 사이에 두고 조화롭게 공존한다. 레스토랑 내부에서 확인할 수 있는 한국의 전통 의식주 양식 역시 모던한 외관과 대조를 이루며 과거와 현재가 공존하고 있음을 느끼게 한다. '온지음'이 운영하는 식문화 연구소이자 레스토랑이기도 한 이곳에서는 조선 왕조 궁중 음식 이수자 조은희 방장과 박성배 연구원, 그리고 이들이 이끄는 젊은 팀원들이 온고지신의 마음으로 한식의 전통을 이어가고 있다. 뚜렷한 사계절을 반영하는 음식에서 한식의 깊은 뿌리를 느낄 수 있고, 오랜 연구 끝에 탄생한 아름다운 음식을 통해 감동을 얻을 수 있는 곳이다.

The elegant stonewalled-path of Gyeongbokgung Palace and a modern residential neighborhood stand directly across from each other. A road is all that lies between Seoul's past and present, coexisting side by side. The same contrast is, again, evident in the modern façade of Onjieum Matgongbang and elements of tradition one discovers inside. Helmed by Cho Eun-hee, certified trainee of Korean royal court cuisine, and researcher Park Seong-bae, the space is both a research institute and restaurant. The food it offers clearly reflects the four distinct seasons and the refined beauty of Korean cuisine.

유 유안
YU YUAN

모던 중국 패션의 절정을 찍었던 1920년대 상하이. 그 화려함을 모티브 삼아 디자인한 중식 전문점 유 유안은 비취색과 금색, 대리석의 은은하고 고급스러운 조화가 매력적인 곳이다. 입구를 지나면서 눈에 들어오는 오리 숙성고는 유 유안이 추구하는 요리의 콘셉트를 잘 보여준다. 광둥식 요리를 앞세우고 있지만, 중국 내 다른 지역의 특색 있는 음식도 함께 선보인다. 이곳의 인기 메뉴는 베이징 덕으로, 반 마리도 주문 가능하다. 주말 브런치도 인기를 끌고 있는데, 유 유안의 수준 높은 딤섬 요리를 맛볼 수 있다.

Inspired by the glitz and glamour of 1920s Shanghai, interior designer André Fu's dining room is drop-dead gorgeous with its alluring jade-colored walls, marbled floors, lavish furniture and refined tableware. The menu features mostly Cantonese dishes, but also offers recipes from other Chinese regions. Highlights include Peking Duck, crispy pork belly and Cantonese-style steamed sea bream. Their weekend dim sum brunch is extremely popular.

중식 • *Chinese*

02-6388-5500

종로구 새문안로 97, 포시즌스 호텔 11층

11F Four Seasons Hotel, 97 Saemunan-ro, Jongno-gu

www.fourseasons.com/seoul/dining/restaurants/yu_yuan

■ **가격 PRICE: ₩₩₩₩**

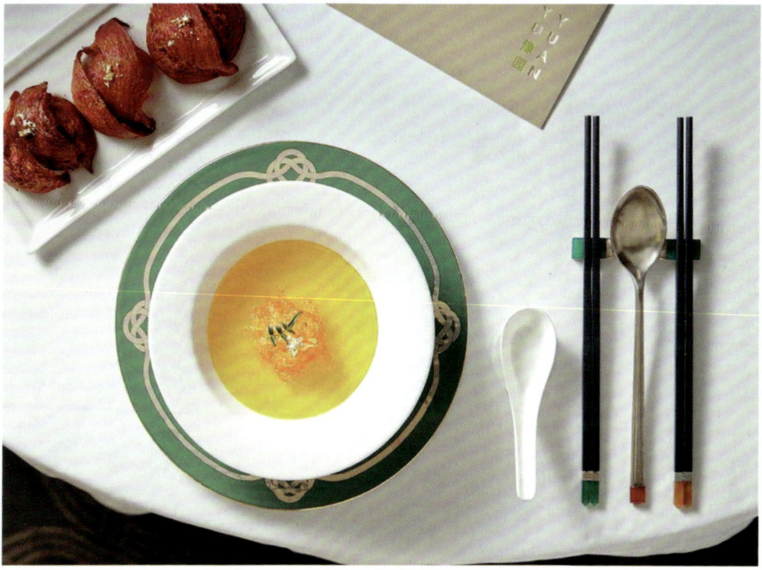

만두 • *Mandu*

02-733-9240

종로구 인사동 10길 11-3

11-3 Insadong 10-gil, Jongno-gu

www.koong.co.kr

■ **가 격 PRICE: ₩**

개성만두 궁

GAESEONG MANDU KOONG

1970년, 개성 출신의 할머니가 시작해 3대째 계승되어온 개성만두 궁은 딸의 손을 거쳐 현재는 손녀가 운영하고 있다. 개성 만두의 특징은 무엇보다 크고 꽉 찬 속인데, 이곳의 만두소는 배추와 숙주나물을 넉넉히 넣어 담백하고 삼삼한 맛이 일품이다. 만둣국과 떡국엔 양지를 고아 만든 육수를 사용하며, 만두소는 매일 신선한 재료로 정성스레 버무린다. 단아한 한옥에서 건강한 음식의 맛을 즐길 수 있다.

Established in 1970 by an elderly Gaeseong native, this restaurant has been serving Gaeseong-style dumplings for three generations. The dumplings here are large, plump and filled with a generous amount of shredded napa cabbage and mung bean sprouts. The soup broth is made with beef brisket, and the owners prepare the dumplings by hand daily with the freshest ingredients. The traditional Korean hanok setting is both charming and elegant.

꽃밥에피다
A FLOWER BLOSSOM ON THE RICE

건강에 민감한 현대인들을 위해 친환경 유기농 재료만을 사용해 정갈한 한 끼 식사를 제공하는 '꽃밥에피다'는 인사동에 위치한 한식 레스토랑이다. 식재료뿐 아니라 인테리어, 담음새 등 구석구석 정성이 가득 느껴지는 이곳은 농인 법인에서 직접 운영하며, 유기농 농장에서만 재료를 납품받는다. 이곳의 대표 메뉴는 노란 달걀 지단 보자기에 단아하게 싸여 나오는 '보자기 비빔밥'. 지단을 걷으면 한 송이 꽃이 피어 있는 듯 밥 위에 곱게 놓여 있는 색색가지 나물들이 눈부터 즐겁게 만든다.

Located in a quiet alley away from the touristy bustle of Insa-dong, A Flower Blossom on the Rice is a restaurant that caters to the health-conscious diner, serving wholesome home-cooked fare using only certified organic ingredients sourced straight from the farm. The signature dish at this restaurant is the Bojagi Bibimbap — a log of cooked rice topped with five different sautéed vegetables in their multi-colored glory, encased in a crépe-thin egg omelet resembling a gift, tied with a seaweed ribbon and presented with a single flower on top.

한식 • Korean

02-732-0276

종로구 인사동 16길 3-6

3-6 Insadong 16-gil, Jongno-gu

www.goodbab.co.kr

■ **가격 PRICE: ₩**

The Chef's commitment:

'꽃밥에 피다'는 식재료의 95%를 유기농과 친환경, 동물복지 인증, 무농약과 유기가공, 바이오다이나믹 인증을 받은 농장과의 직거래를 통해 조달하고 있으며, 이를 통해 건강한 농축산물을 생산하는 농장과 상생을 도모하고 있습니다.
아울러 직접 농업 법인을 설립하여 경북 봉하마을의 유기농 쌀을 비롯해 경남 거창의 콩으로 만든 전통 된장과 간장 같은 친환경 식재료의 전파에도 힘을 쏟고 있습니다.

"The restaurant procures 95% of its ingredients via direct transactions with farms that have been awarded organic, eco-friendly, animal welfare, non-pesticide, organic processing, and biodynamic certifications. Moreover, through its own agricultural entity, the restaurant is striving to popularize eco-friendly ingredients of the region."

도가니탕 • Doganitang

02-735-4259

종로구 사직로 5

5 Sajik-ro, Jongno-gu

■ 가격 PRICE: ₩

대성집

DAESUNGJIP

뽀얗고 맑은 국물에 고기가 붙은 도가니와 쫄깃한 힘줄이 풍성하게 들어 있는 대성집은 해장국집으로 시작해 현재 도가니탕 전문점이 되었다. 진한 국물 속에 가득 담겨있는 도가니에서 소박한 여유와 정감을 느낄 수 있다. 김치와 함께 밥을 가득 말아 특제 간장 소스에 찍어 먹으면 훌륭한 한 끼 식사가 된다. 국내산 식재료만을 고집했지만, 수량이 모자라 현재는 미국산을 조금 섞어 사용한다. 늘 문전성시를 이루며, 선택에 따라 포장도 가능하다.

For a soul-satisfying bowl of ox knee soup, look no further than Daesungjip. Its reputation for quality and consistency has seen generations of loyal patrons come for the rich, hearty signature so thick with ox knee cartilage that you can stand a spoon up in it. Take a bite of the slow-cooked cartilage doused in the special soy dipping sauce and all is right in the world. A long queue is the norm here but, thankfully, takeaways are also possible.

미진
MIJIN

1952년부터 광화문 일대를 지켜온 터줏대감인 미진은 한국식 냉메밀국수 전문점으로, 일본식 소바 쯔유보다 진한 맛의 간장 육수와 더 쫄깃한 식감의 메밀 면발을 선보인다. 식당 지하에 운영하는 공장에서 육수와 면을 직접 생산해 손님들에게 바로바로 제공한다. 한 주전자 가득 담긴 차가운 육수와 테이블마다 인심 좋게 제공하는 메밀국수 고명은 기호에 따라 가감이 가능하다. 숙주와 두부, 신김치와 돼지고기 소로 채운 메밀전병 역시 이 집의 인기 메뉴인데, 1인분의 반인 한 줄씩도 판매한다.

Located in the heart of Gwanghwamun, Mijin has been serving Korean-style cold buckwheat noodles since 1952. The restaurant operates a factory in the basement where the dipping sauce and buckwheat noodles are prepared fresh daily. One portion comes with two stacked tray baskets of noodles, a large kettle of chilled sauce and basic side dishes. Dress your dipping sauce to your desire with grated daikon, light wasabi, crispy seasoned laver and chopped green onions that have already been laid out on the table for you.

메밀국수 •
Memil-guksu

02-730-6198

종로구 종로 19, 르메이에르 종로타운 116-2호

#116-2 le Meilleur Jongno town, 19 Jong-ro, Jongno-gu

■ **가격 PRICE: ₩**

부촌육회

BUCHON YUKHOE

육회 • Yukhoe

02-2267-1831

종로구 종로 200-12

200-12 Jong-ro, Jongno-gu

■ 가 격 PRICE: ₩

국내 최초 사설 시장인 광장시장의 육회 골목 한편에 자리 잡고 있는 부촌육회. 1965년에 부촌 식당으로 개업한 이곳은 1980년대부터 갈비탕과 함께 전라도식 육회를 조금씩 선보이기 시작했다. 고추장 양념에 버무리는 전라도식 육회를 참기름과 배를 넣은 서울식 육회로 바꾼 이유는 손님들의 입맛에 맞추기 위해서다. 매일 아침 공급받는 신선한 국내산 쇠고기를 사용해 고소한 맛이 일품이다. 이곳에선 육회뿐만 아니라 육회 물회, 육회 비빔밥 같은 메뉴도 선보여 한 끼 식사로 즐기기에도 더할 나위 없다. 광장시장의 활기찬 분위기는 덤이다.

Occupying a corner of the well-established raw beef alley of Gwangjang Market, Buchon Yukhoe has been in business since 1965, originally started as Buchon Sikdang selling short rib soup. The founding matriarch's original Jeollado Province-style raw beef, seasoned with red chili paste, gave way to the more popular Seoul-style in the 1980s, seasoned with sesame oil and eaten with matchstick pears. Try the raw beef bibimbap for a more substantial meal. Locally sourced beef is delivered to the restaurant each morning.

삼청동 수제비

SAMCHEONGDONG SUJEBI

삼청동의 역사와 떼려야 뗄 수 없는 삼청동 수제비는 1982년 영업 개시 이래 한자리를 꾸준히 지켜오고 있다. 이곳은 동네 만년 단골손님은 물론 입소문을 듣고 찾아오는 손님들 덕에 늘 문전성시를 이룬다. 이곳의 대표 메뉴인 잡내 없는 깔끔한 멸치 육수에 띄운 얇게 떼어낸 수제비는 부드러운 맛을 자랑하며, 100% 감자만을 이용해 만든 쫄깃한 감자전 또한 또 다른 인기 메뉴다. 줄 서서 기다리기 싫다면 가장 붐비는 정오부터 오후 2시 사이는 피하는 것이 좋지만, 그래도 언제나 늘 만원이다.

This local haunt has been an integral part of Samcheong-dong's history since 1982. The signature dish here is sujebi — rustic hand-pulled dough soup served in a savory anchovy broth. The restaurant is also known for its potato pancakes, made with grated potatoes that are pan-fried until crispy on the outside and pleasantly chewy on the inside. Avoid the lunch rush if you don't want to stand in line, but be warned — the restaurant is always busy.

수제비 • *Sujebi*

02-735-2965

종로구 삼청로 101-1

101-1 Samcheong-ro, Jongno-gu

■ 가 격 PRICE: ₩

안암

ANAM

종로구 성북구

돼지국밥 •

Dwaeji-gukbap

010-6874-8818

종로구 북촌로 5길 10

10 Bukchon-ro 5-gil, Jongno-gu

www.anaminanguk.com

■ **가 격 PRICE: ₩**

북촌에 위치한 작은 공간 안암의 주메뉴는 돼지국밥이다. '보통'과 '고기 많이'로 양이 구분되어 있는데 국밥의 비주얼이 무척 독특하다. 청양고추와 케일로 만든 기름이 깔끔한 육수와 어우러져 풍부한 향을 느끼게 한다. 스페인산 듀록 돼지의 등갈비에 통 목살을 얇게 저민 고기는 굉장히 부드럽고 은은한 육향을 가지고 있어 다채로운 풍미를 즐길 수 있다. 취향에 따라 고수 추가도 가능하니 안암에서 따뜻한 국밥 한 그릇 즐겨 보시기를 권한다.

At this humble diner situated in Bukchon Village, Seoul, the pork and rice soup comes in two sizes: medium and extra-meat. In the soup, a special oil made with Cheongyang chili pepper and kale is drizzled on top of the agreeably clean broth, with their culinary harmony creating a unique visual appearance and rich flavors. Plus, the Spanish Duroc baby pork ribs and thin slices of pork butt that complement the dish are exceedingly tender and boast subtle flavors, raising the gastronomic experience to a new crescendo. Visit Anam and enjoy a warm hearty bowl of its trademark soup. One last thing: Feel free to add cilantro to taste.

THERE IS ETERNITY
IN EVERY BLANCPAIN
The value of authenticity.
Atelier Tourbillon, Blancpain – Le Brassus
Villeret
Collection
A Villeret is for eternity.
Featuring an endless array of watchmaking's most fascinating complications, the Villeret bears authentic testimony to the talent of our watchmakers. Essentials imbued with timeless elegance.
JB
1735
BLANCPAIN
MANUFACTURE DE HAUTE HORLOGERIE
SHINSEGAE GANGNAM · SHINSEGAE MAIN · HYUNDAI COEX · LOTTE AVENUEL WORLD TOWER
HYUNDAI PANGYO · LOTTE AVENUEL · SHINSEGAE DAEJEON · SHINSEGAE CENTUM CITY

용금옥
YONGGEUMOK

1932년에 영업을 개시한 오랜 전통의 추어탕 전문점 용금옥. 종로구에 위치한 한정자 대표의 용금옥은 중구의 용금옥과 한 뿌리를 두고 있으나 현재는 각자의 길을 걷고 있다. 한국의 대표적 보양식인 추어탕을 사시사철 제공하는 이곳에선 서울식 통추어탕과 삶은 미꾸라지를 갈아 넣은 남도식 추어탕을 함께 선보인다. 좋은 재료로 정성껏 준비하는 모든 음식에는 오랜 세월 용금옥을 지켜온 주인장의 애정 어린 손맛이 고스란히 담겨 있다. 계절을 불문하고 많은 이들의 사랑을 받고 있는 따뜻한 추어탕 한 그릇이 아련한 추억을 선사한다.

Since 1932, Yonggeumok has been offering piping hot bowls of loach soup, a popular local dish believed to boost energy, especially during the summer months. This restaurant serves two different versions of the hearty and comforting soup: the chunkier Seoul style with whole loach, and the smoother Jeolla province style with ground loach. Everything on the menu as well as the complimentary side dishes are prepared daily by the longtime owner and chef Han Jeong-ja.

추어탕 • *Chueotang*

02-777-4749

종로구 자하문로 41-2

41-2 Jahamun-ro, Jongno-gu

https://yonggeumok.modoo.at

■ **가 격 PRICE: ₩**

자하 손만두
JAHA SON MANDU

만두 • *Mandu*

02-379-2648

종로구 백석동길 12

12 Baekseokdong-gil, Jongno-gu

www.jahasonmandoo.com

■ 가 격 PRICE: ₩

할머니와 어머니의 요리 솜씨를 이어받은 박혜경 대표의 자하 손만두. 1993년부터 부암동을 지켜온 만두 전문점으로 박 대표가 살던 집을 개조해 만든 레스토랑이다. 이 집 만둣국의 특징은 일체의 조미료를 배제하고 직접 담근 조선간장으로 맛을 낸 삼삼한 국물에 있다. 국내산 밀가루로 만든 쫄깃한 만두피도 빼놓을 수 없다. 정성껏 준비한 건강한 음식을 푸짐하게 대접하고자 하는 자하 손만두의 소신이 느껴지는 대목이다. 한편, 단아한 내부와 인왕산의 절경이 한눈에 들어오는 훌륭한 조망도 이 집의 매력을 한층 높여준다.

For over two decades, this restaurant has been attracting diners with a rustic dumpling recipe passed down from the owner's mother and her grandmother. Although humble by nature, dumpling dishes are always elegantly presented. Their signature dish is mandutguk: plump pork, bean curd and vegetable dumplings nestled in a delicate beef broth, seasoned with homemade soy sauce. The main dining room offers a spectacular view of nearby Inwangsan Mountain.

진중 우육면관
NIROUMIANGUAN

노포들이 즐비한 종각역 부근 청계천로에 위치한 우육면관은 작은 입구에 흰색과 적갈색의 인테리어가 시선을 끌어당긴다. 흔히 우육면은 대만 음식으로 알고 있지만 사실 우육면은 중국 란저우시에서 유래한, 모든 중화권의 대중적인 음식이다. 이곳에서는 셰프가 중국 산동성에서 직접 전수받은 레시피를 사용하여 대만식과는 조금 다른 우육면을 선보인다. 깔끔하고 진하면서 살짝 단맛이 도는 국물에 고수를 듬뿍 올려 먹거나, 라장을 추가하여 좀 더 진한 맛을 즐길 수 있다. 단일 메뉴만 판매하나 중국식 물만두와 오이소채를 곁들여 먹을 수 있으니 참고하길.

Niroumianguan features a memorable juxtaposition of clean white and vibrant rust colors in its décor. Chinese beef noodle soup, a popular delicacy across the Greater China region, is commonly known to have originated from Taiwan, but its real origin is Lanzhou in mainland China. As the chef learned the recipe from a noodle joint in China's Shandong Province, his restaurant serves up fare that is slightly different from the classic Taiwanese style. Add plenty of cilantro to the mildly sweet broth, complete with a clean yet rich taste; or a dab of chili sauce to give your dish deeper flavor.

국수 • *Noodles*

070-4213-5678

종로구 청계천로 75-2

75-2 Cheonggyecheon-ro, Jongno-gu

■ **가 격 PRICE: ₩**

할매집

HALMAEJIP

족발 • *Jokbal*

02-735-2608

종로구 사직로 12길 1-5

1-5 Sajik-ro 12-gil, Jongno-gu

■ 가 격 PRICE: ₩

1975년, 문경자 할머니가 내자동에서 창업한 후 2006년에 현재 위치로 이전했다. 여타 다른 곳과는 달리 고춧가루로 매운맛을 내기 때문에 잡내 없는 깔끔한 맛을 느낄 수 있다. 감자탕도 깻잎과 들깻가루가 아닌 콩나물과 부추만을 사용해 시원하고 알싸한 맛이 일품이다. 여전히 주방 일을 도맡아 하시는 할머님이 테이블마다 돌아다니며 맛있게 먹는 법을 설명해주신다. 지방과 살이 많은 뒷다리와 지방은 적지만 부드러운 앞다리 중 선택은 자유다. 양도 푸짐하므로 여러 명이 함께 가길 추천한다.

The original matriarch who opened this restaurant is still the heart and soul of the kitchen which has been dishing up legendary pork backbone stew and boiled pig's feet since 1975. Chili powder is the only spicy agent used to add the pleasant kick to the taste. It's a common sight to see Mrs. Mun, walking around showing her patrons how to eat her food "the right way. "

호라파
HORAPA

타이 • *Thai*

02-730-0215
종로구 자하문로 37-1, 2층
2F, 37-1 Jahamun-ro, Jongno-gu

■ 가격 PRICE: ₩

태국으로 떠난 짧은 여행. 그곳에서 만난 요리책 한 권은 손승희 셰프의 삶을 크게 바꾸어 놓았고 태국 음식의 매력에 빠져들게 만들었다. 그때부터 손 셰프는 태국 요리에 매진했고 그렇게 쌓은 경험을 레스토랑 호라파에 고스란히 담았다. 숯향과 향신료, 허브의 풍미로 가득한 태국의 거리와 그곳에서 만난 길거리 요리는 셰프에게 큰 영감을 주었고 그의 손을 거쳐 이국적이고 개성 넘치는 호라파만의 요리로 재탄생했다. 손 셰프는 태국 요리의 본질을 지키되 한국에서 나는 양질의 제철 식재료를 사용해 요리에 뚜렷한 개성을 담고자 한다. 그의 이런 철학이 한국에서 재해석된 태국 요리의 새로운 모습을 기대하게 만든다.

A short trip to Thailand and a serendipitous encounter with a local cookbook changed the course of his life and set Son Seung-hee on the path to chefdom. Enamored with the world of Thai cuisine, he has since poured his passion into mastering it, and his culinary dedication has found its culmination in Horapa's fare. The vibrant flavors of spices and herbs amid the wafting aroma of charcoal – this street vibe in Thailand, and the street foods he savored, serve as continued inspiration for the eatery's exotic and exclusive dishes. Chef Son seeks to remain true to the heart and soul of Thai cuisine while maintaining unmistakable originality in his fare by capitalizing on locally produced fine seasonal ingredients. This culinary philosophy leaves us awaiting Korea's novel take on Thai cuisine.

황생가 칼국수
HWANGSAENGGA KALGUKSU

칼국수 • *Kalguksu*

02-739-6334

종로구 북촌로 5길 78

78 Bukchon-ro 5-gil, Jongno-gu

■ 가 격 PRICE: ₩

하루 종일 길게 줄을 서는 이곳은 칼국수와 만두 전문점이다. 2001년에 북촌 칼국수로 시작해 2014년에 황생가 칼국수로 상호를 변경했지만, 예나 지금이나 맛있는 사골 칼국수와 만두를 먹기 위해 이곳을 찾는 손님들의 발걸음은 여전하다. 입구에서 잰 손놀림으로 만드는 왕만두는 매일 아침, 시장에서 선별한 신선한 재료로 그때그때 빚어 더없이 신선하다. 부드러운 칼국수의 면과 깊은 사골 육수의 맛이 일품이고, 옛날식 수육과 여름 한철 선보이는 콩국수도 별미이니 꼭 한번 맛보길 바란다.

No matter what time of day, always expect to see a line outside this beloved establishment, known for their humble noodle soup and dumplings. Originally called Bukchon Kalguksu when it opened in 2001, it changed its name in 2014, but that hasn't stopped the regulars from coming time and again for its freshly made dumplings and silky-soft noodles served in a rich ox bone broth. Boiled beef slices and noodles in cold soybean soup are also popular.

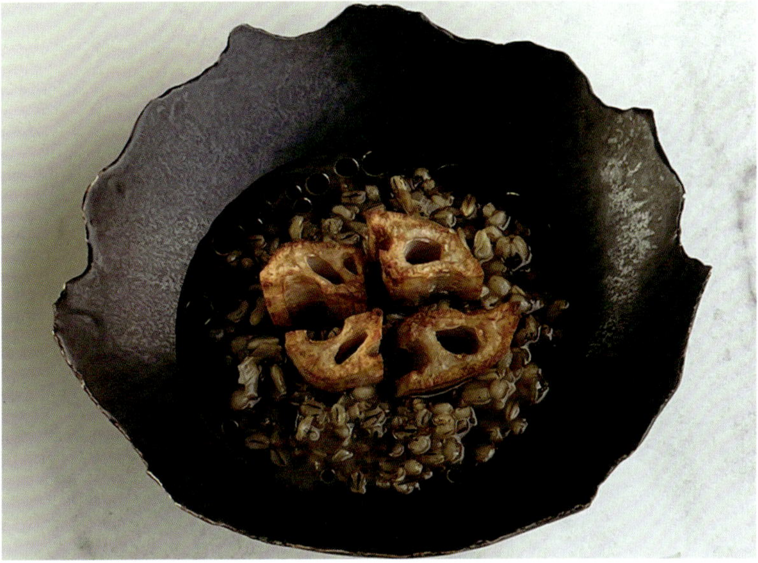

더 그린테이블

THE GREEN TABLE

김은희 셰프의 더 그린테이블은 자연이 키운 식재료를 식탁에 그대로 올리는 것을 의미하는 것으로 베란다에 직접 키우고 있는 옥살리스, 타임 등의 허브를 재배하여 요리에 색감을 더하는 프렌치 식당이다. 곡물과 뿌리채소, 다채로운 재료를 프렌치 조리법에 접목시켜 정갈한 맛을 보여준다. 꾸준히 본인의 색채를 찾아가려는 셰프의 노력이 돋보이는, 따듯하고 정갈한 프렌치를 맛 보시길. 와인 페어링은 셰프의 철학에 따라 내추럴 와인을 사용하니 함께 맛 보시길 바란다.

The Green Table is a French restaurant run by Chef Kim Eun-hee. It also offers seasonal menus featuring seasonal Korean ingredients, delivering ingredients grown by nature to the table directly. On veranda, herbs such as oxalis and thyme are grown to add color to the dishes. By fusing diverse ingredients, such as grains and root vegetables, with French recipes, Chef Kim presents precise flavors. Visit The Green Table for heartwarming yet refined French cuisine imbued with the chef's creativity.

프렌치 • *French*

02-591-2672

종로구 율곡로 83, 아라리오 스페이스 4층

4F Arario Space, 83 Yulgok-ro, Jongno-gu

www.thegreentable.co.kr

■ 가 격 PRICE: ₩₩₩

레스토랑 주은

RESTAURANT JUEUN

한식 • *Korean*

02-540-8580

서울 종로구 경희궁길 36, 경희당 8층

8F Gyeonghuidang, 36 Gyeonghuigung-gil, Jongno-gu

www.restaurantjueun.com

■ **가 격 PRICE: ₩₩₩₩**

경희궁 뒤편에 자리잡은 한식당 '주은'. 한식 공간의 헤드 셰프 출신인 박주은 셰프와 팀 멤버들이 함께 문을 연 공간으로 한국의 미를 곳곳에서 보여주는 디자인을 비롯해 장인들과 함께 만든 아름다운 기물들, 홀의 벽면을 채운 미디어 아트 월 등 정성들여 준비한 흔적이 느껴지는 장소이다. 깨를 이용해 국물을 내고 닭다리살과 방아잎을 넣어 만든 임자수탕, 가리비와 조개, 새우를 듬뿍 넣고 향긋한 해방풍 나물을 넣은 죽까지 한국의 전통을 담은 메뉴들을 만나볼 수 있다. 탄탄한 전통주와 와인 리스트에서 또 다른 즐거움을 만나보시길.

Situated behind Gyeonghuigung Palace, Jueun is a Korean restaurant opened by Chef Park Ju-eun, former head chef at Hansikgonggan, and his team. From design elements imbued with Korean aesthetics to elegant artifacts crafted in partnership with artisans to a media art wall occupying the length of the dining hall's wall, every nook and cranny of the establishment highlights sincere preparation. The menu consists of traditional Korean dishes, ranging from imjasutang, a soup featuring roasted sesame seeds, chicken leg flesh, and Korean mint leaves, to a porridge made with abundant scallops, shellfish, shrimps, and fragrant beach silvertop. The eatery's solid selection of wine and traditional Korean alcohol adds to its culinary delights.

물랑
MOULIN

프렌치 • French

070-4404-7978

종로구 자하문로 16길 8

8 Jahamun-ro 16-gil, Jongno-gu

■ 가 격 PRICE: ₩₩₩

서촌의 한적한 골목에는 주변과 다른 짙은 색의 외관으로 시선을 끄는 프렌치 레스토랑 '물랑'이 있다. 실내에 들어서면 앤틱한 인테리어를 비롯해 셰프가 그동안 수집해온 물랑(후추통) 컬렉션 장식이 시각적인 재미를 선사한다. 프렌치 요리에 계절의 풍미를 담아내려는 윤예랑 셰프의 의도는, 가끔은 섬세하고 때로는 선이 굵은 다양한 디테일과 균형감이 드러나는 요리에서 잘 드러난다. 제철 식재료를 활용하여 꾸준히 만들고 있는 피티비에 시리즈는 그녀의 요리 표현력이 잘 반영된 메뉴이다.

Located on a quiet alley in Seochon, Moulin is a French establishment whose dark-colored frontage draws attention by forming a stark contrast against its surroundings. Once inside, expect to be visually enticed by an antique-style décor and walls adorned with a collection of moulins, or pepper mills, that the chef has amassed over the years. Chef Yoon Ye-rang's desire to impart flavors of the season to her French cuisine is expressed in dishes that celebrate the balance of subtle and bold gastronomic elements. The signature pithivier series that continues to be recreated using seasonal ingredients epitomizes the culinary philosophy.

바비큐 • Barbecue

010-8231-2627

성북구 동소문로 17길 28

28 Dongsomun-ro 17-gil, Seongbuk-gu

■ 가격 PRICE: ₩₩

숙수도가

SOOKSOODOGA

성신여대 인근의 숙수도가는 김새결 셰프의 연구와 노력이 결실을 맺은 한우 바비큐 레스토랑이다. 숙수도가 바비큐의 목표는 간결하다, "최고의 한우로 최고의 숙성육을 만든다". 이를 위해 720시간 동안 숙수도가 만의 매뉴얼로 고기를 온도, 습도, 산소 접촉의 변화에 노출시키고, 건조와 발효를 통해 한우의 감칠맛을 극대화시키는데 집중한다. 이렇게 다듬어진 숙성육은 김새결 셰프의 방식으로 고객의 테이블에서 구워지고, 특유의 풍미를 전한다. 한우 부위에 따른 3가지 코스가 준비되어 있으며, 숙성육의 매력을 전하기 위해 문턱을 낮춘 합리적인 가격 역시 매력적인 요소이다.

Chef's years-long study and mission to "create the best aged beef using the finest Korean meat" according to its own manual, the restaurant dry-ages the meat for 720 hours under varying conditions of temperature, humidity and oxygen for optimal fermentation in order to maximize its umami taste. This aged meat is then grilled on the table using the chef's trademark method, which is known to best bring out the beef's distinct flavor. Depending on the cuts, there are three different course meals available. The restaurant's prices, set affordably to help popularize the appeal of aged beef, add greatly to its attraction.

이문설농탕

IMUN SEOLNONGTANG

1900년대 초, 한국의 첫 음식점으로 공식 기재된 종로구 견지동의 이문설농탕. 100여 년이 넘는 역사를 자랑하는 이곳은 오래전 최초로 개업했을 당시 사용했던 '설농탕'이라는 이름을 지금까지 고수하고 있다. 큰 무쇠솥에 17시간 동안 사골을 고아 기름을 말끔히 제거한 후 남은 뽀얗고 맑은 국물 맛이 이 집의 자존심이라 할 수 있다. 전성근 대표는 "좋은 재료로 대중음식점에 걸맞은 단순하지만 맛있는 음식을 제공하는 것이 목표"라고 말한다. 원하는 고기 양에 따라 보통 혹은 특을 선택할 수 있다.

Still going strong after more than 100 years of being in business, Imun Seolnongtang was the first eatery in Korea to officially register for a restaurant license when it opened in 1904. To this day, it honors the tradition of boiling ox bones for 17 hours until the broth turns rich and opaque. Other cuts of beef are later added to the intensely flavorful broth, served with a generous portion of sliced beef and soft wheat noodles.

설렁탕 • *Seolleongtang*

02-733-6526

종로구 우정국로 38-13

38-13 Ujeongguk-ro, Jongno-gu

https://imun.modoo.at

■ 가격 PRICE: ₩

Yido Kum/Getty Images Plus

중구
JUNG-GU

라연

LA YEON

중구

한식 • *Korean*

02-2230-3367

중구 동호로 249, 신라호텔 23층

23F Shilla Hotel, 249 Dongho-ro, Jung-gu

www.shilla.net/seoul/index.do

■ **가격 PRICE: ₩₩₩₩**

품격 있는 한식 정찬을 선보이는 라연은 전통 한식을 현대적인 조리법으로 세련되게 표현해낸다. 전망 좋은 신라호텔 23층에 자리해 시원한 남산 경관을 감상할 수 있는 이곳은 한국의 전통 문양을 활용한 기품 있는 인테리어가 인상적이다. 우아하고 편안한 식사 경험을 제공하기 위해 구비한 고급 식기와 백자를 형상화한 그릇은 레스토랑이 지향하는 또 다른 차원의 섬세함을 잘 드러낸다. 현대적으로 재해석한 메뉴에 와인을 조합해 즐길 수 있으며, 요구하지 않아도 세심한 배려가 돋보이는 서비스는 이곳의 또 다른 매력이다.

Time-honored traditions of Korean cuisine are given a contemporary touch at La Yeon. Located on the 23rd floor of The Shilla Hotel, this refined dining space offers stunning vistas over Namsan Park. It's the detail here that are noteworthy, from the fine tableware to the attentive service. Hansik and wine pairings elevate the dining experience to another level.

라망 시크레
L'AMANT SECRET

''비밀스러운 연인'을 뜻하는 '라망 시크레'. 레스케이프 호텔 26층에 자리 잡고 있는 이곳은 그 이름처럼 비밀스러운 분위기의 공간에 세련된 인테리어로 손님들을 맞는다. 미국에서 오랜 경력을 쌓고 돌아온 손종원 셰프는 '한국 스타일의 제철 재료를 이용한 양식'을 현대적으로 풀어 낸다. 한국의 다양한 식재료를 서양 요리의 테크닉과 접목시켜 만들어 내는 음식은 신선하면서도 사뭇 익숙하게 다가온다. '라망 시크레'에서는, 좋은 재료와 그 재료를 공급하는 생산자의 마음이 주방을 거쳐 손님에게 전달되는 소통 과정을 중시하는 셰프의 마음을 느낄 수 있다.

Located on the 26th floor of L'Escape Hotel, L'Amant Secret (French for secret lover) is an intimate space inspired by Parisian sensibilities. Chef Son Jong-won, who honed his culinary chops in the United States, strives for a style which he refers to as Korean-style Western cuisine with Korean seasonal ingredients. His modern interpretations are based on local ingredients blended with Western cooking techniques, resulting in creations that are both original and familiar, respectful of the symbiosis between the producer and the ingredients as well as the kitchen and the diner.

컨템퍼러리 •
Contemporary

02-317-4003

중구 퇴계로 67, 레스케이프 호텔 26층

26F L'Escape Hotel, 67 Toegye-ro, Jung-gu

www.lescapehotel.com/dining/lamantsecret

■ 가 격 PRICE: ₩₩₩₩

JUNG-GU

기가스
GIGAS

지중해식 • Mediterranean Cuisine

02-3448-9929

중구 퇴계로 6가길 30, 3층

3F, 30 Toegye-ro 6ga-gil, Jung-gu

■ 가 격 PRICE: ₩₩₩

The Chef's commitment:

'레스토랑에서 사용하는 야채의 95%는 유기농 재배와 노지 생산을 하는 셰프 아버지의 직영 농장에서 공급받고, 나머지 5% 역시 선별된 유기농 생산자로부터 조달하고 있다. 레스토랑 내에서는 일회용 플라스틱 용품을 일절 사용하지 않고 있으며, 식재료 보관상 유리나 스테인리스 용기만을 사용하기 어려운 경우에는 재활용이 용이한 HDPE나 PP 재질의 제품을 사용한다. 이처럼 현장의 작은 부분부터 친환경을 실천하려는 그의 의지를 레스토랑 곳곳에서 확인할 수 있다.

" The restaurant's fare features exclusively organic produce, with 95 percent of it supplied from a farm directly run by the chef's father and the remaining five percent from select organic producers. What's more, no single-use plastics are utilized within this eatery. Food ingredients are stored either in glass or stainless-steel containers. If such storage is not feasible, high-density polyethylene (HDPE) or polypropylene (PP) products are used instead as they are easily recycled. As described, the chef's meticulous commitment to sustainability can be felt in every nook and cranny of this establishment. "

국내에서는 접하기 쉽지 않은 정통 지중해 요리를 선보이는 레스토랑이다. 식재료를 구하기 쉽지 않아 지중해식 퀴진을 국내에서 온전히 구현하는 일은 쉬운 일이 아니다. 하지만 셰프는 직접 밭을 일구어 100% 친자연적으로 생산된 식재료를 이용해 지중해 요리의 전통이 반영된 레시피를 구현했고, 이를 통해 고객들은 또 다른 완성도와 방향성이 드러나는 매력적인 지중해 요리를 즐길 수 있다. 자연주의와 지속 가능성을 깊이 고민하고 요리를 통해 이를 실천하고자 하는 정하완 셰프의 철학이 담긴 기가스의 도전이 즐거운 다이닝 경험을 제공한다. 앞으로 그의 요리가 이 도시 안에서 어떤 방향으로 성장할지 귀추가 주목된다.

This authentic Mediterranean restaurant is a rarity in the Korean culinary landscape. Recreating bona fide Mediterranean cuisine in Korea is not an easy feat to achieve because of the scarcity of particular ingredients. Nevertheless, using purely organic ingredients grown on his family's farm, Chef Jung Ha-wan has managed to present fascinating Mediterranean fare with authenticity and direction that reflect the region's culinary tradition. What drives Gigas forward and ensures gastronomic pleasure is the chef's dedication to sustainability. How this restaurant will take on this challenge and grow amidst Seoul's culinary landscape is something that sparks our curiosity as much as the pleasant dining experience it offers.

소수헌 N

SOSUHEON

서울 중심부의 가장 한국적인 공간에서 박경재 셰프의 스시를 즐길 수 있는 소수헌. 기품 있는 한국의 미로 가득한 전통 공간이 주는 감성과 셰프의 정교한 솜씨가 빚어 내는 스시와 일식의 조합은 누구도 상상해본 적이 없을 것이다. 그만큼 공간과 맛이 조화를 이루는 이곳에서의 미식 경험은 특별하다. 제철의 시작과 정점, 그리고 피날레를 향해 가는 양질의 다양한 해산물을 한자리에서 셰프의 정교한 솜씨를 통해 즐길 수 있다는 점이 늘 기대와 흥분을 선사한다. " 최고의 공간에서, 최고의 직원들과, 최고의 식재료로, 최고의 손님들을 보실 수 있어 영광이다."라는 확신에 찬 셰프의 말에서 일식 요리사로서 걸어 온 그의 지난 여정의 정수를 느낄 수 있다. 이 곳에서 즐기는 다이닝은 감성과 감각을 채워주는 매력적인 식사 경험이 될 것이다.

스시 • Sushi

010-9694-3368

중구 만리재로 21길 8

8 Mallijae-ro 21-gil, Jung-gu

■ 가 격 PRICE: ₩₩₩₩

JUNG-GU

Enjoy Chef Park Kyung-jae's sushi at Sosuheon, located in the heart of Seoul and boasting an unmistakably Korean vibe. The combination of the elegant traditional Korean venue and the chef's precise sushi-crafting skills creates a truly special experience. At Sosuheon, the space and flavors of the food harmonize to elevate the dining experience. Guests can savor the excitement of enjoying premium seafood at their season's beginning, peak, and finale. The chef's confident statement, "It's an honor to host the best guests with the best ingredients, in the best space, with the best staff," reflects the essence of his journey as a chef specialized in Japanese cuisine. Dining at Sosuheon will be an unforgettable experience that delights both the emotions and senses.

중구

호빈
HAOBIN

중식 • *Chinese*

02-2270-3141

중구 동호로 287, 앰배서더 서울 풀만 2층

2F, Ambassador-Pullman Hotel, 287 Dongho-ro, Jung-gu

www.ambatel.com

■ **가 격 PRICE: ₩₩₩₩**

호빈은 후덕죽 셰프가 운영하는 중식 레스토랑이다. 후덕죽 셰프는 자타 공인 한국 중식의 산증인이자 수십 년간 광동식 중화 요리의 고급화에 앞장서 온 인물이다. '귀한 손님'을 뜻하는 상호 '호빈'은 고객과 함께 요리의 길을 걸어온 셰프가, 자신의 고객 존중의 마음을 표현한 것이다. 어향통해삼, 팔진초면 등 호빈을 대표하는 요리는 여럿 있지만 국내에서 최초로 선보인 불도장이야말로 빼놓을 수 없는 메뉴다. 불도장은 지금도 그를 대표하는 요리일 정도로 상징성이 있다. "신선한 식재료를 활용하여 재료 본연의 맛을 살려 조리한다."는 셰프의 말은 요리의 기본이 되는 명제임에도 남다른 무게가 느껴진다. 호빈에서는 다양한 요리와 더불어 제철 식재료를 활용한 보양식도 제공한다.

Haobin is a Chinese restaurant helmed by Chef Hu Deok-juk, celebrated as a living legend of Korean-Chinese cuisine and a trailblazer who led the refinement of Cantonese cuisine. The restaurant's title, which means "precious guests" in Chinese, reflects the chef's respect for his diners. Haobin boasts a vast repertoire of signature dishes, including braised whole sea cucumber with Sichuanese sauce and fried noodles with stir-fried seafood. Yet, its best-known offering is the classic soup poetically dubbed "Buddha Jumps Over the Wall," which was first introduced to Korea by Chef Hu and has remained the icon of his cuisine. "I strive to highlight the genuine flavors of the ingredients from the freshest ingredients." This quote by the chef carries exceptional weight although it merely reiterates the time-tested principle of culinary art. In addition to diverse gastronomic delights, the establishment also offers various vigor-boosting dishes made with seasonal ingredients.

광화문 국밥
GWANGHWAMUN GUKBAP

광화문 국밥은 박찬일 셰프가 운영하는 돼지국밥 전문점으로, 흰색 간판의 정갈한 이미지가 그의 음식과 꼭 닮아 있다. 흑돼지 엉덩이 살과 듀록 돼지 어깨 살로만 맛을 내는 이곳의 돼지국밥은 맑고 깨끗한 동시에 은은한 향과 깊은 맛을 자랑한다. 국밥이지만 국물과 밥을 따로 내는 이유는 갓 지은 밥맛을 최대한 살리기 위해서라고 한다. 거기에 넉넉하게 올려 내는 부추 고명이 육수에 향긋함을 더해준다. 편안하게 한 끼 식사를 즐기기에 안성맞춤인 곳이다.

The restaurant's clean white signage says it all. Chef Park Chan-il's dwaeji-gukbap or pork and rice soup looks and tastes unadulterated. Prepared simply by boiling black pork ham and Duroc pork shoulder cuts, the clear broth is fragrant and profoundly flavorful. Although 'gukbap' is commonly served with rice already mixed into the hot soup, Park serves the two separately, to preserve the taste of freshly steamed rice. The heaping of chopped chives added to the soup just before it is served renders the broth wonderfully aromatic.

돼지국밥 •
Dwaeji-gukbap

02-738-5688
중구 세종대로 21길 53
53 Sejong-daero 21-gil, Jung-gu

■ 가 격 PRICE: ₩

금돼지식당

GEUMDWAEJI SIKDANG

바비큐 • *Barbecue*

010-4484-8750

중구 다산로 149

149 Dasan-ro, Jung-gu

■ **가 격 PRICE: ₩**

신당동 길가에 자리한, 흰색 타일에 황금색 간판이 눈에 띄는 금돼지식당은 식사 시간이 아닌데도 문밖으로 길게 줄 서 있는 풍경이 낯설지 않을 만큼 인기가 높다. 이곳의 대표는 살코기의 풍부한 육즙, 탄력 있고 쫄깃한 식감, 그리고 지방의 풍미가 잘 살아 있는 돼지 품종을 찾기 위해 오랜 시간을 투자했는데, 이전에 YBD에서 최상급 선별육으로 변경해 풍미를 더욱 끌어올렸다. 갈비뼈가 붙어 있는 본삼겹과 등 목살 등의 특수 부위를 연탄불에 달군 주물 판에 구우면 고기가 타지 않고 맛있게 익는다. 그 흔한 돼지고기지만, 한번 맛보면 절대 잊을 수 없을 것이다. 예약은 받지 않는다.

Located along a main road in Sindang-dong, Geumdwaeji Sikdang can be easily spotted by its gold-on-white-tile signage and the queue outside the door long after peak dining hours. The establishment used to serve fine cuts of YBD pig, and recently upgraded the meat quality by switching to premium-grade cuts, enhancing overall standards. The texture of the pork is firm and meaty, with a good balance of flavorful fat that renders the meat supremely juicy. Items are is cooked on a cast-iron grill over coal briquettes that help keep the temperature constant. The restaurant does not accept reservations.

만족오향족발
MANJOK OHYANG JOKBAL

예로부터 한국인들의 대중적인 사랑을 받아온 족발을 '최고의 맛으로 제공하자'는 일념하에 달려온 만족오향족발은 철저한 위생 관리는 물론, 중앙 공급 시스템과 통합 물류 시스템을 체계적으로 운영해 전 매장에서 균등한 품질의 족발을 제공한다. 국내 최초로 온족을 개발한 이곳은 묵묵히 한길을 걸어온 전문점답게 품질 만족도가 높은 편이다. 현재 세 곳의 직영점을 운영하고 있다.

At Manjok Oyhang Jokbal, the beloved Korean braised pig's feet dish is impeccably crafted with the utmost dedication and care to hygiene and quality. The restaurant, armed with a systematic central distribution system, offers consistent quality at all of its franchised locations. Here, the popular pork dish can be enjoyed warm until the very last piece, thanks to the specially designed hotplates installed into the tables.

족발 • *Jokbal*

02-753-4755

중구 서소문로 134-7

134-7 Seosomun-ro, Jung-gu

www.manjok.net

■ 가 격 PRICE: ₩

명동 교자

MYEONGDONG KYOJA

중구

칼국수 • *Kalguksu*

02-776-5348
중구 명동 10길 29
29 Myeongdong 10-gil, Jung-gu
www.mdkj.co.kr/en

■ **가 격 PRICE: ₩**

1966년에 개점한 명동교자는 전통 조리법을 고수하는 칼국수 전문점으로 가족 경영 음식점이다. 선보이는 메뉴는 4가지 품목으로 단출하지만, 만두와 칼국수는 오랫동안 이곳을 대중들에게 알린 대표 메뉴라 할 수 있다. 소박한 서비스와 인테리어, 합리적인 가격 덕에 명동교자 밖에는 항상 손님들이 줄지어 문전성시를 이룬다. 한편, 같은 구역에 본점과 동일한 메뉴를 제공하는 2호점을 운영하고 있다.

Myeongdong Kyoja is a family-owned place in operation since 1966. The restaurant, which offers only four items on the menu, specializes in dumplings and noodle soup. An impressive number of patrons flock here daily, largely because all the dishes, including its signature garlic-laden kimchi, are made in-house. Simple décor and service come with hefty portions at affordable prices. It has a sister operation in the same area of Myeong-dong.

서령 N

SEORYUNG

홍천에서 시작된 이경희, 정종문 부부의 공간은 강화의 서령을 거쳐 서울 남대문의 서령으로 이어졌고, 그 여정은 자연스럽게 이들의 면 요리를 사랑하는 식도락가의 발걸음을 이끌었다. 서울에 터전을 잡은 뒤에는 전보다 많은 좌석과 쾌적한 식사 공간을 확보하고, 정성과 진정성을 쏟아 면과 육수를 준비해 고객과의 접점을 넓혀 가고 있다. 모든 면은 면장 정종문 셰프의 관리하에 100% 순 메밀면으로 만들어 낸다. 서령 순면, 비빔 순면, 들기름 순면으로 맛에 변주를 주어도 고유의 메밀 맛을 유지할 수 있는 비결이다. 정갈하게 담긴 면에 곁들여 나오는 만두와 항정 제육이 더욱 풍성한 느낌을 선사한다.

메밀국수 •

Memil-guksu

02-318-8766

중구 소월로 10

10 Sowol-ro, Jung-gu

■ **가 격 PRICE: ₩**

The couple, Lee Gyeong-hee and Jeong Jong-mun's Seoryung, began its journey in Hongcheon, moved via Ganghwa, and finally settled in Namdaemun, Seoul. The restaurant has drawn foodies, especially those who appreciate noodle dishes, wherever it relocated. After putting down roots in Seoul, they secured more tables, created a comfortable dining space, and expanded their connection with customers by preparing noodles and broths with dedication and authenticity. All of their noodles are made purely from buckwheat which is lovingly sourced and prepared by noodle master chef Jeong. This is the secret to the fragrant buckwheat flavor that shines through in all their variations of noodle dishes, like the Seoryung noodles, bibim noodles, and perilla oil noodles. The mandu and jeyuk, made from the most tender part of the pork shoulder served alongside the neatly presented noodles, provide an even more satisfying experience.

우래옥
WOO LAE OAK

냉면 • *Naengmyeon*

02-2265-0151

중구 창경궁로 62-29

62-29 Changgyeonggung-ro, Jung-gu

■ 가격 PRICE: ₩

서울 시내 최고의 평양식 냉면 전문점 중 하나로 손꼽히는 우래옥은 1946년 개업한 이래 꾸준히 전통을 이어오고 있는 유서 깊은 레스토랑이다. 이 집의 대표 메뉴는 전통 평양냉면과 불고기. 오랜 세월에 걸쳐 습득한 노하우와 국내산 재료만을 사용하는 뚝심으로 한결같은 맛을 자랑하는 냉면과 고품질의 한우를 제공한다. 레스토랑 내부가 상당히 넓은 편이라 많은 손님들이 몰리는 바쁜 시간에도 효율적인 좌석 배치가 가능하지만, 그럼에도 문 앞엔 항상 긴 줄이 늘어서 있다.

Lauded as one of the best Pyeongyang cold buckwheat noodle restaurants in the city, Woo Lae Oak has been serving consistently stellar food since 1946. The family-operated establishment is tucked away in the back alleys of Euljiro 4-ga, a bustling business hub. The restaurant interior is spacious and spotlessly clean. Indulge in their legendary Pyeongyang cold buckwheat noodles, served in broth or in a spicy sauce, and their bulgogi, grilled tableside.

중구

유림면
YURIMMYEON

서소문동에서 50년 이상 영업을 이어온, 오랜 역사를 지니고 있는 유림면. 1980년에 지금의 자리로 이전해 3대째 운영하고 있는 가족 경영 식당이다. 이곳에선 신안의 비금도 소금과 봉평 메밀만을 이용해 면을 직접 만드는데, 미리 숙성시켜 놓은 면을 주문과 동시에 삶아 낸다. 김민경 대표는 이렇게 숙성 과정을 거친 면은 글루텐 형성이 최소화되어 식감이 훨씬 부드럽고 소화가 잘 된다고 설명한다. 메뉴 중 나물과 지단, 그리고 달콤한 양념을 올려 내는 비빔 메밀국수는 든든한 한 끼 식사로 충분하다. 또한 깔끔한 국물이 매력적인 메밀국수와 어묵을 푸짐히 담아 내는 가락국수도 이곳의 인기 메뉴다.

For over 50 years, this family-run eatery has been serving bowls of noodles to those seeking comforting nourishment. The fresh buckwheat noodles, one of its bestsellers, are made from scratch, daily, using premium salt from Bigeumdo Island in Sinan County, and buckwheat flour from Bongpyeong. Topped with seasoned vegetables, thin strips of egg garnish, and a dollop of sweet and spicy sauce, a bowl of these noodles makes for a satisfying meal. Garak-guksu, wheat noodles in piping hot broth, comes with a generous serving of fishcake.

메밀국수 •
Memil-guksu

02-755-0659

중구 서소문로 139-1

139-1 Seosomun-ro, Jung-gu

■ **가 격 PRICE: ₩**

JUNG-GU

중구

필동면옥
PILDONG MYEONOK

냉면 • *Naengmyeon*

02-2266-2611

중구 서애로 26

26 Seoae-ro, Jung-gu

■ 가 격 PRICE: ₩

중구 필동에 자리하고 있는 남산골 한옥마을 인근의 평양냉면 레스토랑. 내로라하는 평양냉면 전문점 중 하나인 필동면옥은 오랜 세월 많은 이들에게 사랑받아왔다. 자칫 특징 없이 밍밍하다고 느낄 수 있을 만큼 깔끔한 맛을 자랑하는 이곳 육수에서 나는 섬세한 육 향과 은은한 감칠맛에 중독되어 단골이 된 손님들도 많다고. 두툼하면서도 부드럽고 촉촉한 돼지 수육은 이 집의 또 다른 명물이다. 정통 평양냉면을 선보이는 곳들 중에서도 특유의 섬세함을 가장 잘 표현해낸다는 평을 받는 곳이기도 하다.

Located near Namsangol Hanok Village by Chungmuro subway station, this restaurant is a Pil-dong landmark that has been serving Pyeongyang cold buckwheat noodles for decades. The restaurant's chilled broth has a delicate beef flavor, its subtlety both loved and disputed among cold buckwheat noodle aficionados. Another highlight of the restaurant is the buttery and tender boiled pork slices, served in thick slices with a dipping sauce. Homemade dumplings are also popular.

나인스 게이트
THE NINTH GATE

서울 프렌치 퀴진의 발전과 흐름을 논할 때 빼놓을 수 없는 나인스 게이트가 역동적인 서울 외식업계의 흐름에 발맞춰 제2막을 시작했다. 중후한 클래식 프렌치를 기반으로 하는 점은 여전하지만, 새 단장 후 한층 세련된 느낌의 요리를 선보인다. 노련한 소믈리에의 감각이 돋보이는 와인 리스트와 서비스는 이곳에서의 식사를 더욱더 풍요롭게 해준다. 변화와 기존 정취를 모두 다 느낄 수 있어서인지 단골손님들의 발길도 여전하다. 밤 10시 이후 바 테이블에서 선보이는 다양한 와인 테이스팅 프로그램 역시 매력적이다.

It would be challenging to discuss the evolution of French dining in Seoul without mentioning The Ninth Gate. Keeping up with Seoul's ever-transforming restaurant scene, a newer and better The Ninth Gate reopened its doors to the delight of fans both old and new. While the food is still reflective of the classic French style from the days before its facelift, there is also greater sophistication that makes the restaurant more relevant than ever before. Wine-tasting programs are offered at the bar counter after 10 pm.

프렌치 • *French*

02-317-0366

중구 소공로 106, 웨스틴 조선 호텔 1층

1F The Westin Chosun Hotel, 106 Sogong-ro, Jung-gu

www.josunhotel.com/intro.do

■ **가 격 PRICE: ₩₩₩**

남포면옥

NAMPO MYEONOK

냉면 • *Naengmyeon*

02-777-3131

중구 을지로 3길 24

24 Eulji-ro 3-gil, Jung-gu

■ 가 격 PRICE: ₩

남포면옥은 사람들의 발길이 끊기지 않는 오피스 빌딩 밀집 지역의 활기 넘치는 좁은 골목에 위치한 이북식 냉면집이다. 평양식 냉면, 어복쟁반, 전 요리를 전문으로 하는 남포면옥은 남녀노소를 불문하고 오랜 세월에 걸쳐 대중적인 사랑을 받아왔다. 늘 손님들로 분주한 분위기 속에서도 군더더기 없는 서비스와 한결같이 밝은 종업원들의 응대가 매력적인 남포면옥은 테이블식 좌석과 방석식 테이블의 룸으로 구성되어 있다.

Tucked away in a small alley among densely populated office buildings that sees a constant stream of foot traffic, the main building of this long-standing institution recently underwent a major facelift. A longtime favorite among patrons of all ages for its authentic Pyeongyang cold buckwheat noodles and beef hot pot, Nampo Myeonok continues to charm with its consistently good food and friendly service. Chair seating and floor seating are both available.

도림

TOH LIM

롯데호텔 37층에 자리한 차이니즈 레스토랑 도림은 중식 고급화의 첨단을 보여주는 곳으로, 식재료 본연의 맛을 잘 표현해내기로 유명하다. 광둥식 요리를 비롯해 다양한 중식을 소개하고 있으며, 이곳의 음식은 정통의 맛과 멋을 존중하며, 창의성까지 겸비한 훌륭한 중식으로 평가받는다. 요리의 품격은 고급스러움과 현대적인 감각이 녹아 있는 인테리어로 인해 한층 더 격상된다. 이곳엔 다양한 규모의 별실이 마련되어있어 돌잔치, 비즈니스 및 가족 식사 등 각종 모임 장소로도 각광받고 있다.

Located on the 37th floor of the Lotte Hotel, Toh Lim offers a state-of-the-art Chinese fine dining experience. The restaurant is acclaimed for its expert handling of ingredients, whose natural flavors shine through in the individual dishes. Led by a highly respected veteran of Korea's culinary industry, the team serves up a wide array of Chinese, with a special focus on Cantonese-style cuisine. Private rooms are available.

중식 • *Chinese*

02-317-7101

중구 을지로 30, 롯데호텔 37층

37F Lotte Hotel, 30 Eulji-ro, Jung-gu

www.lottehotel.com/seoul-hotel/ko/dining/restaurant-toh-lim.html

■ **가격 PRICE: ₩₩₩₩**

중구

한식 • *Korean*

02-317-7061

중구 을지로 30, 롯데호텔 38층

38F Lotte Hotel, 30 Eulji-ro, Jung-gu

www.lottehotel.com/seoul-hotel/ko/dining/restaurant-mugunghwa.html

■ **가격 PRICE: ₩₩₩₩**

무궁화

MUGUNGHWA

소공동 롯데 호텔 38층에 위치한 파인 다이닝 레스토랑 무궁화. 동양의 멋과 현대적 감성이 공존하는 공간으로 모던한 한식을 만나볼 수 있다. 제철 식재료의 맛과 효능에 대해 끊임없이 연구하는 이곳은 약과 음식은 근원이 같다는 '약식동원' 사상에 기반을 둔 건강식을 선보인다. 계절에 따라 변화하는 무궁화의 깊이 있는 요리는 정통 한식의 맛과 멋을 느끼기에 충분하다. 38층에서 내려다보는 서울의 도심 전망 또한 근사하다.

Located on the 38th floor with sweeping views of Seoul's dynamic urban jungle below, Mugunghwa is a modern Korean restaurant. The cooking is based on the basic principle that dictated Eastern medicine — that food and medicine are essentially the same. Creating modern cuisine firmly rooted in traditional Korean fare, the chef is constantly studying to bring the tastiest yet also the healthiest dishes to the table.

서울 다이닝

SEOUL DINING

서울의 특징을 요리에 반영한다? 서울 다이닝 요리는 고객에게 서울만의 미식 경험을 느끼게 할 수는 없을까, 라는 셰프의 자문에서 시작한다. 이 모티브를 바탕으로 제철 식재료와 셰프의 창의성이 결합되어 서울 다이닝만의 재치 있는 요리들이 고객의 식탁에 오른다. 다양한 식문화가 공존하는 서울의 특징을 고려해 곳곳에 다양한 풍미를 느낄 수 있는 재료와 소스를 사용한 것도 서울 다이닝만의 묘미다. 모던하고 활기찬 다이닝 공간 역시 재기 발랄한 요리 스타일과 절묘한 조화를 이룬다.

A culinary journey that captures the essence of Seoul? The fare at this destination sprang from the chef's own question of 'Is there a way to bring the unique gastronomic experience that Seoul embodies to restaurant patrons?" Based on this philosophy, the establishment combines seasonal ingredients with a great deal of creativity to bring brilliant, one-of-a-kind dishes to the table. Adding to its appeal is the use of ingredients and sauces that deliver a wide variety of flavors, a gesture that reflects the co-existence of diverse food cultures in Seoul. The contemporary and vibrant dining space also creates a sense of harmony worthy of its buoyant dishes.

컨템퍼러리 • *Contemporary*

02-6325-6321

중구 동호로 272, 디자인하우스 2층

2F Designhouse, 272 Dongho-ro, Jung-gu

www.seoul-dining.com

■ 가 격 PRICE: ₩₩

콘티넨탈

CONTINENTAL

프렌치 • *French*

02-2230-3369

중구 동호로 249, 신라호텔 23층

**23F The Shilla Hotel,
249 Dongho-ro, Jung-gu**

www.shilla.net/seoul/index.do

■ 가 격 PRICE: ₩₩₩₩

신라호텔 23층에 자리한 클래식 프렌치 레스토랑. 내부 인테리어와 테이블웨어 역시 모던하기보다는 고전적인 분위기가 돋보인다. 이곳에선 두 가지 세트 메뉴를 선보이는데, 훌륭한 식재료로 만든 정통 프렌치 요리의 고급스러운 플레이팅과 뛰어난 맛은 좋은 인상을 남기기에 충분하다. 한마디로 서비스, 분위기, 맛이라는 세 가지 요소를 모두 충족시키는 기본이 탄탄한 레스토랑이라 할 수 있다. 서울 시내가 한눈에 내려다보이는 탁 트인 전망 역시 콘티넨탈이 제공하는 즐거움 중 하나다.

If you are looking for a refined French restaurant with all the elements of classic French luxury, Continental is a solid bet. Perched on the 23rd floor of The Shilla Seoul, the restaurant is decorated in rich colors, with large tables and French empire chairs. What's more, the bright dining room offers diners a fantastic view of the city. The meticulously prepared food is beautifully plated and served on two different set menus of your choice.

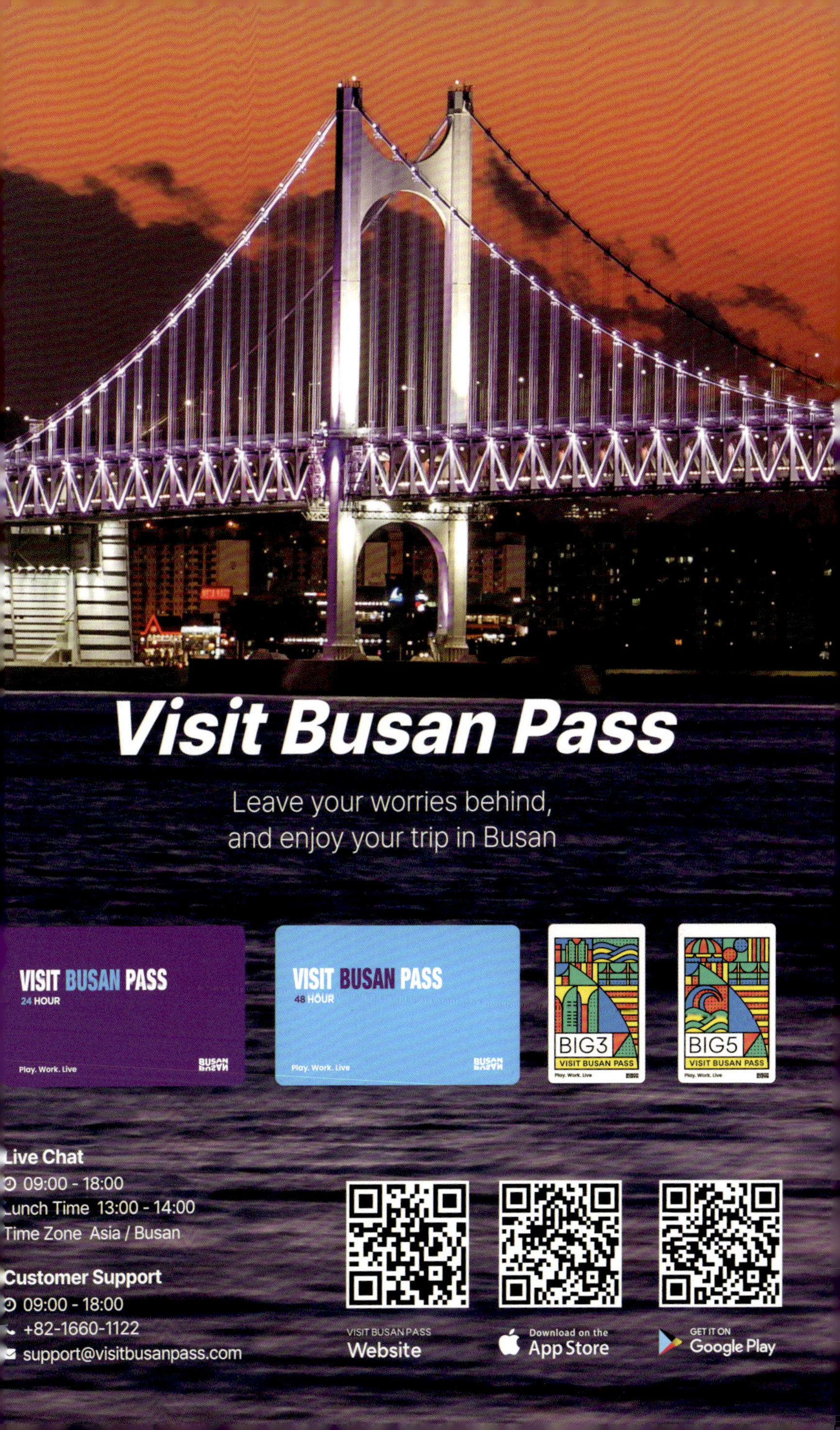

Visit Busan Pass
Leave your worries behind,
and enjoy your trip in Busan
VISIT BUSAN PASS
24 HOUR
Play. Work. Live
VISIT BUSAN PASS
48 HOUR
Play. Work. Live
BIG3
VISIT BUSAN PASS
BIG5
VISIT BUSAN PASS
Live Chat
09:00 - 18:00
Lunch Time 13:00 - 14:00
Time Zone Asia / Busan
Customer Support
09:00 - 18:00
+82-1660-1122
support@visitbusanpass.com
VISIT BUSAN PASS
Website
Download on the
App Store
GET IT ON
Google Play

크리스탈 제이드

CRYSTAL JADE

아시아와 미국 등지에 다수의 지점을 운영하고 있는 크리스탈 제이드는 싱가포르에서 광둥식 요리를 전문으로 선보이는 중국식 체인 레스토랑이다. 레스토랑, 딤섬 전문점, 익스프레스점 등 현재 우리나라에만 10여 곳의 매장을 운영하고 있다. 상하이식 요리와 광둥식 요리, 홍콩식 딤섬 등 다양한 지역의 음식을 제공하는 이곳의 대표 메뉴로는 XO 소스에 조리한 새우 관자 요리와 짜장 소스 치킨 요리 등을 꼽을 수 있다. 이곳에선 모던 하면서도 중국의 정취를 느낄 수 있는 쾌적한 다이닝 공간에서 식사를 즐길 수 있다.

Crystal Jade first opened its doors in Singapore in 1991 as a Cantonese restaurant. More than two decades later, the restaurant chain operates in many countries across Asia, including Korea with more than 10 locations. Their mission is to serve high-quality regional cuisine from China. Classics like Hong Kong-style dim sum, sautéed prawns and scallops in XO sauce, and sautéed chicken in black bean sauce are perennial highlights.

중식 • *Chinese*

02-3789-8088

중구 남대문로 7길 16, 지하 1층

B1F, 16 Namdaemun-ro 7-gil, Jung-gu

www.crystaljade.co.kr

■ 가 격 PRICE: ₩₩

JUNG-GU

중구

중식 • *Chinese*

02-317-4001

중구 퇴계로 67, 레스케이프 호텔 6층

6F L'Escape Hotel, 67 Toegye-ro, Jung-gu

www.lescapehotel.com

■ 가 격 PRICE: ₩₩₩

팔레드 신

PALAIS DE CHINE

우아한 프렌치 감성이 물씬 풍기는 레스케이프 호텔에서 유일하게 동양의 맛과 멋을 느낄 수 있는 곳, 중식당 '팔레드 신'이다. 가장 화려했던 시절에 상하이가 가지고 있던 아름다움을 모던한 다이닝 공간으로 풀어 냈다. '팔레드 신'은 전통 중식의 맛을 추구하지만 때로는 현대적인 색깔을 과감하게 요리에 입히기도 한다. 이곳에서는 중국의 지역적 특색이 반영된 요리를 다양하게 즐길 수 있는데 그 중 하나가 바로 딤섬이다. 지역색이 뚜렷한 북경 오리 역시 인기 메뉴다.

Located inside the Parisian Belle Époque-inspired L'Escape Hotel, Palais de Chine is the only space within the hotel that offers Eastern tastes and sensibilities. Inspired by designs from Shanghai's own belle époque, the modern space offers both authentic and modern interpretations of Chinese cuisine. There is a good range of dishes on the menu that stay true to their regional eccentricities, including the dim sum selection. Palais de Chine prides itself on its Peking duck, another celebrated Chinese dish with regional distinctiveness.

평양면옥

PYEONGYANG MYEONOK

장충동에서 3대째 평양냉면의 전통을 이어오고 있는 평양면옥은 서울의 유서 깊은 레스토랑으로 무더운 여름철, 입구에 길게 줄지어 있는 냉면 애호가들의 행렬로도 유명한 곳이다. 유난히 맑고 투명한 이 집의 냉면 육수는 은은한 육 향을 품고 있으며, 자극적이지 않고 깔끔한 맛이 일품이다. 냉면 외에도 다양한 메뉴를 선보이는데, 만두소를 푸짐하게 넣은 평양식 손만두와 얇게 썰어 따뜻하게 내오는 제육도 인기 메뉴다.

This establishment has been open for three generations, serving some of the finest bowls of Pyeongyang cold buckwheat noodles in the city. The long queue outside the entrance constitutes a part of the street's daily scenery during the sweltering summer months. The clear meat broth is delicately seasoned and the buckwheat noodles have a pleasant texture, firm and not too chewy. Steamed dumplings and boiled pork slices, served warm, are also standout dishes.

냉면 • *Naengmyeon*

02-2267-7784

중구 장충단로 207

207 Jangchungdan-ro, Jung-gu

■ **가 격 PRICE: ₩**

프렌치 • *French*

02-317-7181

중구 을지로 30, 롯데호텔 35층

35F Lotte Hotel, 30 Eulji-ro, Jung-gu

www.lottehotel.com/seoul-hotel/ko/dining/restaurant-pierre-gagnaire-a-seoul.html

■ 가 격 PRICE: ₩₩₩₩

피에르 가니에르

PIERRE GAGNAIRE

소공동 롯데 호텔 신관 최상층에 위치한 이곳은 프랑스 파리 출신의 세계적인 셰프 피에르 가니에르가 2008년 오픈한 프렌치 파인 다이닝 레스토랑이다. 고급 인테리어와 우아한 다이닝 공간을 자랑하는 이곳은 피에르 가니에르 셰프의 팀이 한국의 식재료를 바탕으로 만들어 내는 모던한 프랑스 요리를 선보이고 있다. 250여 종 이상의 고급 와인이 준비되어 있는 유리 와인 저장고와 모든 룸에서 내려다보이는 멋진 도심 경관은 시각적 즐거움도 충족시켜 준다. 정중하고 전문적인 서비스도 매력적이다.

Internationally celebrated French Chef Pierre Gagnaire opened his eponymous contemporary fine dining restaurant on top of Lotte Hotel's New Wing in 2008. The elegant dining space, adorned with Murano chandeliers and gold trim walls, exudes classic French luxury. The artfully presented food, made with 80% local ingredients, is respectful of the Paris-based chef's creative style. With more than 250 labels, the wine cellar display also impresses.

중구

하동관

HADONGKWAN

1939년부터 한결같은 맛으로 명성을 유지해온 명동의 터줏대감 하동관. 오랜 세월의 노하우가 고스란히 담긴 이곳의 곰탕은 깔끔하면서도 깊은 맛을 자랑한다. 곰탕 한 그릇에 양지, 내포, 양 등 소의 다양한 부위를 골고루 푸짐하게 내오는 것이 이 집의 특징이다. 맑은 고깃국물에 밥을 토렴해 내오는 곰탕에 다진 파를 넉넉하게 얹어 서울식 깍두기와 함께 먹으면 든든한 한 끼 식사로 그만이다. 분주한 아침과 점심시간에는 줄 서서 기다려야 하며, 다른 손님들과 합석하는 경우도 빈번하다. 이곳은 그날 준비한 분량을 모두 소진하면 영업을 종료한다. 계산은 선불제이고, 포장도 가능하다.

This beloved family-owned culinary landmark, located on a busy side street in Myeong-dong, has been serving rustic bowls of beef bone soup since 1939. The version here is served in traditional brass bowls with rice already submerged in the hot soup. The broth is pure and rich with an unmistakable sweetness that can only result from boiling large amounts of beef for a long period of time. This old-fashioned, no-fuss eatery opens early in the morning and closes when its soup vats run dry.

곰탕 • *Gomtang*

02-776-5656

중구 명동 9길 12

12 Myeongdong 9-gil, Jung-gu

■ **가 격 PRICE: ₩**

홍연

HONG YUAN

중식 • Chinese

02-317-0494

중구 소공로 106, 웨스틴 조선 호텔 1층

1F The Westin Chosun Hotel, 106 Sogong-ro, Jung-gu

www.josunhotel.com/intro.do

■ **가 격 PRICE: ₩₩₩₩**

강렬한 붉은 톤의 인테리어가 눈길을 사로잡는 차이니즈 레스토랑 홍연은 광둥식 요리 전문점으로 우아한 분위기에서 중식 정찬의 진수를 맛볼 수 있다. 노련한 주방 팀이 만들어내는 요리는 맛도 훌륭하지만 영양학적으로도 조화로운 건강식이다. 무겁지 않은 해산물, 두부, 채소 요리에 중점을 두고 있으며, 다소 시간이 걸리더라도 고객의 건강을 최우선으로 생각하는 조리법으로 음식을 준비한다. 매일 저녁 선보이는 라이브 뮤직도 즐거운 식사 환경에 한몫한다.

Instantly memorable with its crimson décor, this high-end restaurant at The Westin Chosun Seoul, specializes in Cantonese cuisine. The elegant space offers a taste of the best in Chinese-style formal dining, with its classic yet innovative dishes. Hong Yuan's commitment to using the freshest ingredients to make healthy and tasty food is unparalleled, as seen in its heavy use of seafood, tofu and vegetables. Live music during dinner service.

부산
BUSAN

Prasit Rodphan/Alamy/hemis.fr

Namhae Expressway
Namhae Expressway
Nakdongbuk-ro
Dongseo-daero
Hogye-ro
Seonakdong-ro
Jungang Expressway
북구
BUK-GU
강서구
GANGSEO-GU
Nakdonggang
Jedo-ro
Gonghang-ro
Gangbyeon-daero
김해국제공항
Gimhae International Airport
Joman-ro
Garak-daero
사상구
SASANG-GU
Namhae Expressway
Dongseo Expressway
Gangbyeon-daero
Gonghang-ro
Nakdong-daero
서구
SEO-GU
Nakdongnam-ro
Nakdongnam-ro
Myeongjigukje 1-ro
Nakdong-daero
Nakdong-daero
JUNG-
BIFF Square
감천문화마을
Gamcheon Culture Village
Jagalchi Market
Renault Samsung-daero
Eulsukdo-daero
Eulsukdo-daero
사하구
SAHA-GU
Wonyang-ro
Namhang
Dadae-ro
Gamcheonhang-ro
Dasong-ro
Dadae-ro

금정구
GEUMJEONG-GU
Bansong-ro
기장군
GIJANG-GUN
Chungnyeol-daero
동래구
DONGNAE-GU
Beonyeong-ro
Suyeonggangbyeon-daero
해운대구
HAEUNDAE-GU
Chungnyeol-daero
부산아시아드주경기장
Asiad Stadium
연제구
YEONJE-GU
Geoje-daero
Haeun-daero
Donghae Expressway
부산시립미술관 본관
Busan
Museum of Art
Mangmibeonyeong-ro
영화의전당
Busan
Cinema Center
Jangsan-ro
부산진구
JSANJIN-GU
Gwangan-daero
부산 아쿠아리움
Sea Life
Busan Aquarium
수영구
SUYEONG-GU
해운대해수욕장
Haeundae Beach
롯데백화점
Lotte Department Store
광안리 해수욕장
Gwangalli Beach
동백섬
Dongbaek
Island
광안대교
Gwangan Bridge
Beonyeong-ro
Busan Museum
부산광역시립박물관
Dongseo Expressway
남구
NAM-GU
부산역
san Station
Igidae Park
Bukhang-ro
dusan Park
Haeyang-ro
영도구
YEONGDO-GU
N
태종대
Taejongdae Park
부산시
BUSAN
0
3km
0
1mile
태종대 전망대
Taejongdae Observatory

tupungato/Getty Images Plus

해운대구
HAEUNDAE-GU

모리

MORI

일식 • *Japanese*

051-731-9889

해운대구 해운대해변로 298번길 24, 팔레드시즈 2층 2-4호

#2-4, 2F, 24 Haeundaehaebyeon-ro 298 beon-gil, Haeundae-gu

■ **가 격 PRICE: ₩₩₩**

일본에서 수학한 셰프와 그의 일본인 아내가 함께 운영하는 모리. 정갈한 정통 가이세키 요리를 즐길 수 있는 곳으로, 눈과 입이 모두 즐거운 곳이다. 부산의 신선한 해산물과 제철 채소를 이용해 섬세한 요리를 만들어 내는 김완규 셰프는 식재료의 조화와 코스의 리듬감을 잘 조절하는 균형 감각이 탁월하다. 아내의 세심하고 유려한 서비스와 셰프의 정성스런 요리를 맛볼 수 있는 따뜻한 공간에서 정통 일식을 즐겨 보시길 바란다.

Co-owned by a Korean chef trained in Japan and his Japanese wife, Mori offers nicely presented authentic Japanese kaiseki dining that will delight both your eyes and palate. Chef Kim Wan-gyu crafts delicate dishes using the fresh seafood and seasonal produce of Busan. He has an unmatched sense of culinary balance as manifested by the perfect harmony of ingredients and a well-controlled sense of rhythm that characterizes Mori's course meals. Enjoy authentic Japanese cuisine in this cozy space, where the chef's sincerely crafted cuisine is complemented by the smooth and attentive service of his wife.

팔레트
PALATE

프렌치 퀴진을 기반으로 자유롭게 구성에 변화를 준 현대적 요리를 선보이는 팔레트. 팔레트의 감각적인 요리 결과물은 김재훈 셰프가 경험한 요리 문화의 다양성이 바탕이 되었다. 고향 부산에서 당차게 팔레트를 오픈한 이후 요리적으로 다양한 도전과 레스토랑의 컨셉 변화를 시도한 결과, 그가 그린 팔레트의 발전적인 모습이 현재의 요리에 담겨져 있다. 다이닝만큼은 옛것을 고수하려는 부산의 다이닝 씬에서 변화무쌍한 시도를 하는 그의 요리가 어떠한 형태로 발전하게 될지 기대가 된다.

Palate offers contemporary French cuisine that is free-spirited and adventurous in style. Its sensuous fare is based on the culinary diversity experienced by Chef Kim Jae-hoon. Ever since he boldly opened this diner in Busan, his hometown, the chef has been taking up diverse epicurean challenges while injecting freshness into the restaurant's concept. This progressive aspect of Palate is well reflected in the cuisine it serves today. When it comes to dining, Busan has much respect for the old and traditional. This urban dining landscape makes one wonder how the chef's ever-evolving culinary experiments will translate into gastronomic revolutions.

컨템퍼러리 •
Contemporary

051-626-2364

해운대구 달맞이길 65번길 154, 3층

3F, 154 Dalmaji-gil 65 beon-gil, Haeundae-gu

www.palatebusan.com

■ 가 격 PRICE: ₩₩

HAEUNDAE-GU

피오또
FIOTTO

이탈리언 • *Italian*

해운대구 좌동순환로 432, 4층
4F, Jwadongsunhwan-ro 432, Haeunedae-gu, Busan, South Korea

■ 가 격 PRICE: ₩₩

The Chef's commitment:

'피오또는 레스토랑에서 사용하는 채소와 과일의 90% 이상을 부모님의 농장에서 조달한다. 셰프 부부는 자신들의 요리 철학에 걸맞은 건강한 식재료를 얻기 위해 부모님의 농사일에도 적극 참여하고 있다. 이들은 공산품 식재료의 사용을 최소화하는 대신 자연에서 난 식재료를 사용한 뒤 이를 다시 자연으로 돌려보내는 환경 친화적 선순환에 집중한다. 셰프 부부의 농사 이야기와 식재료의 출처를 듣는 것도 피오또의 요리만큼이나 흥미로운 다이닝 경험을 선사한다.

"Helmed by a chef couple, Fiotto sources more than 90 percent of its vegetables and fruits from their parents' farm. To obtain healthy ingredients aligned with their culinary philosophy, the chefs remain active farmers as well. With minimal reliance on the use of processed ingredients, they focus on a virtuous green cycle, where natural ingredients are returned to nature after use. Hearing about their fascinating stories of life on the farm and the sources of their ingredients is almost as intriguing as the dining experience at Fiotto."

달맞이 고개에서 부부가 운영하는 아담한 공간 피오또. 파스타 코스를 제공하는 곳인데 코스가 파스타로만 구성되어 있다고 고개를 갸웃할 수도 있다. 하지만 직접 경험해 보면 다양한 파스타의 다채로운 맛을 즐기는 일이 무척 즐겁다는 것을 알게 될 것이다. 여러 종류의 생면부터 생햄, 부모님과 함께 운영하는 농장의 채소로 준비하는 재료와 콤부차로 만든 식초, 시럽 등 거의 모든 식재료를 직접 만들어 준비하고 피오또만의 자연적인 맛과 색을 입혀 낸다. 그렇기에 파스타로만 짜여진 코스임에도 속이 부담스럽지 않다.

Located on Dalmaji Hill, Fiotto is a cozy little bistro run by a couple that serves tasting course featuring pasta and more. The menu highlights fresh vegetables from the couple's family farm, premium Jirisan pork, heirloom rice, and other locally sourced ingredients. Nearly every component, from various types of fresh pasta and cured ham to kombucha-based vinegar and syrups, is made in-house. These elements are crafted with care to bring out Fiotto's unique, natural flavors and colors. For those who wish to experience the meticulous preparation and pure taste of nature, making a reservation is essential.

해운대구

나가하마 만게츠
NAGAHAMA MANGETSU

해리단길 안쪽으로 깊숙이 들어가면 긴 줄이 보인다. 1960년대에 후쿠오카 나가하마에서 시작한 라멘 전문점이 부산에 처음 지점을 연 곳이다. 이곳의 라멘은 돈 사골을 오랜 시간 고아 낸 국물에 비법 간장을 넣어 진하면서도 무겁지 않은 맛을 낸다. 취향에 따라 면의 삶기 정도를 선택할 수 있고 생마늘이나 매운 소스를 첨가해 즐길 수도 있다. 짜게 느껴진다면 국물을 더 요청할 수도 있으니 망설이지 말고 취향껏 추가해 먹어볼 것을 권한다.

Tucked deep within the Haeridan-gil area, this establishment stands out with a long line of diners waiting to be seated. This ramen joint in Busan is the first Korean outpost of a restaurant that started during the 1960s in the Nagahama area in Fukuoka, Japan. The ramen is prepared by simmering pig bones for hours until the broth becomes milky and smooth. Combined with a secret homemade soy sauce, the broth tastes rich, but never heavy. You may request your noodles be cooked to your liking, or add raw garlic or a spicy sauce. If you find your new broth a little too salty, feel free to ask for additional broth to savor your dish to the fullest.

라멘 • *Ramen*

051-731-0886

해운대구 우동 1로 57

57 Udong 1-ro, Haeundae-gu

■ **가 격 PRICE: ₩**

부다면옥

BUDA MYEONOAK

냉면 • *Naengmyeon*

051-746-8872

해운대구 중동 1로 36, 2층

2F, 36 Jungdong 1-ro, Haeundae-gu

■ **가 격 PRICE: ₩**

반여동의 부다밀면에 익숙한 분들이라면 부다면옥이라는 이름이 생소하지 않을 것이다. 지난 2021년에 이곳 해운대로 자리를 옮긴 부다면옥은 100% 순 메밀면으로 만든 평양냉면을 판매한다. 뚝뚝 끊길 것 같지만 제법 탄력도 있고 씹을수록 고소한 순면, 그리고 한우를 우린 국물에 채수를 섞어 구수하고 슴슴한 감칠맛이 풍부한 국물이 일품이다. 새콤달콤한 무와 얼갈이, 오이 같은 고명이 따로 나오는데 취향에 따라 얹어 먹으면 그 맛에 중독될 것이다.

For those familiar with Buda Milmyeon in Banyeo-dong, the name Buda Myeonoak may ring a bell. Relocated to the present location near Haeundae Beach in 2021, this noodle haven offers Pyeongyang cold buckwheat noodles made out of 100% buckwheat flour. Unexpectedly resilient, the pure noodles reveal additional nutty flavor with each bite. The broth, made from Korean beef and mixed with vegetable broth, is earthy and mild yet full of umami. When topped with your choice of garnishes that are served separately, such as sweet and sour radish, winter cabbage, and cucumber, the noodles are sensationally addictive.

해목

HAEMOK

외지인과 현지인의 발걸음이 꾸준히 이어지는 해목은 대중적인 일식 요리를 선보인다. 파란색 담장과 어딘가 이국적인 구조물이 주변과는 또 다른 분위기를 자아낸다. 원목 베이스의 인테리어와 다다미 좌석 역시 이국적 정취를 느끼게 하는 데 한몫한다. 해목은 일본식 덮밥 서너 가지와 사시미, 튀김, 타다끼 요리 등을 제공하지만 대표 메뉴는 뭐니뭐니 해도 히츠마부시이다. 그윽한 훈연의 풍미와 감칠맛 나는 소스의 맛을 머금은 우나기는 고슬고슬하게 지은 밥과 잘 어울린다. 해목은 부산 본점 외에 서울에서도 분점을 운영 중이다.

Popular among both tourists and local regulars, Haemok offers accessible Japanese fare. Its blue fence and inexplicably exotic edifice create a vibe that makes this spot stand out in the neighborhood. Its wood-based décor and tatami floor also add to the exotic ambiance. Haemok's menu includes a few selections of Japanese rice bowls, sashimi, tempura, and tataki dishes. But its signature item is unarguably hitsumabushi (Nagoya-style grilled eel). Coated with umami-rich sauce, the eel features bottomless flavor and is a perfect accompaniment to the rice cooked to perfection. And just so you know, Haemok also has outposts in Seoul.

일식 • *Japanese*

051-746-3730

부산 해운대구 구남로 24번길 8

8 Gunam-ro 24 beon-gil, Haeundae-gu

■ 가 격 PRICE: ₩₩

복어 •

Fugu / Pufferfish

051-742-3600

해운대구 중동 1로 43번길 23

23 Jungdong 1-ro 43 beon-gil, Haeundae-gu

■ 가 격 PRICE: ₩₩

금수복국

KUMSU BOKGUK

금수복국은 본점인 해운대를 필두로 서울과 부산에 여러 지점을 둔 복어 요리 전문점이다. 1970년에 금수식장으로 문을 열어 50년 넘게 대를 이어 영업 중이다. 네 가지 종류의 복을 선택하여 먹을 수 있는데 은복은 쫄깃하고 고소하며 밀복은 크기가 큰 커서 매운탕에 많이 쓰인다. 까치복은 단맛이 나서 찜이나 수육으로 먹고, 참복은 가장 큰 사이즈로 식감이 단단하여 회로 먹기에 좋다고 한다. 복어 조리사 자격증 소지자만 수십 명에 달할 정도로 관리에 만전을 기하고 있다고 하니 본점을 찾아가 즐겨 보시는 건 어떨까.

Kumsu Bokguk in Haeundae District is the head restaurant of a chain that has many outposts in Seoul and Busan. For more than 50 years since 1970, and across multiple generations, this eatery has delighted seafood lovers as a specialized puffer fish restaurant. It offers four types of puffer fish. Brown-backed puffer is chewy and has a nutty flavor. Globe puffer is large and often made into a spicy stew. Yellowfin puffer is sweet, so it is usually steamed or boiled. Ocellate puffer is the largest variety of the fish. Its firm texture makes the fish more suitable to be served raw. Safety is the first priority at this head restaurant as demonstrated by the hiring of dozens of chefs, all licensed to prepare puffer fish. So why not rest assured and visit this time-tested establishment for a gastronomic adventure?

딤타오
DIM TAO

'마음에 점을 찍다'라는 의미의 딤섬은 중국 광둥 지역의 대표 음식이다. 배를 가득 채우기 위함이 아닌 간소하게 먹는 음식이라는 뜻이 담겨 있다. 딤섬은 종류가 무수히 많지만 딤타오에서는 그 중 가장 유명한 몇 가지를 선보인다. 육즙이 가득한 샤오롱바오, 통통한 새우살과 부추를 듬뿍 채운 교자를 비롯해 원톤수프나 바베큐번 등도 만나볼 수 있다. 예로부터 딤섬은 차와 함께 먹었다고 하니 보이차나 재스민차와 곁들여 먹어 보기를 추천한다. 해리단길에서 긴 줄을 찾다 보면 금세 발견할 수 있다.

Dim sum, a representative Cantonese dish, literally means "touch the heart," implying that it's not intended to fill your stomach, but is supposed to be a simple meal. Dim Tao focuses on the most famous dim sum dishes among its countless varieties, including juicy xiao long bao (soup dumplings); a dumpling filled with plump shrimp and chives; wonton soup; and barbeque pork buns. Traditionally, dim sum is served with tea. We recommend the pu'er and jasmine teas. A long line of customers outside makes this popular establishment in the Haeridan-gil area impossible to miss.

딤섬 • *Dim Sum*

051-741-3638

해운대구 우동 1로 25

25 Udong 1-ro, Haeundae-gu

■ 가 격 PRICE: ₩

컨템퍼러리 •
Contemporary

051-747-8522

해운대구 마린시티 3로 37, 2층

2F, 37 Marine city 3-ro, Haeundae-gu

www.ledorer.com

■ 가 격 PRICE: ₩₩₩

르도헤
LE DORER

마린시티에 위치해 아름다운 바다의 조망을 자랑하는 르 도헤. 이곳의 상호 르 도헤는 '금빛으로 물들인다'는 뜻의 프랑스어로 고급스럽고 아름다운 경험을 제공하겠다는 의지가 담겨 있다. 이전에는 한식당으로 운영했으나 지금은 프렌치와 일식의 터치를 가미한 컨템퍼러리를 지향한다. 다양한 종류와 리스트를 자랑하는 와인 셀러를 보유하고 있으며, 와인과의 마리아주에 집중할 수 있도록 코스 메뉴 외에 단품 메뉴 및 와인과 칵테일을 곁들일 수 있는 바 메뉴도 선보이고 있다.

Le Dorer's Marine City location offers a gorgeous seascape. Dorer is a French word that means "to coat with gold." The restaurant's name therefore symbolizes its resolve to provide a swanky and beautiful dining experience. Le Dorer started off as a Korean restaurant, but now serves contemporary fare with a touch of French and Japanese cuisine. It also features a wine cellar that boasts a wide range of vintages and varietals. For those who prefer to focus on the union of food and wine, Le Dorer also offers an a la carte menu and a bar menu with a wine and cocktail list.

머스트루
MUSTRUE

부산을 대표하는 파인다이닝 중 하나인 머스트루. 부산 토박이 정재용 셰프의 공간으로, 달맞이길 골목에 비밀스레 위치해 있다. 금빛 문을 열고 들어가면 셰프가 바 테이블에서 음식 조리부터 서빙까지 모든 것을 능수능란하게 컨트롤한다. 유러피안 음식을 기반으로 하지만 당귀 씨나 참나물 소스를 이용하는 등 재료에 변화를 주어 한국 재료와의 조화를 중시하는 셰프의 진심이 늘 한결같다. 머스트루라는 이름처럼.

Mustrue is one of the representative fine dining spots in Busan. Helmed by Chef Jung Jae-yong, a Busan native, it is covertly tucked away in a back alley of Dalmaji-gil Road. Open the golden door, and you'll be greeted with a bar counter, where the chef masterfully handles everything from cooking to serving. By using unique local ingredients, such as Korean angelica seeds and short-fruit pimpinella, he creates European cuisine with a Korean twist. Chef Jung is passionate about maintaining the harmony between his culinary creations and Korean ingredients. And his passion is uncompromising – just as Mustrue, the eatery's name, suggests.

유러피언 • *European*

051-747-2369

해운대구 좌동순환로 433번길 29

29 Jwadongsunhwan-ro 433 beon-gil, Haeundae-gu

■ **가 격 PRICE: ₩₩**

본 앤 브레드 N

BORN AND BRED

스테이크하우스 •

Steakhouse

051-749-2400

해운대구 해운대해변로 296
파라다이스호텔 지하 1층

B1F, Paradise Hotel, 296
Haeundaehaebyeon-ro,
Haeundae-gu

www.bamdb.co.kr

■ 가 격 PRICE: ₩₩₩₩

마장동의 최고급 한우를 이제 부산에서도 즐길 수 있다. 베테랑 직원들이 매일 경매에서 최상급 암소(1++BMS9 등급)만을 수급하고 이를 숙성, 정형해 최적의 두께로 준비한 고기는 그야말로 다채로운 맛을 낸다. 본앤브레드에서는 모든 부위를 즐길 수 있는 맡김차림도 경험할 수 있는데 기본적으로 15~19 가지 정도의 부위를 참숯에 구워 낸다. 이 외에도 소고기 사시미나 소고기 타코 등 다양한 시도를 한 요리들이 코스에 가득하다. 배가 너무 부를 수 있으니 적당히 속을 비우고 가기를 추천한다.

Premium-grade hanwoo is now served in Busan. Only top-grade female cattle (1++BMS9 grade) are hand-picked daily by highly experienced staff, aged and trimmed to a perfect thickness to create a multi-faceted flavor profile. Born and Bred also offers an omakase-style experience where diners can taste 15 to 19 different cuts of charcoal-grilled beef. The menu is filled with creative dishes like beef sashimi and beef tacos. Make sure you arrive ready to indulge yourself.

소공간
SOGONGGAN

'작은(小) 공간' 또는 '소고기를 다루는 공간'이라는 중의적인 뜻의 소공간은 한식이 기본이 되는 정성스러운 메뉴를 선보인다. 셰프는 오랜 기간 양식 요리를 하다 한식으로 전환했다. 그는 드디어 맞춤옷을 입은 듯 편한 마음으로 즐겁게 요리하고 있다고 말하는데 그 즐거운 마음이 요리에 고스란히 녹아 있다. 미려한 플레이팅과 독창적 요리. 여기에 직접 48시간 동안 끓인 곰탕과 솥밥 등 세련된 한식을 맛볼 수 있는, 결코 '작지 않은 공간'이다.

Sogonggan is a double entendre that can be read as "a small space" or "a space dealing with beef." Its thoughtfully crafted menu is rooted in Korean cuisine. The chef spent many years perfecting his Western cuisine before making the switch to its Korean counterpart. He says the switching has made cooking more enjoyable and comforting as if he were finally wearing a tailored suit. Indeed, his sense of happiness is genuinely reflected in the fare. With Sogonggan's elegant plating, original dishes, and refined Korean menu lineup, such as beef bone soup simmered in-house for 48 hours and pot rice, the "small space" moniker is unquestionably a misnomer.

한식 • Korean

010-5191-9002

해운대구 해운대해변로 298번길 47, 4층

4F, 47 Haeundaehaebyon-ro 298 beon-gil, Haeundae-gu

■ 가 격 PRICE: ₩₩

일식 • *Japanese*

010-8543-3356

부산 해운대구 해운대해변로 209번길 13, 2층

2F, 13 Haeundaehaebyeon-ro 209 beon-gil, Haeundae-gu

■ 가 격 PRICE: ₩₩

이와
IWA

생선 숙성 특허를 보유한 셰프는 분명한 의도를 가지고 숙성 식재료를 준비한다. 여기서 나오는 안정적인 맛의 다양한 구성이 즐거움을 준다. 식재료의 수급 상황과 셰프의 구상에 따라 스시와 사시미, 일식 요리의 비중을 그때그때 조절한다. 셰프는 모든 생선을 기본적으로 4일 이상 숙성하며 생선의 종류와 특성, 컨디션에 맞춰 최적의 숙성 시기를 찾기 위해 식재료에 세심한 주의를 기울인다. 합리적인 가격과 풍미 깊은 숙성 식재료의 다양한 일식을 한 자리에서 즐기는 것은 또 다른 재미를 준다.

The chef, who holds a patent for the aging of fish, prepares aged ingredients with clear intent. Such meticulous preparation, combined with diverse selections, produces stable flavors and gastronomic delights. Depending on the ingredients available and the chef's tactics, the proportion of sushi, sashimi, and other Japanese dishes in the omakase can vary. All fish here are aged at least four days, and the chef carefully selects an optimal aging period for each fish based on its type, characteristics, and conditions. At Iwa, customers can enjoy at one sitting a wide variety of Japanese dishes, each prepared with aged ingredients with full-bodied flavors. And reasonable prices make this culinary feast all the more special.

차오란
CHAORAN

중식 • *Chinese*

051-922-1250
해운대구 달맞이길 30, 시그니엘 부산 5층
5F Signiel, 30 Dalmaji-gil, Haeundae-gu

■ 가 격 PRICE: ₩₩₩₩

시그니엘 5층에 위치한 차오란. 정통 광둥식 음식을 내는 중식당으로 정확히는 홍콩식에 가깝다. 홍콩식은 광둥식을 기반으로 하면서도 다양한 문화를 가진 지역의 특색이 만들어 낸 새로운 맛들이 조화롭게 섞인 것이 특징이다. 딤섬만 하더라도 오징어 먹물로 색을 낸 만두피에 금박을 올린 하가우, 트러플을 비롯한 각종 버섯과 아스파라거스를 넣은 야채교자, 말린 가리비와 XO 소스를 넣고 날치알을 올린 딤섬 등 화려하고 맛있는 메뉴가 다양하게 준비되어 있다. 대표 메뉴인 꿀 소스 바베큐와 바삭한 크리스피 삼겹살은 촉촉한 고기에 바삭한 껍질과 과하지 않은 양념 맛이 일품이다. 1920년대 홍콩을 재연한 듯한 실내에서 해운대를 조망하며 음식을 음미해 보기를 바란다.

Situated on the fifth floor of Signiel Busan, Chaoran serves authentic Cantonese cuisine – more precisely its Hong Kong variety, which is based on the former yet characterized by the harmony of new flavors resulting from the city's culturally diverse geographical contexts. Take, for example, the dim sum: It consists of a gamut of splendid and scrumptious dishes, including har gow (shrimp dumplings), characterized by skin colored with squid ink and topped with gold leaf; a vegetable dumpling filled with truffle, other mushrooms, and asparagus; and a seafood dumpling stuffed with dried scallops in XO sauce and decorated with flying fish roe. Pork Barbeque with Honey Sauce and Crispy Pork Belly, the signature dishes, boast juicy meat and crispy skin accompanied by mild flavors conjured up by seasonings. Its décor, reminiscent of Hong Kong in the 1920s, and its spectacular view of the Haeundae area make this fine diner an optimal location to savor a delectable meal.

토라후구가
TORAFUGUGA

복어 •
Fugu / Pufferfish

051-743-5432
해운대구 좌동순환로 480
480 Jwadongsunhwan-ro, Haeundae-gu

■ 가 격 PRICE: ₩₩

해운대 중동사거리 대로변에 토라후구(참복)가 헤엄치는 작은 수족관과 옛스러운 나무 디자인의 외관이 유독 눈에 띄는 이곳. 주인장 정승훈 셰프가 직접 붓글씨로 쓴 작은 상호명 외에 따로 간판은 없지만 이러한 시각적 요소만으로도 복어 요리 전문점임을 알 수 있다. 셰프의 정교한 손놀림을 통해 참복이 가진 다채로운 맛의 매력이 고객의 테이블 위로 쉼 없이 전해지고, 유비키와 텟사, 가라아게, 지리, 죠스이 등 기본에 충실한 각종 일본식 복어 요리가 알차게 코스를 구성한다. 복어를 취급하는 곳은 많아도 일본 스타일의 요리를 구현하고자 하는 곳은 많지 않다. 그런 점에서 복어를 다루고 요리해 손님 상에 올리는 셰프의 진지함에서 요리에 대한 그의 진심이 느껴진다.

Located on a boulevard near Jungdong Intersection in the Haeundae District, Torafuguga stands out with its quaint wooden exterior and a small aquarium with live torafuku (tiger puffer) at the front. The eatery has no sign except for a small calligraphy of its name penned by the owner-chef Jung Seung-hun himself. Yet, these visual elements are enough to let you know that it's a specialist puffer fish restaurant. Here, the chef's precise hand movements bring out the variegated flavors of tiger puffer and deliver them, nonstop, to customers at the tables. Torafuguga's Japanese-style puffer fish course features a wide array of faithful dishes that are parboiled, served raw in slices, fried, made into a soup, or crafted into a porridge. There are many restaurants that handle puffer fish, but few show commitment to presenting it in authentic Japanese style. In light of this, the chef's earnestness in preparing and serving puffer fish testifies to his passion for culinary art.

해운대 암소갈비집 N
HAEUNDAE RIB BARBECUE RESTAURANT

1964년부터 한 자리를 한결같이 지켜온 부산의 명물. 100년 넘은 고택에서 현대적인 건물로 탈바꿈한 해운대 암소갈비집은 3대째 이어져 온 이곳은 이름에서 알 수 있듯 암소의 갈비와 불고기만을 내는 곳으로 그 역사와 전통을 자랑한다. 꽃갈비만 사용하는 생갈비와 은은하면서도 자꾸만 당기는 맛의 양념갈비가 있는데, 생갈비는 수량이 정해져 있어 점심이 지나면 거의 품절되는 일이 다반사다. 쫄깃한 감자면 사리와 구수한 갈빗대가 들어간 뚝배기 된장을 함께 먹어볼 것. 살살 녹는 갈비와 함께 입이 즐거울 것이다. 주말 및 성수기에는 대기 시간이 다소 길어질 수 있고 생갈비는 방문 1주일전 미리예약이 가능하니 꼭 먹어볼 것.

바비큐 • *Barbecue*

051-746-0033

해운대구 해운대해변로 333

333 Haunedahaebyeon-ro, Haeundae-gu

■ 가 격 PRICE: ₩₩

A landmark of Busan's culinary scene, Haeundae Rib barbecue restaurant has stood steadfast since 1964, transitioning from a century-old traditional house to a modernized building while maintaining its rich heritage. Now run by the third generation, this renowned restaurant specializes in just two dishes: fresh ribs and marinated ribs, both exclusively made from cow ribs, as the name suggests. The fresh ribs, crafted only from prime cuts, are limited in quantity and often sell out by lunchtime. The marinated ribs are equally enticing, with a subtle sweetness and depth of flavor that leaves you craving more. Pair your meal with a hearty bowl of bean paste stew, complete with tender rib bones and chewy potato noodles, for a perfectly balanced and satisfying dining experience. Fresh ribs can be reserved up to a week in advance, ensuring you don't miss out on this specialty.

Photo Seagull/Getty Images Plus

수영구
SUYEONG-GU

뉴러우멘관즈

NIUROU MIAN GUAN ZI

타이완 • Taiwanese

051-623-0251

수영구 수영로 388번길 25-4

25-4 Suyeong-ro 388 beon-gil, Suyeong-gu

■ 가 격 PRICE: ₩

남천동의 한 골목, 노란 차양 아래에 길게 이어진 줄. 뉴러우멘관즈를 찾는 데는 그리 오랜 시간이 걸리지 않는다. 칼칼한 대만식 '홍샤오 우육면'과 '완탕면', 대만식 비빔면 '량멘', 그리고 완탕면에 곁들임으로 들어가는 만두에 매운 기름 홍유를 얹은 홍유초수와 '마라깐양' 등 메뉴는 단출하지만 그 맛은 깊다. 간장으로 맛을 낸 큼직한 소고기에 청경채와 배추갓 절임을 올리고 라유로 매운 맛을 낸 우육면 한 그릇이면 겨울에도 땀이 난다. 달달한 망고맥주와 함께 먹으면 제격이다.

A long line under a yellow awning makes spotting this bustling Taiwanese eatery a breeze. Its streamlined menu features homely yet delectable dishes, including pleasantly spicy Taiwan-style braised beef noodle soup, wonton soup, Taiwanese cold noodles, spicy wonton in chili oil, and tripe in mala sauce. The signature braised beef noodle soup features large chunks of beef, bok choy, pickled leaf mustard, and some chili oil for a spicy twist. And a bowl of this particular soup will make you sweat even in the depths of winter. When paired with sweet-flavored mango beer, it's a match made in heaven.

동경밥상

TOKYO BABSANG

부산의 정취가 돋보이는 광안리 해수욕장의 익숙한 거리 분위기에서 벗어나 레스토랑의 정문에 이르면 사뭇 차분하고 정적인 분위기가 감돈다. 일본의 대표적인 장어 덮밥인 우나쥬와 히츠마부시를 선보이는 동경 밥상의 모습이다. 김태우 셰프의 손을 거친 동경 밥상의 음식에서 이 요리의 정통성을 표현하고자 하는 그의 노력이 엿보인다. 두툼하게 씹히는 우나기는 본연의 풍미가 도드라지고 감칠맛 나는 소스와 잘 어우러진다. 무엇보다 최근 도정을 원칙으로 하는 윤기 나는 쌀밥과의 조화가 입맛을 당긴다. 전통성 있는 레시피를 존중하며 디테일하게 자신만의 맛을 더해가는 모습이 요리에 대한 신뢰로 이어진다.

장어 •

Unagi / Freshwater Eel

070-7576-1428

수영구 남천바다로 34-6

34-6 Namcheonbada-ro, Suyeong-gu

■ 가 격 PRICE: ₩

The familiar vibrant vibe of Gwangalli Beach, a landmark attraction in Busan, will have given way to that of calm and peace by the time one arrives at the door of Tokyo Babsang, which specializes in unaju (grilled eel over rice) and hitsuma-bushi (Nagoya-style grilled eel), the two representative Japanese eel dishes. The fare at this diner mirrors Chef Kim Tae-woo's dedication to authenticity. Each bite of the thick and chewy eel, which stands out with its inherent flavor, goes perfectly with the accompanying sauce brimming with umami. But above all, its harmony with the glossy steamed rice, normally made from newly polished rice, heightens the appetite. The chef's respect for authentic recipes, coupled with his sensitive culinary creativity, is what keeps the joint's fare trustworthy.

수영구

러브얼스
LOVEURTH

비건 • *Vegan*

070-4647-2420

수영구 광안로 49번길 32-1

32-1 Gwangan-ro 49 beon-gil, Suyeong-gu

■ 가 격 PRICE: ₩

광안초등학교 뒤편 골목에 위치한 러브얼스는 비건 요리 전문 레스토랑이다. 친숙한 일상의 메뉴를 비건 스타일로 선보이는 곳으로 캐주얼한 요리에서 한 끼 든든히 즐길 수 있는 요리까지 러브얼스는 요리의 경계를 정하지 않고 다양한 시도를 하고 있다.. 김한솔, 정명원 대표는 덮밥과 파스타, 우동, 수프 같은 일상의 요리를 온전히 비건식으로 선보이기 위해 비건 메뉴에 대한 자신들의 경험과 고민을 재기 발랄한 아이디어로 풀어 낸다. 여건상 다양한 메뉴를 제공하기는 어렵지만 주기적으로 메뉴에 변화를 줌으로써 비건식의 다양성과 미식의 즐거움을 손님들에게 선사하고 있다.

Tucked away in a back alley near Gwangan Elementary School, Loveurth is a vegan restaurant that serves vegan versions of familiar foods. From casual dishes to filling, hearty meals, this innovative diner continues to embark on diverse experiments that transcend culinary boundaries. Building upon their experience and insight into vegan food, Co-CEOs Kim Han-sol and Jung Myeong-won transform familiar classics, such as rice bowls, pastas, udon dishes, and soups, into vegan equivalents with a fun and playful twist. Since offering an extensive vegan menu is no easy feat, Loveurth instead tweaks its menu every once in a while so that it can better provide customers with gastronomic pleasure derived from a diverse compendium of vegan cuisine.

백일평냉 N
100.1.PYEONGNAENG

백일평냉은 딱 100일만 운영하는 냉면집으로 2023년 하반기에 큰 주목을 받았던 곳이다. 냉면 맛에 대한 확신이 분명했던 곽동훈 대표는 2024년 3월 3일 '뛰어날 백'과 '편안할 일'을 합친 '백일'이라는 이름의 평양냉면집을 정식으로 오픈했다. 전국 각지를 돌며 유명 평양냉면집의 맛을 연구한 끝에 백일평냉 고유의 맛을 완성시킬 수 있었다. 섬세하며 은은한 감칠맛이 느껴지는 육수 한 모금에서 이곳의 냉면 맛을 충분히 엿볼 수 있다. 냉면 외에도 접시 불고기, 어복쟁반, 만두 같은 한식 메뉴가 다양하게 준비되어 있어 술자리로도 안성맞춤이다.

냉면 • *Naengmyeon*

051-625-5515

수영구 남천바다로 10번길 29

29 Namcheonbada-ro 10 beon-gil, Suyeong-gu

■ **가 격 PRICE: ₩**

100.1.Pyeongnaeng was a naengmyeon restaurant that ran for exactly 100 days and grabbed the attention of foodies in the latter half of 2023. With a strong passion for cold noodle flavors, Kwak Dong-hoon officially opened the Pyongyang-style naengmyeon restaurant on March 3, 2024. Kwak developed his own Pyongyang naengmyeon recipe after touring naengmyeon restaurants all over Korean in search for the bowl of noodles. A single sip of the delicate, subtle broth is all you need to see the restaurant's mastery in crafting naengmyeon. They also offer various Korean dishes like bulgogi, eobokjaengban, and mandu, which perfectly compliment any occasion that calls for alcoholic beverages.

SUYEONG-GU

비비재 N
BIBIJAE

비빔밥 • *Bibimbap*

070-8287-1035

수영구 남천바다로 10번길 45

45 Namcheonbada-ro 10 beon-gil, Suyeong-gu

■ 가 격 PRICE: ₩

비빔밥은 그 식재료의 구성에 따라 다양한 맛의 변화를 만들어 낼수 있는 매력적인 한식이다. 비비재는 이처럼 다양한 식재료의 조합을 통해 색다른 맛의 비빔밥을 선보이는 곳이다. 기본이 되는 전통적 비빔밥 외에 제철 식재료를 독창적으로 조합해 만든 비빔밥 등 익숙하지만 흥미로운 비빔밥 메뉴를 경험할 수 있다. 또 하나, 모든 비빔밥 메뉴를 따끈따끈한 돌솥 비빔밥으로 변경할 수 있어 기호에 맞게 즐길 수 있다는 것도 장점이다. 평범한 비빔밥에 다양한 맛의 색채를 입히고 있는 비비재의 노력이 흥미롭다.

Bibimbap is a versatile Korean dish with flavors that can drastically change depending on the ingredients. Bibijae offers bibimbap dishes made with creative combinations of ingredients and flavors. Diners can not only enjoy classic bibimbap but also enjoy creative twists with seasonal ingedients. There's more - for those who prefer piping hot bibimbap, all dishes can be upgraded to a hot stone bowl. It is exciting to see what new flavor profiles Bibijae adds to the humble bibimbap.

안목
ANMOK

우리가 기억하는 돼지 국밥의 맛이나 멋과는 다른, 새로운 형태의 돼지 국밥을 제안한 안목. 안목은 단순히 기존의 국밥과 형태만 달리한 것이 아닌, 고개가 끄덕여지는 돼지 국밥의 맛을 선사한다. 돼지 국밥은 특유의 풍미를 가지고 있지만 그 안에서 한국의 다른 국물 음식을 떠올리게 하는 오묘한 맛이 있다. 돼지 국밥의 일번지라 할 부산에서 수많은 유명 돼지 국밥과 맛에 있어 확실한 차별화를 꾀하면서도, 요리는 다양한 방향성을 갖고 변화하고 발전한다는 느낌을 주는 레스토랑이다. 개개인의 취향 차이가 있겠지만 다대기나 새우젓을 넣지 않고 이곳만의 돼지 국밥을 있는 그대로 즐겨 보는 것도 좋을 것 같다.

돼지국밥 •
Dwaeji-gukbap

070-8778-0519

수영구 광남로 22번길 3

3 Gwangnam-ro 22 beon-gil, Suyeong-gu

■ 가 격 PRICE: ₩

Anmok's unique take on dwaeji-gukbap, or pork and rice soup, may surprise customers with novel flavors and charm that defy their memories of the dish. The soup is not merely unconventional. It'll make you nod in appreciation. The dish also has a distinct flavor that evokes those of many other Korean soups. Indeed, the diner has successfully differentiated itself from countless other famed restaurants in Busan, the capital of dwaeji-gukbap, giving the impression that it continues to change and evolve while exploring diverse culinary directions. Though everyone has different preferences, we recommend you savor Amok's soup offerings as they are prepared without adding chili sauce or salted shrimp.

SUYEONG-GU

수영구

피리피리
PILI PILI

타이 • *Thai*

010-7997-4143

수영구 무학로 33번길 54

54 Muhak-ro 33 beon-gil, Suyeong-gu

■ 가격 PRICE: ₩

광안동을 걷다가 슬쩍 보면 여기가 태국인지 부산인지 헷갈릴 정도의 실내와 외관을 갖춘 피리피리가 있다. 피리피리는 태국식 다이닝바로, 태국 음식과 이국적인 칵테일을 맛볼 수 있는 곳이다. 힙한 분위기는 물론이고 턴테이블에서 흐르는 음악과 푸짐한 정통 태국 음식이 현지를 여행하는 듯한 느낌을 준다. 엄청난 비주얼의 푸팟퐁 커리와 함께 타이 하이볼 한 잔 어떨지.

Take a stroll around Gwangan-dong, and you'll come across a restaurant whose exterior and interior design will make you ask yourself whether you are in Busan or Thailand. Piri Piri is a Thai-style dining bar that serves Thai cuisine and exotic cocktails. Its hip vibes, music resonating from a turntable, and generous servings of authentic Thai dishes evoke a magical feeling of traveling in that exotic country. So why not come and indulge in the visual feast of the spectacular Poo Pad Phong Curry (stir-fried crab in curry powder) while imbibing a Thai highball?

한월관 N
HANWOLGWAN

한월관의 곰탕 한 그릇에는 식재료에 대한 자부심과 그 맛을 살리기 위한 노력이 담겨 있다. 한월관에서는 식용으로 키운 미경산 한우 암소만을 사용한 덕분에 곰탕 국물에서 특유의 은은한 육향을 즐길 수 있다. 이곳의 곰탕은 맑은 고기 육수 또는 진한 사골 육수 중에서 선택할 수 있다. 이뿐만 아니라 곰탕에 올라가는 양지와 차돌, 도가니를 기호에 맞게 선택할 수 있어 곰탕 한 그릇만으로도 다양한 한우의 맛을 즐길 수 있다. 유기그릇에 정갈하게 제공되는 김치를 비롯한 기본 찬들도 곰탕의 맛과 잘 어울린다.

A bowl of gomtang at Hanwolgwan is served with generous helpings of their pride in the ingredients and a deep commitment to bring out the best flavors. Hanwolgwan exclusively uses heifer hanwoo beef, which imparts a delicate beef aroma to the broth. Diners can select either a clear meat broth or a rich bone broth, topped with various cuts of beef like brisket, chuck, and knee joint to ensure that they experience a wide selection of hanwoo flavors from one single bowl of gomtang. The elegantly plated kimchi and side dishes in bangjja yugi, or hand-forged bronze tableware, complement the gomtang perfectly.

곰탕 • *Gomtang*

051-711-7025

수영구 광안로 62번길 10

10 Gwangan-ro 62 beon-gil, Suyeong-gu

■ 가 격 PRICE: ₩

프렌치 • *French*

010-9406-3135

수영구 광안해변로 284번길 38 3층

3F, 38 Gwanganhaebyeon-ro 284 beon-gil, Suyeong-gu

■ **가격 PRICE: ₩₩₩**

램지
RAMSEY

클래식 프렌치 퀴진을 베이스로 삼고 식재료를 활용한 여러 시도를 보여주는 이규진 셰프의 램지. 램지는 최근 다양한 스타일의 레스토랑이 속속 생겨나는 민란동의 다이닝 격전지에서 매력적인 프렌치 요리로 그 존재감을 드러내고 있다. 다양한 풍미를 조합하여 맛의 변주를 이끄는 아뮤즈 부슈부터 안정적 쿠킹 능력이 돋보이는 생선 및 고기 요리까지 프렌치 코스 요리의 요소를 갖추고 있으며, 소스의 맛을 잘 활용한 요리에 중점을 두고 있다. 레스토랑의 아늑한 분위기를 만끽하며 차분한 서비스와 함께 편안하게 식사를 즐겨 보시기 바란다.

Helmed by Chef Lee Gyu-jin, Ramsey pushes the boundaries of its classic French cuisine through inventive use of ingredients. Located in Millak-dong, the highly competitive dining battleground where eateries of diverse varieties keep popping up, this bistro is set apart from the pack with its alluring French fare. From the amuse-bouche, which combines diverse flavors to create culinary variations on a theme, to fantastic fish and meat dishes that highlight the chef's seasoned cooking skills, Ramsey is well-versed in every element of a French course meal and focuses on fare that makes good use of sauce flavors. Come and enjoy a cozy meal at Ramsey accompanied by attentive and discreet service while relishing its inviting vibe to the fullest.

레썽스
L'ESSENCE

남천역 인근의 한적한 골목에 위치한 프렌치 레스토랑이다. 레썽스의 전지성 셰프는 우리나라의 제철 식재료와 진한 소스를 조합하여 맛과 향의 조화가 뛰어난 프렌치 요리를 선보인다. 아울러 이따금 장아찌나 젓갈 같은 발효 식품을 요리에 더해 포인트를 주기도 하는데 녹진한 프렌치 요리의 풍미 속에서 한국적인 맛을 찾는 재미가 있다. 기본적으로 단품 요리만 제공하지만 늦어도 방문 하루 전에 주문한다면 좀더 다양하게 구성된 코스 요리도 즐길 수 있다.

L'Essence is a French restaurant set in a quiet alley near Namcheon Station. Here, Chef Jeon Ji-seong combines seasonal local ingredients with vibrant sauces to present French cuisine offering an outstanding balance of taste and aroma. Sometimes, the chef uses fermented ingredients, such as pickled vegetables and salted seafood, to add verve to his dishes, providing diners with the fun of spotting Korean flavors hidden amidst his delicate French cuisine. Though L'Essence usually offers only an a la carte menu, customers can enjoy its multi-course meal with a reservation at least a day in advance.

프렌치 • *French*

010-9585-7050

수영구 광남로 22번길 17, 3층

3F, 17 Gwangnam-ro 22 beon-gil, Suyeong-gu

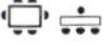

■ **가 격 PRICE: ₩₩**

수영구

이탤리언 • *Italian*

010-2981-8078

수영구 수영로 522번길 55

55 Suyeong-ro 522 beon-gil, Suyeong-gu

www.vignetobusan.com

■ **가 격 PRICE: ₩**

비네토

VIGNETO

비네토는 알마요리학교에서 이탈리아 요리를 배우던 주인장 부부가 결혼 후 부산에 정착해 문을 연 레스토랑이다. 레스토랑 건물은 이들 부부가 집과 식당으로 쓰기 위해 지었는데 천장과 가구가 나무로 되어 있어 아늑하고 포근한 분위기를 선사한다. 이탈리안 와인바 비네토는 정통 이탈리아 음식은 물론, 쉽게 접하기 힘든 이탈리안 내추럴 와인까지 곁들일 수 있으며 파스타와 햄을 모두 직접 만들어 식감과 풍미가 뛰어나다. 편안한 분위기에서 맛있는 음식과 와인을 즐기고 싶다면 예약은 필수다. 예약은 30분 단위로 받는다.

Vigneto is the very first restaurant by an owner-chef couple who settled in Busan after studying Italian cuisine at ALMA, the renowned culinary school in Italy. The building is both their home and restaurant, with the wooden ceiling and furniture in the interior creating a cozy and warm vibe. An Italian wine bar, Vigneto combines authentic Italian cuisine with a rare Italian natural wine pairing. In particular, its pastas and hams, all housemade, boast exceptional textures and flavors. For foodies who seek to revel in food and wine amidst Vigneto's snug ambiance, we recommend reservations (which are set at 30-minute intervals).

아웃트로 바이 비토
OUTRO BY VITO

유러피언 • *European*

051-758-7123

수영구 민락본동로 19번길 18

18 Millakbondong-ro 19 beon-gil, Suyeong-gu

www.vito.kr

■ **가격 PRICE: ₩₩**

해리단길에서 광안리로 이전 오픈한 아웃트로 바이 비토. 달라진 이름처럼 외관과 실내를 현대적이고 세련되게 단장하고 내추럴 와인과 음식을 제공한다. 하지만 그 본질인 파스타 요리는 달라지지 않고 더욱 맛있어졌다. 자가 제면 파스타는 밀가루의 함량을 높여 숙성 후에 뽑아 내는데 차진 식감은 물론 소스와도 잘 어우러져 맛을 배가시킨다. 여러 종류의 파스타 외에도 샐러드나 고기 요리 등 메뉴가 다양하게 준비가 되어 있다. 셰프가 음식에 맞춰 추천하는 내추럴 와인과 함께 세련된 분위기에서 즐겨 보시기를.

With the new name Outro by Vito, the restaurant relocated from a location in the Haeridan-gil area to this spot near Gwangalli Beach. Not only did this fine purveyor of natural wine and cuisine change its name, but it also revamped its exterior and décor with a touch of contemporary elegance. Regardless, its pasta dishes, the quintessential offerings, have remained the same – only with enhanced flavors. The diner's housemade pasta now features higher flour content and undergoes fermentation. The glutinous texture and impeccable pairing with the sauce make the pasta even more appetizing. In addition to a diverse array of pasta dishes, the menu features salads, meat, and various other scrumptious dishes. Come on down and savor your meal with a chef-recommended natural wine replete with a cultured vibe.

야키토리 해공
YAKITORI HAEGONG

야키토리 • *Yakitori*

051-758-8333
수영구 민락본동로 19번길 30-5
30-5 Millakbondong-ro 19 beon-gil, Suyoeng-gu

■ **가 격 PRICE: ₩₩**

조용한 주택가 골목 한 켠의 분홍색 건물에 '해공'이라고 적힌 작은 간판이 걸려 있다. 토종닭 야키토리를 맛볼 수 있는 곳이다. 2022년 10월, 지금의 자리로 이전 오픈하면서 야키토리를 좀 더 고급스럽게 즐길 수 있도록 변화를 꾀했다. 특히 해공의 특제 부산 곰장어 구이는 입에 꽉 차는 크기와 풍성한 육즙에 바다맛 미네랄리티와 탱탱한 식감을 모두 맛볼 수 있으니 꼭 경험해 볼 것. 세련된 실내 디자인이 돋보이는 조용한 분위기에서 부산의 야키토리를 즐길 수 있는 곳이다.

In an alley of a quiet residential neighborhood is a pink building with an unexpected tiny little sign that reads "Haegong." This Japanese eatery specializes in yakitori (grilled chicken skewers) made with native Korean chicken. As part of the relocation to its present location in October 2022, some upgrades were made to its space to ensure a more sophisticated dining experience. Grilled hagfish, another gem of this establishment, is not a dish to miss, with each mouthful piece brimming with juice, oceanic minerality, and delightfully firm texture. Yakitori Haegong is a rare gem in Busan to savor yakitori in a serene vibe accentuated by its refined interior décor.

언양불고기 부산집

EONYANG BULGOGI BUSANJIP

흔히 부산집으로 불리는 이곳은 오랜 시간 광안리 앞을 지켜 온 터줏대감으로 늘 문전성시를 이룬다. 수십 년을 운영하던 곳을 떠나 2018년에 지금의 위치로 이전했다. 육수를 넣고 자작하게 끓여 내는 서울식 불고기와는 달리 언양식은 양념한 고기를 석쇠에 올려 굽거나 직화 구이 방식을 이용한다. 서울식이 달달한 맛이라면 언양식은 단맛이 적고 한우 등심의 고소한 맛을 더 강조하며 소스에서 나오는 산미가 상큼함을 더한다. 부산집에서는 불고기 외에 다양한 특수 부위도 맛볼 수 있다. 오늘은 광안리 앞바다를 보면서 흰밥에 고기 한 점 드셔 보시길.

More commonly known as just Busanjip, this eatery at Gwangalli Beach has long been a popular spot, always bustling with customers waiting to get in. After decades of business in its previous location, the restaurant moved to this location in 2018. Unlike Seoul-style bulgogi, where meat is cooked in broth, the Eonyang style features marinated meat grilled on a gridiron or over a fire. As for flavor, Seoul bulgogi tends to be sweet, whereas Eonyang bulgogi is less so, with more emphasis on the nutty taste of Korean beef sirloin enhanced by the acidic flavor of the sauce. In addition to its namesake dish, Busanjip serves up a diverse range of special beef cuts. Come and relish the beauty of the coastal waters off Gwangalli today – with each scrumptious bite of beef topped on rice!

불고기 • *Bulgogi*

051-754-1004

수영구 남천바다로 32

32 Namcheonbada-ro, Suyeong-gu

■ **가 격 PRICE: ₩**

수영구

국수 • Noodles

051-758-6011
수영구 광안해변로 277번길 10
10 Gwanganhaebyeon-ro 277 beon-gil, Suyeong-gu

■ 가 격 PRICE: ₩

융캉찌에
YONGKANGZZIE

융캉찌에는 광안리 인근 민락골목시장으로 이어지는 골목 초입에 위치한 우육탕면 레스토랑이다. 외관에서부터 실내까지 일관된 디자인과 디테일한 장식이 대만 현지의 분위기를 제대로 살렸다. 대만식을 지향하는 따끈한 우육탕면 한 그릇이 캐주얼하고 이국적인 식당의 분위기와 잘 어울린다. 은은한 산미와 함께 감칠맛이 나는 우육탕면 국물과 식감 좋은 두툼한 면발은 사시사철 언제든지 편하게 즐길 수 있는 맛이다. 주메뉴인 우육탕면 외에 다른 중국식 면 요리와 부대 메뉴도 준비되어 있어 기호에 맞게 선택할 수 있다. 자체 주차 공간이 없으니 차량 이용 시 참고하시기 바란다.

Situated near Gwangalli Beach at the beginning of an alley leading to Millak Golmok Market, Yongkangzzie is a Taiwanese spot best known for its beef noodle soup. The consistent design concepts that permeate both exterior and interior spaces, as well as the detailed décor, have done a remarkable job of reproducing a vibe that evokes Taiwan. The warmth of the signature soup goes well with the eatery's casual and exotic ambiance. The broth, which offers up subtle sour flavors and umami, and the thick, pleasantly textured noodles make this iconic soup a comforting choice in any season. In addition to this signature dish, Yongkangzzie serves other noodle and side dishes that are guaranteed to please the palate. Please note that the restaurant has no parking lot.

으뜸 이로리바타
EUTTEUM IRORIBATA

'이로리', 즉 화로를 활용하여 오마카세를 제공하는 남천역 인근의 레스토랑이다. 비록 일본의 전통 이로리는 아니지만 요리에서 쓰이는 역할을 잘 표현했다. 꼬치에 끼워져 이로리에 가지런히 놓인 제철 생선의 시각적 효과와 풍미는 요리를 즐기는 또 다른 재미이다. 이 레스토랑은 일식 요리사 정으뜸 셰프의 경험과 개인적 기호가 어우러진 공간으로, 다양한 생선구이 요리를 즐기기에 제격이다. 솥밥을 비롯해 오마카세에 포함된 각종 요리들도 하나같이 일식의 정갈한 맛을 오롯이 전해 준다.

Located near Namcheon station, this Japanese diner specializes in omakase dining prepared using irori (traditional Japanese hearth). Though not as authentic as the ones in old Japanese houses, the irori here is faithful to its role as kitchen equipment. The visual and aromatic appeal of grilling seasonal fish skewers, arranged in a row in front of the irori, adds to the diner's culinary delight. An embodiment of Chef Jung Eu-tteum's experience with Japanese cuisine and his personal gastronomic affinities, the eatery is a perfect haven to relish a diverse array of grilled fish. Clay pot rice and other dishes served during the omakase course boast a range of refined flavors that often characterize Japanese cuisine.

일식 • *Japanese*

010-6640-2884

수영구 수영로 408번길 20

20 Suyeong-ro 408 beon-gil, Suyeong-gu

■ 가 격 PRICE: ₩₩

SUYEONG-GU

제로 베이스
ZERO BASE

일식 • *Japanese*

070-8803-0318

수영구 민락로 33번길 17, 2층

2F, 17 Millak-ro 33 beon-gil, Suyeong-gu

■ 가 격 PRICE: ₩₩₩

제로 베이스는 일식 이자카야 '유노우'로 고객들에게 좋은 반응을 얻었던 유병찬 셰프의 일식 레스토랑이다. 유노우를 운영하면서 깊이 있는 일식 요리에 대한 갈증을 느꼈던 그가 제로 베이스에서 새로운 요리를 발전시키며 또 한 번 손님들과 교감하고 있다. 탄탄한 조리 솜씨를 바탕으로 식재료를 다양하게 활용하는데, 클래식한 방식이지만 셰프의 감각이 돋보이는 시도들이 눈에 띈다. 손님을 대접하기 위해 제철 식재료를 엄선하는 데 큰 비중을 두는 것은 당연하다. 현대적 디자인의 내부 공간이 클래식한 요리 스타일과 대비를 이루며 묘한 이질감을 느끼게 한다.

Zero Base is a new Japanese restaurant by Chef Yu Byeong-chan, who previously ran the izakaya Yoo No Woo with a stellar reputation. The chef's unrelenting thirst for classy Japanese cuisine, which had never been fully quenched at his former spot, drove him to present his newly evolved cuisine at this up-and-coming eatery. His solid culinary skills turn ingredients into sumptuous variations on a classic theme, in a way that accentuates his sensibilities. The eatery pays special attention to selecting the freshest of seasonal ingredients. And it simply makes sense. The delicate juxtaposition between Zero Base's contemporary décor and classic cuisine conjures up an exclusive vibe.

KatkaGrofova/Getty Images Plus

연제구
북구
부산진구
YEONJE-GU
BUK-GU
BUSANJIN-GU

담미옥
DAMIOK

냉면 • *Naengmyeon*

010-7704-5318

부산진구 복지로 15, 개금포르투나 상가 103호

#103, 15 Bokji-ro, Busanjin-gu

■ 가 격 PRICE: ₩

개금동에 소담히 자리잡은 담미옥. 그 이름처럼 담백한 맛을 추구하는 평양냉면 전문점이다. 소와 돼지, 닭으로만 육수를 내어 잡내가 없고 기름기가 적어 깔끔한 맛을 자랑한다. 자가 제면한 메밀면을 쓰는데 입맛에 따라 100% 순면을 선택할 수도 있다. 좀더 고소한 맛을 느낄 수 있으니 도전해 볼 것. 냉면 외에 곰탕과 어복쟁반 같은 부대 메뉴도 준비되어 있다.

Quietly nestled in Gaegeum-dong, Damiok specializes in Pyeongyang cold buckwheat noodles. As its name suggests, the establishment focuses on presenting refreshingly light and clean flavors. The broth tastes pure and non-greasy, without unpleasant flavors, as it is made only from simmered beef, pork, and chicken. The noodles are housemade, and you have the added option of selecting 100 percent buckwheat noodles, which taste nuttier and may titillate more adventurous palates. In addition to the signature dish, Damiok offers beef bone soup and Pyeongyang-style beef hot pot.

바오하우스
BAO HAUS

최행락 셰프는 자신의 고향 부산에 바오하우스를 오픈하고 해외에서 활동하며 쌓은 경험을 요리로 풀어 내고 있다. 바오하우스는 대만식 요리를 기반으로 삼아 캐주얼하고 심플한 요리를 선보인다. 셰프는 이처럼 요리의 문턱을 낮춤으로써 친숙하면서도 이국적인 중화권 요리를 편하게 즐길 수 있게 한다. 바오하우스에서는 대만식 찐빵 '바오'와 대만식 간장 소스 삼겹살 덮밥 '루로우판', 마파두부, 어향가지튀김 등 음식 본연의 풍미와 셰프의 아이디어가 접목된 요리를 가볍게 즐길 수 있다. 레스토랑의 공간이 넓지 않고 예약을 받지 않으므로 대기 시간이 있을 수 있다.

When Chef Choi Haeng-rak opened Bao Haus here in his hometown of Busan, his extensive overseas training at last found a place to flourish. His restaurant offers simple and casual Taiwanese-style dishes. By lowering the threshold for fine cuisine, the chef ushers diners into the familiar yet exotic world of the different variations of Chinese cuisine. The menu features dishes loaded with inherent flavors and executed with Chef Choi's novel twists, including bao (Taiwanese steamed buns), lu rou fan (Taiwanese braised pork rice bowl), mapo tofu, and deep-fried eggplant. Since the eatery is housed in a compact space, the wait can be long without a reservation.

타이완 • *Taiwanese*

010-4888-1041

부산진구 서전로 38번길 62-9, 2층

2F, 62-9 Seojeon-ro 38 beon-gil, Busanjin-gu

■ 가 격 PRICE: ₩

슌사이 쿠보
SHUNSAI KUBO

장어 •
Unagi / Freshwater Eel

051-365-2959
북구 양달로 4번길 17
17 Yangdal-ro 4 beon-gil, Buk-gu

■ 가 격 PRICE: ₩

이재욱 셰프의 슌사이 쿠보는 히츠마부시 전문점이다. 일본에서 수련한 셰프는 히츠마부시의 맛과 품질을 자신이 추구하는 명확한 기준까지 끌어올리기 위해 정진하고 있다. 이곳에서는 자포니카종인 생물 풍천 장어만을 사용한다. 정성껏 소스를 발라 구운 장어의 그윽한 향과 씹는 맛을 살린 식감이 고슬고슬 잘 지어진 밥과 어우러져 조화로운 맛을 준다. 어린이용 장어 덮밥도 준비하여 아이를 동반한 가족 손님에 대한 배려도 잊지 않았다. 또한 과거 슌사이 쿠보의 갓포 요리를 기억하는 손님들을 위해 기본에 충실한 가벼운 안줏거리도 제공하고 있다.

Shunsai Kubo is a hitsumabushi (Nagoya-style grilled eel) restaurant helmed by Chef Lee Jae-wook. Trained in Japan, the chef is continually striving to raise the bar on the flavor and quality of his signature dish made only with live Japanese eels (Anguilla japonica). The rich aroma of the eels, rubbed with a special sauce and carefully grilled, creates a delightful gastronomic harmony with the rice cooked to just the right texture. The restaurant serves a hitsumabushi menu for children, a considerate gesture that caters to families. Shunsai Kubo also offers authentic light bar snacks for long-time regulars with fond memories of its former Japanese kappo cuisine.

야키토리 온정
YAKITORI ONJUNG

부부가 운영하는 작은 야키토리 식당 온정. 서울에서 경험을 쌓고 부산에서 첫 식당을 열었다. 토종닭을 사용하면서도 크기가 적당한 것을 골라 육질이 부드럽다. 벽돌집 아치 안에 자리한 듯한 편안한 분위기와 채도 낮은 조명이 다양하게 준비되어 있는 니혼슈와 위스키의 맛을 한층 배가 시킨다. 야키토리와 함께 한 잔 즐겨 보는 것은 어떨까?

Onjung is a small yakitori bistro run by a couple, who opened their first restaurant here in Busan after acquiring culinary experience in Seoul. Though their yakitori is made with Korean native chicken, the meat is soft in texture as they use poultry appropriately sized for the dish. The brick-arched entrance and low-saturation lighting create a cozy ambiance that accentuates the flavors of this bistro's wide selection of nihonshu (Japanese sake) and whisky. Why not come and indulge in a drink or two with yummy skewers of yakitori?

야키토리 • *Yakitori*

010-2281-9293

부산진구 동천로 108번길 9-7

9-7 Dongcheon-ro 108 beon-gil, Busanjin-Gu

■ **가 격 PRICE: ₩**

코르 파스타바

COR PASTA BAR

이탤리언 • *Italian*

010-2366-4570

부산진구 동성로 25번길 13, 2층

2F, 13 Dongseong-ro 25 beon-gil, Busanjin-gu

■ 가 격 PRICE: ₩

전포동의 힙한 골목길로 들어서 2층의 두꺼운 철문을 열고 들어서면 10석 남짓한 작은 공간이 있다. 파스타 바(Bar)라는 이름처럼 직접 제면한 파스타 메뉴를 제공하는 곳으로 파스타를 종류별로 다양하게 맛볼 수 있다. 진한 소스의 새우 비스크 소스 스파게티, 성게와 어란을 사용한 보타르가 파스타, 토마토 소스를 넣은 한우 양 벌집 트리파를 직접 구운 포카치아나 와인과 함께 즐겨보시길.

Walk into a hip alley in Jeonpo-dong, and there is a thick steel door on the second floor of a glass-walled building, behind which is an elegant ten-seater diner. As the name Pasta Bar suggests, this eatery offers a wide selection of its namesake dishes made with fresh housemade pasta. Visit Cor Pasta Bar and treat yourself to its shrimp spaghetti with rich bisque sauce; bottarga pasta with sea urchin and fish roe; or roman-style Korean beef honeycomb tripe in tomato sauce – with its house-baked focaccia or your favorite wine.

굿모닝홍콩
GOOD MORNING HONGKONG

홍콩 음식이 그립다면, 홍콩의 바이브를 느껴 보고 싶다면 차찬텡 컨셉의 이곳을 주목하자. 그저 홍콩이 좋아 오픈했다는 오너는 정통 홍콩식보다는 한국인의 입맛에 맞게 약간 변형시킨 음식을 제공한다. 그럼에도 그 맛이나 비주얼만큼은 현지 음식에 뒤지지 않는다. 토마토와 햄이 듬뿍 들어간 칼칼한 토마토 국수를 비롯해 연유와 시럽을 아낌 없이 넣은 빵, 달달한 밀크티인 나이차나 레몬 홍차인 똥랭차 등을 맛볼 수 있다. 홍콩스러운 비주얼은 덤이다.

If you pine for Hong Kong cuisine and want to experience a uniquely Hong Kong vibe, this diner deserves your full attention as it is inspired by cha chaan teng, or a Hong Kong-style café. The owner says he opened this joint merely out of his love for Hong Kong. It serves less-than-authentic Hong Kong dishes, slightly modified to suit the Korean palate. Still, their flavors and visuals are no less spectacular than those of the local Hong Kong cuisine. Signatures include pleasantly spicy tomato noodle soup with plenty of tomato and ham; bread generously glazed with condensed milk and syrup; sweet nai cha (milk tea); and dong ning cha (iced lemon tea). The diner's Hong Kong-style visuals are a plus!

중식 • *Chinese*

010-6444-3724
부산진구 서전로 47번길 19
19 Seojeon-ro 47 beon-gil, Busanjin-gu

■ 가 격 PRICE: ₩

델리봉

DELIBONG

프렌치 • *French*

연제구 신금로 25, 노블레스 스퀘어 110호

#110 Noblesse square, 25 Singeum-ro, Yeonje-gu

■ **가 격 PRICE: ₩₩**

직접 만든 샤퀴트리(수가공 햄)로 구성된 코스라니, 도대체 궁금하지 않은가? 델리봉의 주인장 박정봉 셰프는 오랜 시간 프렌치 다이닝을 운영하다가 이곳에 새롭게 둥지를 틀었다. 10석 남짓한 작은 공간에 아담한 바 좌석과 테이블, 어두운 조명에 간판이 없어 처음에는 찾기 어려울지 모른다. 코파, 잠봉, 리예트, 프로슈토 등 시간을 들여 정성스럽게 염장과 건조를 거쳐야 하는 가공육들과 이를 이용한 세련된 요리들이 기다리고 있다. 예약을 꼭 하고 가시길 바란다.

A charcuterie course consisting of housemade meat products – doesn't that pique your interest? After many years of running a French dining spot, the owner-chef Park Jeong-bong finally opened this little gem with a bar counter and tables that can seat only about ten people. With dim lighting and no sign, Delibong may be difficult for first-timers to find. Processed meats that require lengthy, meticulous curing and drying processes, as well as the polished dishes crafted with them, such as coppa, jambon, rillettes, and prosciutto, await. Aren't you just a little bit curious? Reservations strongly advised.

레땅
L'ÉTANG

연지동의 한 도로변에 홀로 자리를 지키고 있는 프렌치 레스토랑 레땅. 레땅은 정동원 셰프가 혼자서 요리와 서비스를 전담하는 1인 셰프 다이닝이다. 식재료 준비부터 조리와 서비스까지 요리의 전 과정에 셰프의 손길이 닿는다. 레땅은 제철 식재료를 사용하여 계절별로 메뉴에 변화를 줌으로써 계절의 풍미를 셰프의 프렌치 요리에 올곧이 담아 낸다. 기본에 충실하면서도 간결하고 담백한 프렌치 퀴진을 즐길 수 있는 곳이다. 주방을 마주보는 카운터 테이블은 좌석이 넉넉지 않으니 방문하기 전 예약을 권장한다.

L'étang is a French bistro located on one of the main roads in Yeonji-dong. Here, the owner-chef Jung Dong-won does everything single-handedly, from preparing the ingredients to cooking and serving. By revamping its menu every season to reflect seasonal ingredients, L'étang incorporates the flavors of the season into its French cuisine characterized by adherence to culinary basics and traditions as well as fresh and mild flavors. Since the bar counter facing the kitchen features limited seating, reservations are recommended.

프렌치 • *French*

051-807-3636

부산진구 성지로 22

22 Seongji-ro, Busanjin-gu

■ 가 격 PRICE: ₩₩

오스테리아 어부
OSTERIA ABOO

이탤리언 • *Italian*

051-802-8858
부산진구 동천로 58
58 Dongcheon-ro, Busanjin-gu

■ 가 격 PRICE: ₩₩

전포동에 위치한 오스테리아 어부. 특이하게 음주 양식당이라는 상호를 내걸고 있는 이곳은 해산물이 풍부한 이탈리아 남부 정통 요리를 추구하는 곳으로 2017년부터 이 자리를 지켜 왔다. 알 덴테로 익힌 파스타에 짭짤하다고 느낄 정도의 간으로 신선한 딱새우를 풍부하게 넣은 비스크 파스타나 새로 추가된 마레(바다) 코스를 맛보는 것도 좋은 선택이 될 것이다. 셰프가 직접 추천하는 와인과 함께 곁들여 보시길. 진한 이탈리아의 맛을 느낄 수 있다.

As its sign suggests, Osteria Aboo in Jeonpo-dong oddly labels itself a Western gastropub. Since 2017, this establishment has strived to offer authentic Southern Italian cuisine, a cuisine characterized by ample use of seafood-based ingredients. Among all the exquisite items on the menu, we are partial to the bisque pasta, featuring al dente noodles and a sumptuous amount of fresh and savory red-banded lobster, as well as the newly added Mare ("sea") course. When paired with a chef-recommended wine, the cuisine will astonish you with the rich flavors of Italy.

차애전 할매 칼국수
CHA AE JEON HALMAE KALGUKSU

칼국수 • *Kalguksu*

051-751-9639

연제구 과정로 191번가길 70

70 Gwajeong-ro 191 beonga-gil, Yeonje-gu

■ 가 격 PRICE: ₩

차애전 할매 칼국수는 1982년 개업 이후 변함없는 꾸준함을 무기로 오랜 시간 지역민들에게 소박하고 따뜻한 칼국수를 제공해왔다. 어디서든 쉽게 접할 수 있는 칼국수이지만 이곳의 칼국수는 소박함에서 나오는 옛스러운 스타일이 눈에 띈다. 걸쭉한 국물과는 달리 마일드하고 라이트한 맛, 김치 대신 나오는 독특하고 매콤한 맛의 김치양파 다대기 등 이곳만의 특징적 요소들이 있다. 처음에는 다대기를 풀지 말고 슴슴한 국물과 면을 즐긴 다음 국물에 다대기를 풀어 먹으면 얼큰함이 잔잔하게 올라온다. 이 밖에도 할매칼국수와 비빔칼국수, 여름에만 판매하는 맷돌콩칼국수 등 칼국수의 여러 변형된 메뉴를 즐길 수 있다. 칼국수 양을 고를 수 있어 식사량에 따라 합리적으로 선택도 가능하다.

Since 1982, this establishment has faithfully and unwaveringly continued to serve local customers with the simple yet hearty dish of kalguksu (hand-cut noodle soup). Though this humble dish can be found anywhere, the eatery's variant has distinctive old-fashioned charm derived from its unpretentiousness. The broth is not thick, but mild and light. And instead of serving kimchi as a side dish, it is offered in the form of a uniquely spicy garnish mixed with onion. It is these and other intricacies that give this joint's menu a singular flair. For an optimal dining experience, first, enjoy the mild broth and noodles in their natural state. Then, add in the garnish for a pleasant spiciness that slowly builds up. The menu features several varieties of kalguksu, including Halmae Kalguksu, the restaurant's namesake signature dish; bibim (spicy cold) kalguksu; and kalguksu in cold soybean soup made from stone-ground soybeans, its summer special. Plus, you can even select the portion sizes that suit your mood.

Sanga Park/Getty Images Plus

중구
남구
영도구
사하구
JUNG-GU
NAM-GU
YEONGDO-GU
SAHA-GU

중구 남구 영도구 사하구

아르프
ARP

비건 • *Vegan*

010-5588-1368
영도구 태종로 99번길 35
35 Taejong-ro 99 beon-gil, Yeongdo-gu

■ 가 격 PRICE: ₩

100% 비건 음식만을 서빙하는 아르프. Around Plant에서 앞 글자를 따 만든 이름인데 둥그런 지구의 긍정적이고 윤리적인 식탁과 채소 요리의 무한한 가능성을 표현한 상호라고 한다. 쌀로 직접 만든 와인과 함께 고기가 들어가지 않은 음식을 만나볼 수 있는데 '비건 요리는 맛없다'는 편견을 단박에 깨뜨린다. 시그니처 메뉴인 고사리 파스타는 고사리와 버섯을 말려 식감을 극대화해 쫄깃하고 고소한 맛을 느낄 수 있고, 비건 치즈는 코코넛 오일로 만들었지만 체다치즈와 똑같은 맛을 낸다. 동물성 재료 없이도 빼어난 맛을 내는 음식을 아름다운 공간에서 즐겨 보시길.

ARP offers a 100 percent vegan menu. An acronym formed from the phrase "Around Plants," the eatery's name symbolizes the positive, ethical kitchen table of the round Earth and the unlimited possibilities inherent in veggie cuisine. Here, customers can enjoy a diverse range of non-meat dishes paired with housemade wine made of rice. And these offerings immediately debunk the common misconception that vegan food is not delicious. For instance, the signature bracken pasta features dried bracken and mushrooms for a maximally chewy texture and pleasant nutty flavors. The vegan cheese, though made from coconut oil, tastes exactly like cheddar cheese. Come and relish the gastronomic charm of ARP's delectable non-animal-based fare in this elegantly designed space.

정짓간 N
JEONGJITGAN

'정짓간'은 '부엌'의 경상도 방언이다. 2011년 문을 연 정짓간은 부산식 돼지국밥 전문점이다. 국밥에 들어가는 육수를 매일 직접 끓여 준비하는데 진한 사골국같이 뽀얀 국물은 깔끔하고 고소하면서도 담백한 맛이 일품이다. 국밥에 듬뿍 올라가 있는 얇고 부들부들한 고기와 부속 고기, 순대 등 원하는 재료를 선택해서 즐길 수 있다. 항정살로 만든 수육과 막국수도 이곳의 대표 메뉴. 24시간 운영한다.

Jeongjitgan is the Gyeongsang-do dialect word for kitchen. Opened in 2011, Jeongjitgan specializes in Busan-style dwejigukbap, or pork soup. The rich, milky broth, which is reminiscent of a clean, savory beef bone broth is prepared fresh daily. Diners can choose the toppings they like from thinly sliced, tender meat, offal, and sundae. Suyuk made from pork shoulder, and makguksu, or cold buckwheat noodles, are also signature dishes. Jeongjitgan is open 24 hours, which means that it's always the perfect time to visit.

돼지국밥 •
Dwaeji-gukbap

051-293-2900
사하구 비봉로 6
6 Bibong-ro, Saha-gu
www.busangukbap.modoo.at

■ 가격 PRICE: ₩

합천국밥집
HAPCHEON GUKBAPJIP

부산을 상징하는 음식 돼지 국밥은 시대와 식성의 변화와 함께 다양한 모습으로 변모해 왔다. 이러한 변화 속에서도 합천국밥집의 돼지 국밥은 오랜 시간 원칙을 고수하며 한결같이 매력적인 맛으로 손님의 발길을 이끈다. 합천국밥집은 특유의 고기 토렴 노하우로 잡내를 잡아 돼지고기의 풍미를 살리는 것이 특징이다. 특히 감칠맛과 깔끔한 맛이 동시에 느껴지는 맑은 국물은 시간이 지날수록 다시 생각나는 맛이다. 또 다른 인기 메뉴인 수육은 수량이 정해져 있어 서두르지 않으면 맛보기 힘들다. 11시부터 1시까지는 1인 식사가 되지 않는다는 점도 참고하시기 바란다.

돼지국밥 • *Dwaeji-gukbap*

051-628-4898

남구 용호로 235

235 Yongho-ro, Nam-gu

■ 가 격 PRICE: ₩

Dwaeji-gukbap (pork and rice soup), the representative culinary delight of Busan, has continued to evolve with changing times and dietary trends. Amid this evolution, the variant served at Hapcheon Gukbapjip has long adhered to the original recipe, delighting customers with its time-tested flavors. Here, pork is repeatedly covered with broth and drained right before it is included in the soup and served. This technique eliminates unpleasant zests while enhancing the meat's rich flavor. The clear broth, on the other hand, is brimming with umami and clean flavors; they will be etched in your memory and reverberate every now and then. Another signature item, boiled pork slices, is often unavailable due to limited daily portions, so arrive early. Solo diners are advised to avoid peak lunch hours from 11 am to 1 pm.

나막집
NAMAKZIP

부산은 돼지 국밥의 도시답게 국밥의 스타일도 다양하다. 돼지 국밥 고유의 맛은 유지하면서도 가게마다 국물을 내는 방식을 조금씩 달리하는 점이 특징이다. 나막집은 고기 육수에서 채수의 비율을 높여 진득한 맛보다는 가벼우면서도 깔끔한 국물 맛을 즐길 수 있다. 주메뉴인 돼지 국밥 외에 국밥 육수를 사용한 고기칼국수와 생면칼국수, 수육과 삼겹구이 등 부대 메뉴도 선택이 가능하다. 모던한 느낌의 공간에서 뒷맛이 깔끔한 돼지 국밥을 즐기기에 안성맞춤이다.

Busan offers a wide variety of dwaeji-gukbap (pork and rice soup), befitting its position as the origin of this dish. Every restaurant adds its own twist to the soup's broth while staying true to its authentic flavors. At Namakzip, the meat broth features a higher proportion of vegetable broth, so it tastes light and clean rather than heavy. In addition to this iconic soup, the menu includes kalguksu (hand-cut noodle soup) with meat; kalguksu with fresh noodles, both featuring meat broth from dwaeji-gukbap; boiled pork slices; and grilled pork belly. For those wishing to enjoy, amidst a modern dining space, a satisfying dwaeji-gukbap with a minimal aftertaste, Namakzip is the way to go.

돼지국밥 •

Dwaeji-gukbap

051-746-4882

남구 분포로 145, W 스퀘어 A동 1068호

#1068 A, W square, 145 Bunpo-ro, Nam-gu

■ **가격 PRICE: ₩**

컨템퍼러리 • *Contemporary*

010-4585-6607

중구 중구로 23번길 12

12 Junggu-ro 23 beon-gil, Jung-gu

■ 가 격 PRICE: ₩₩

쉐프곤
CHEF GON

자갈치 시장 근처 골목에 위치한 이곳은 오랫동안 호텔에서 근무하던 셰프가 독립해 만든 공간이다. 셰프가 직접 아침마다 신선한 재료를 시장에서 구해다 계절에 맞게 그날의 메뉴를 준비한다. 그래서 코스 이름도 '자갈치 셰프 코스 스페셜'이다. 주방 쪽 테이블에 앉으면 재료에 대한 설명을 들으며 요리하는 모습을 직접 감상할 수 있다. 해산물뿐만 아니라 고기 요리도 다양하며 단품도 준비되어 있으니 수준급 와인과 함께 자갈치의 정수를 즐겨 보시길 바란다.

Situated in an alley near Jagalchi Market, this joint is run by a former hotel chef with years of experience. Every morning, the chef visits the market to buy fresh ingredients, with which he prepares the day's seasonal menu. For this reason, the restaurant's course meal is called "Jagalchi Chef's Course Special." Diners sitting near the kitchen can watch the chef in action while listening to his explanations about the ingredients. In addition to seafood offerings, the menu features a wide range of meat and a la carte dishes, as well as a well-balanced wine list, all of which await your indulgence.

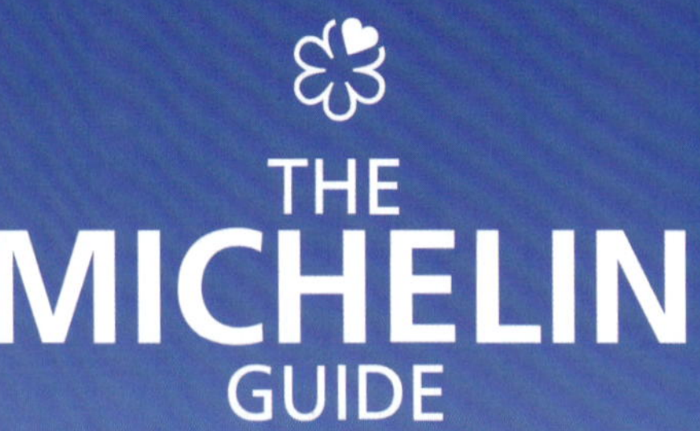
THE
MICHELIN
GUIDE

For over 120 years, the MICHELIN Guide has been committed to identifying high-quality gastronomic experiences. We're now applying that same level of passion and expertise to hotels. Our experts have scoured the earth to find accommodations that stand out for their style, service, and personality — with options for all budgets.

Visit the MICHELIN Guide website and download the app to book the best hotels you can imagine.

Download on the App Store

GET IT ON Google Play

Banyan Tree Club & Spa Seoul | Seoul, Korea

인덱스

INDEX

스타 레스토랑
STARRED RESTAURANTS

서울 SEOUL

부산 BUSAN

빕 구르망 레스토랑
BIB GOURMAND RESTAURANTS

부산 BUSAN

요리 유형별 레스토랑 분류
RESTAURANTS BY CUISINE TYPE

서울 SEOUL

게장 Gejang

곰탕 Gomtang

국수 Noodles

냉면 Naengmyeon

도가니탕 Doganitang

돼지국밥 Dwaeji-gukbap

두부 Dubu

딤섬 Dim Sum

라멘 Ramen

만두 Mandu

메밀국수 Memil-guksu

멕시칸 Mexican

바비큐 Barbecue

베지테리안 Vegetarian

불고기 Bulgogi

비건 Vegan

설렁탕 Seolleongtang

소바 Soba

수제비 Sujebi

스시 Sushi

스테이크하우스 Steakhouse

아시안 Asian

야키토리 Yakitori

우동 Udon

육회 Yukhoe

이노베이티브 Innovative

이탤리언 Italian

일식 Japanese

족발 Jokbal

중식 Chinese

지중해식 Mediterranean Cuisine

추어탕 Chueotang

칼국수 Kalguksu

컨템퍼러리 Contemporary

쿠시아게 Kushiage

타이 Thai

테판야키 Teppanyaki

프렌치 French

한식 Korean

BUSAN

곰탕 Gomtang

국수 Noodles

냉면 Naengmyeon

돼지국밥 Dwaeji-gukbap

딤섬 Dim Sum

라멘 Ramen

바비큐 Barbecue

복어 Fugu / Pufferfish

불고기 Bulgogi

비건 Vegan

비빔밥 Bibimbap

스테이크하우스 Steakhouse

야키토리 Yakitori

유러피언 European

이탤리언 Italian

일식 Japanese

장어 Unagi / Freshwater Eel

중식 Chinese

칼국수 Kalguksu

컨템퍼러리 Contemporary

타이 Thai

타이완 Taiwanese

프렌치 French

한식 Korean

영문 알파벳 순서별 분류
ALPHABETICAL LIST OF RESTAURANTS

D

E-F

G

H

I

J

LIST OF RESTAURANTS

N

O

P

V-W

Y-Z

CREDITS

Page 4, from top to bottom: bong hyunjungn/Getty Images Plus - Photomick/ Getty Images Plus • **Page 5, from top to bottom:** Mlenny/Getty Images Plus - Prasit Rodphan/Alamy/hemis.fr

All other photos by Michelin, or with the kind permission of the establishments mentioned in this guide.

MANUFACTURE FRANCAISE DES PNEUMATIQUES MICHELIN

Simplified joint stock company with a share capital of 504 000 004 €
23, Place des Carmes Dechaux, 63000 Clermont-Ferrand (France)
R.C.S Clermont-Ferrand 855 200 507

Legal deposit : 02-2025
Printed in China - 02-2025
New Central Printing
Block A22, Fusheng 8th Road, New Industry
Fu Cheng Ao, Longgang District
Shenzhen 518111

Graphic design: Ici Barbès
Typesetting: Michelin éditions, Voluntari (Romania)

Our editorial team has taken the greatest care in writing this guide and checking the information in it. However, practical information (prices, addresses, telephone numbers, internet addresses, etc) is subject to frequent change and such information should therefore be used for guidance only. It is possible that some of the information in this guide may not be accurate or exhaustive as at the date of publication. We therefore accept no liability in regard to such information.